GRAPHIC DESIGN IN GERMANY 1890—1945

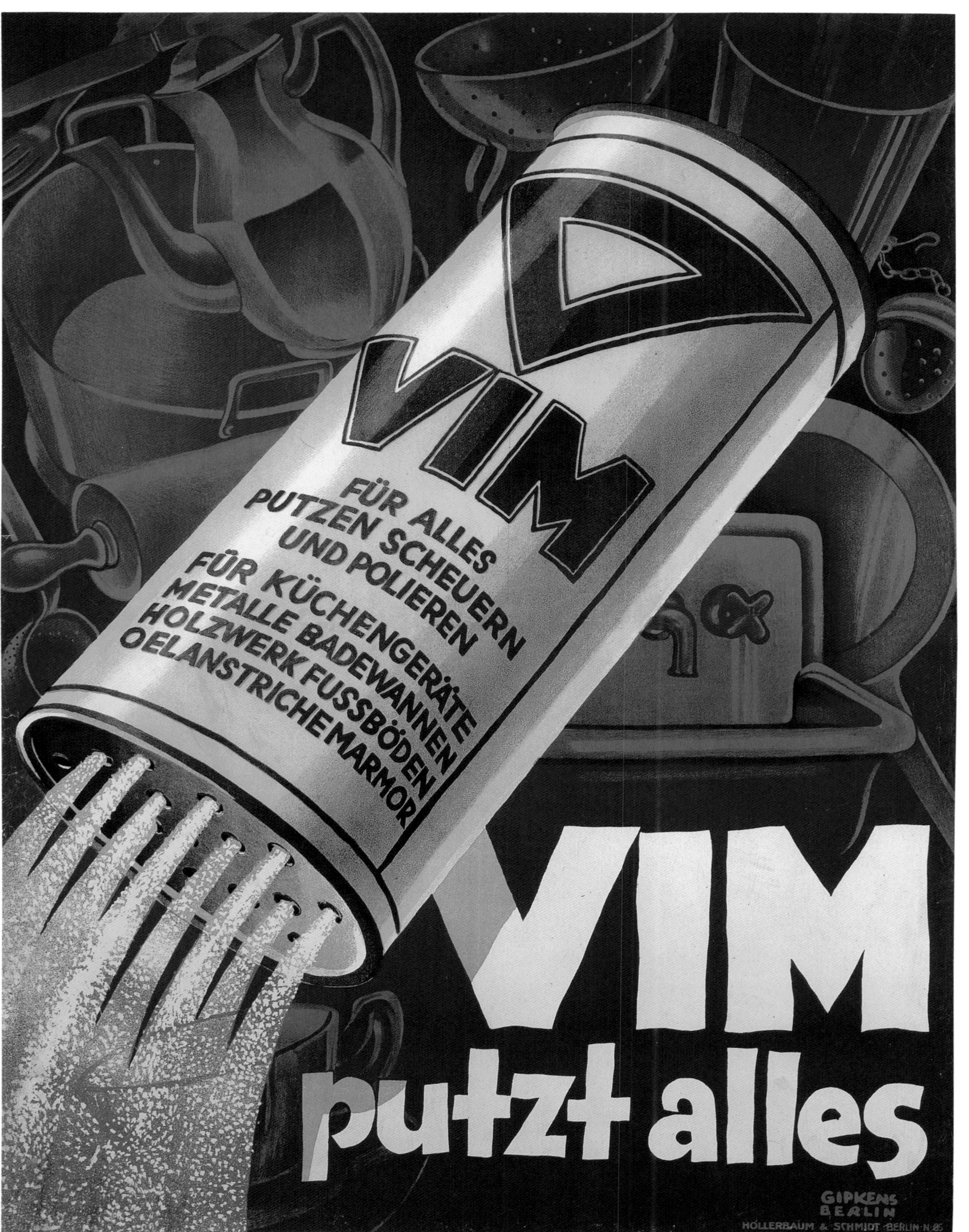
VIM
FÜR ALLES
PUTZEN SCHEUERN
UND POLIEREN
FÜR KÜCHENGERÄTE
METALLE BADEWANNEN
HOLZWERK FUSSBÖDEN
OELANSTRICHE MARMOR
VIM
putzt alles
GIPKENS
BERLIN
HOLLERBAUM & SCHMIDT BERLIN N.65

Jeremy Aynsley

GRAPHIC DESIGN IN GERMANY 1890—1945

With 253 illustrations, 152 in colour

Frontispiece
Vim Putzt Alles
(Vim cleans everything)

Designed by Julius Gipkens
Poster
About 1920

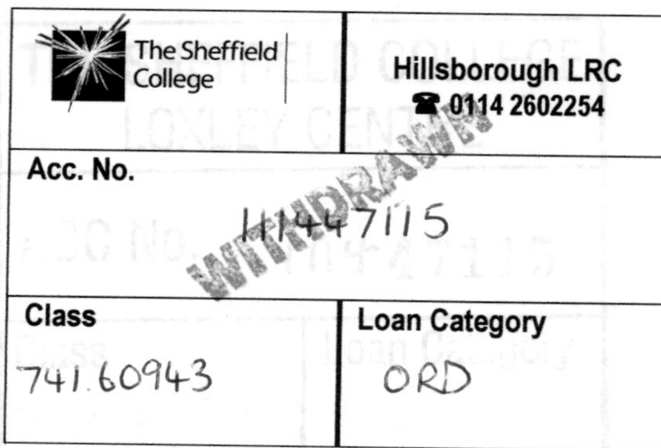

For my parents

First published in the United Kingdom in 2000
by Thames & Hudson Ltd, 181A High Holborn,
London WC1V 7QX

British Library Cataloguing-in-Publication Data
A catalogue record for this book is available from the British Library

ISBN 0-500-51007-5

Printed and bound in Hong Kong by C&C Offset

This book is published on the occasion of the exhibition, *Print, Power and Persuasion: Graphic Design in Germany 1890–1945*, presented at The Wolfsonian-Florida International University, 27 September 2000–29 April 2001. The exhibition, organized by The Wolfsonian–FIU and drawn entirely from its collection, was curated by Dr Jeremy Aynsley of the Royal College of Art, London, and Wolfsonian curator Marianne Lamonaca.

Dr Aynsley's collaboration with The Wolfsonian–FIU began in 1996 when he conducted research on the museum's rich collection of German-language graphic design. He examined a wide range of materials, from postage stamps to posters, exploring the profound changes that occurred in graphic and typographic design from the 1890s to the1940s.

In recognition of the author's important work, The Wolfsonian–FIU provided the photography for more than 125 objects from its collection which are reproduced in the book.

The Wolfsonian–FIU is a museum and research centre that promotes the examination of modern material culture and design to enhance the understanding and appreciation of objects as agents and reflections of social, political, and technological change.
The organization's focus is its extraordinary collection of North American and European decorative, propaganda, and fine arts of the 1885–1945 period, donated to Florida International University in 1997 by Mitchell Wolfson, Jr.

Contents

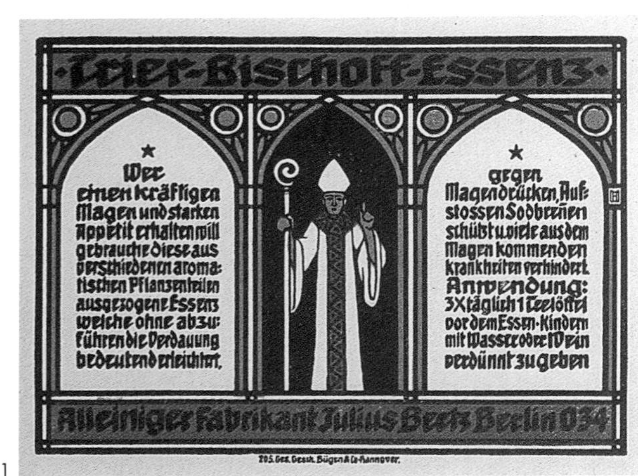

0.1

0.1 *Trier Bischoff Essenz*

Designed by Max Hertwig
Label for bottle
About 1910

Introduction

German graphic and typographic design in the first half of the 20th century represents an extraordinarily rich and diverse aspect of the history of visual culture. It marks the moment of recognition that the world was becoming increasingly dependent on a modern and commercialized system of communication in which the designer was to play a major role. An unprecedented scale of attention was devoted to printed matter, whether as designs for graphic ornament, typefaces and logos in books and advertisements, or magazines, posters, signage and exhibitions.

This book represents the first account in the English language of the emergence of German graphic design between 1890 and 1945. The aim in selecting material has been to provide a broad range from across a stylistically diverse field. While some of the individual designers such as Peter Behrens, Lucian Bernhard, Jan Tschichold, Herbert Bayer and John Heartfield are well known, many others have not received such attention, possibly because they do not easily fit within the stylistic criteria adopted by many earlier publications.

In the first decades of the 20th century graphic design was a newly self-aware profession, initially not even recognized by a single term. There were many good reasons for Germany to lead in the field of print culture. Historically it was a country that had been associated since the Middle Ages with the arts of the book and printing, and many of the new design developments in the 20th century grew from that base. The industrialization of printing in the 19th century and the advent of mass circulation –in the form of advertising, books, magazines and packaging – separated the activity of designing from its base in the crafts. Design had formerly been integrated as part of a daily workshop activity, but with the increasing division of labour under mechanization, instructions were given at a distance for the practical aspects of print. Graphic designers might be employed by an advertising agency, or work freelance, or be taken on by major manufacturing companies and organizations in design departments.

Many designers sought to raise the standards of printed culture by integrating experimental ideas from avant-garde art. This was the case for the generation of *Jugendstil* designers, for instance, who adapted Symbolist ideas of representing literary themes to advertising posters. At a later stage, the new typography and the new photography recognized the power of abstract composition and new forms of juxtaposition in experimental photomontage to provide a graphic language for industrial clients.

This study examines a time in German design history marked by political and social turbulence. At its broadest, the period falls into three contrasting stages of Modernity. Germany's position as a world power and an aggressive international competitor was asserted from the unification of the country in 1871 until the outbreak of the First World War in 1914. Following Germany's defeat, social experiment took place during the Weimar Republic, a period from 1919 to 1933, when designers joined forces with other cultural figures in the hope of establishing an international exchange of ideas. The third broad stage, which opened with the appointment of Adolf Hitler as Chancellor in January 1933, led to the control of all forms of artistic life by official National Socialist Party politics.

These distinct political stages have been used here as a way to define cultural change among broad groups of graphic designers. Firstly, the rich exchange

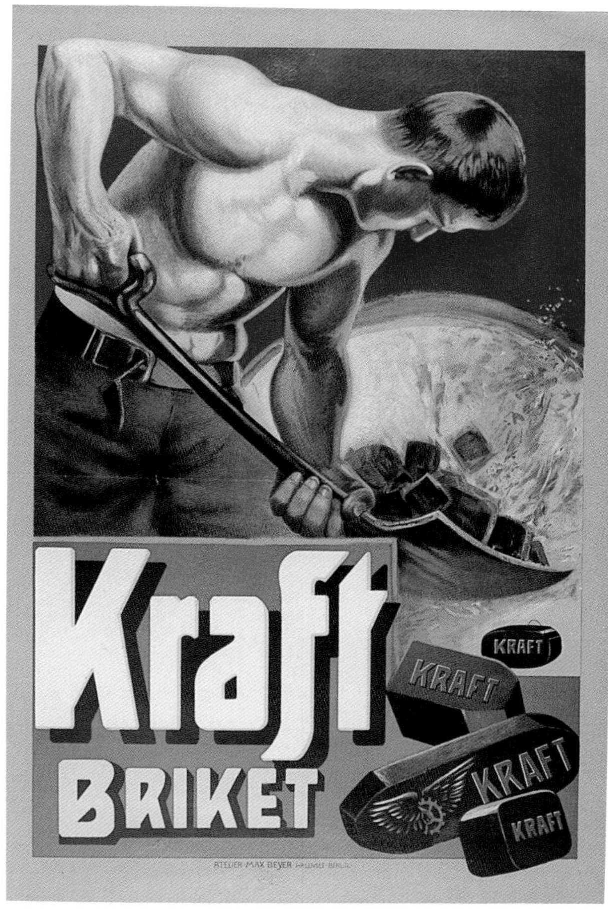

0.2

0.3

0.2 *Kraft Briket*
(Kraft coal briquettes)

Designed by Max Beyer
Poster
About 1930

0.3 *Das Deutsche Lichtbild*
(The German photograph)

Designed by Georg Trump
Poster
1930

0.4

0.4 *30. Januar 1933 Adolf Hitler gründet das Dritte Reich!* (Adolf Hitler founds the Third Reich!)

Poster
1933

between the applied and fine arts that was characterized as *Jugendstil* (the style of youth). Secondly, the radicalized cultural experiment of abstraction and constructivism in design, usually associated with the broader phenomenon of Modernism. Finally, the National Socialist period, when cultural reaction and authoritative control of the arts supported a preference for figuration and tradition. While following these political demarcations, I am concerned to reveal examples of continuity between periods that question the conventional interpretation of the relationship between artistic style and political ideology.

For the historian of graphic design, categories of style remain meaningful. However, they are not the only way of approaching the subject. To consider graphic design as deeply connected with other forms of visual and material culture often means extending research on design as part of a complex system. In an ideal world, the historian would be in a position to retrieve examples of correspondence between designers and clients, surviving business papers or other unpublished sources, leading to a sense of the scale of a print run or the circulation of particular designs. This research has inevitably been affected by the disruptions of history. Furthermore, the removal of companies from one city to another has meant that few intact archives remain.

By contrast to this situation, the museum and art and design school collections provide an extremely valuable source of information on the education of the new

graphic designers, with examples of teaching and student work held at the Berlin Kunstbibliothek, the Bauhaus Archiv in Berlin, and the Leipzig Akademie. Accordingly, emphasis is given to the rich debate on the appropriate teaching of the graphic designer.

The research towards this book has taken place over a number of years and witnessed the shifting nature of parallel enquiry. At the outset, few secondary commentaries existed; since then other scholars have added to the subject in many ways, through a greater number of exhibitions, monographs on distinctive individuals and thematic interpretations of graphic culture. Also during the period of my research, priorities in history have moved in many other ways. Postmodernism has altered the way we look at much early 20th-century culture which did not fit into the canon of Modernism; it has offered new ways of thinking about historicism or figurative design, for example.

Throughout the period, great concern was expressed in the more polemical design literature as to how national and international tendencies could be embodied in specific examples of design. Lobbies were formed on behalf of particular points of view, whether for typefaces, posters or publications. During the Nazi period, however, extreme tensions regarding design as a 'national' culture surfaced and legislation was put in place to control it. But there were inherent contradictions in these policies.

A great deal of debate was devoted to where graphic design stood in relation to other arts and business practices. Was it indeed an art or commerce? Was it moral or immoral? Could it be national, or were its implications inevitably international? I am suggesting in this book that the examples from the history of German graphic design indicate it was all these things. This design depended on its ability to satisfy the expectations of different contexts, to be diverse and, at times, contradictory. To impose a more consistent interpretation would be to lose the complexity of graphic design's ambiguous character to act as signs of both art and commerce.

GROSSE BERLINER
KUNST·AUSSTELLUNG
1902
LANDES-AUSSTELLUNGS-GEBAEUDE AM LEHRTER BAHNHOF
DAUER VOM 3. MAI BIS 28. SEPTEMBER EINTRITT 50 PF. MONTAGS 1 MK.

M. FISCHER, KUNSTVERLAGSANSTALT BERLIN W.35.

1.1

1.1 *Grosse Berliner Kunst Ausstellung* (Great Berlin Art Exhibition)

Designed by T. Lucius
Poster
1902

1.2 Photograph of Fritz Hellmut Ehmcke about 1914.

1 From Applied Art to Graphic Design 1890–1914

'Commercial Graphics, this is a collective term, which fifteen years ago did not exist, although what it describes is ancient. That a particular group of this kind of graphic achievements has been pushed to the foreground of interest has to do with the expansion of the whole of economic and commercial life, with the enormous growth in power of industry and factors which determine the face of politics and culture even more than ever today.'[1]

F. H. EHMCKE

1.2

German graphic art and design flourished in the first half of the 20th century, undergoing a significant change in scale and category. At any single point it could range from the smallest piece of ephemera to the most public poster, or from an artist's print portfolio to the brand identity of Germany's main electrical industries. When grouped collectively, the examples of graphic design were extremely diverse, as was their destination or use. Nevertheless, they often indicated shared stylistic and technical characteristics, while in some cases they were the work of the same person. According to the prominent designer and teacher Fritz Ehmcke, as quoted above, the term commercial graphics, or 'graphics for use' (as *Gebrauchsgraphik* can be translated), was still relatively new even in 1927.

He suggests that whereas the activity had existed for a long time, the word was being used to characterize a new configuration of interests at the beginning of the century. Germany held an important place in this change in terminology.

Design as a self-conscious, professionalized and autonomous activity is largely a modern phenomenon that arose from an increasing division of labour. As with many specialist terms, the demarcations of what we now call graphic design were never clear-cut at any one time. At the turn of the century, however, traditions from publishing, the fine arts and the graphic arts fruitfully collided and brought together designers of different backgrounds to shape them in new ways. Driving this was a belief that the various practices held something in common, and that, more than previously, such interconnections could benefit modern commercial practice just as much as they could promote artistic innovation.

Division of Labour and New Names

The derivation of the term 'graphic design' is usually attributed to the American designer William Addison Dwiggins, who first used it in 1922. Dwiggins was distinguishing three categories when he adopted the terms fine art printing, utilitarian printing and printing for purpose. It was the latter that he called 'graphic design'.[2] In the USA, this was to become a generic term covering letter design, typography, book design, design for packaging, printed ephemera, posters and press advertisements. A large and unwieldy category, the activities of graphic design were importantly distinguished from the longer-standing tradition of book typography which had an established history by this time. By contrast, graphic design was regarded as emerging with the formation of mass-circulation magazines, advertising and modern retail distribution, and was largely overlooked as a topic for serious study.

Significantly, the traditional terms for design for print in the German language were those of the fine arts, as it was deemed to arise from academic rather than from business spheres. This was most obviously signalled by the predominant use

1.3

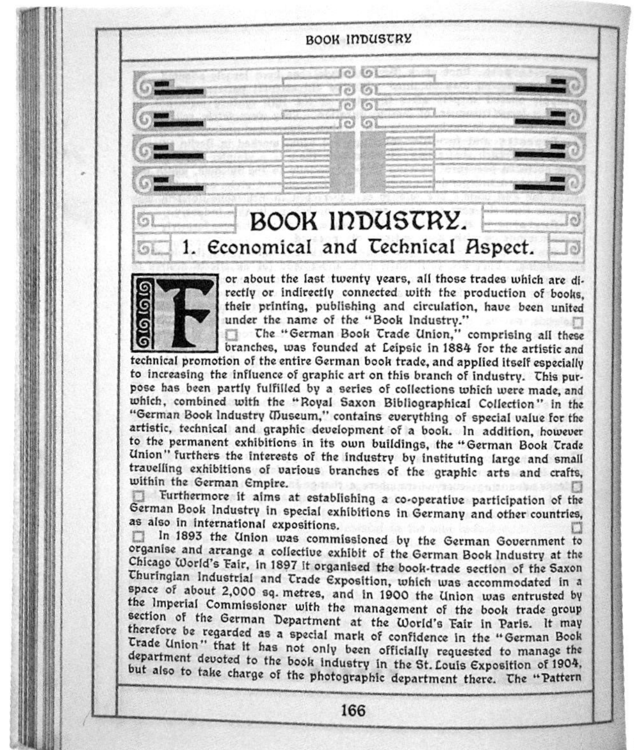

BOOK INDUSTRY

BOOK INDUSTRY.

1. Economical and Technical Aspect.

For about the last twenty years, all those trades which are directly or indirectly connected with the production of books, their printing, publishing and circulation, have been united under the name of the "Book Industry."

The "German Book Trade Union," comprising all these branches, was founded at Leipsic in 1884 for the artistic and technical promotion of the entire German book trade, and applied itself especially to increasing the influence of graphic art on this branch of industry. This purpose has been partly fulfilled by a series of collections which were made, and which, combined with the "Royal Saxon Bibliographical Collection" in the "German Book Industry Museum," contains everything of special value for the artistic, technical and graphic development of a book. In addition, however to the permanent exhibitions in its own buildings, the "German Book Trade Union" furthers the interests of the industry by instituting large and small travelling exhibitions of various branches of the graphic arts and crafts, within the German Empire.

Furthermore it aims at establishing a co-operative participation of the German Book Industry in special exhibitions in Germany and other countries, as also in international expositions.

In 1893 the Union was commissioned by the German Government to organise and arrange a collective exhibit of the German Book Industry at the Chicago World's Fair, in 1897 it organised the book-trade section of the Saxon Thuringian Industrial and Trade Exposition, which was accommodated in a space of about 2,000 sq. metres, and in 1900 the Union was entrusted by the Imperial Commissioner with the management of the book trade group section of the German Department at the World's Fair in Paris. It may therefore be regarded as a special mark of confidence in the "German Book Trade Union" that it has not only been officially requested to manage the department devoted to the book industry in the St. Louis Exposition of 1904, but also to take charge of the photographic department there. The "Pattern

166

1.4

1.3 and 1.4 Official catalogue of the Exhibition of the German Empire: International Exposition, St. Louis, 1904

Designed by Peter Behrens
Cover and chapter opening
1904

of the word artist, as in *Schriftkünstler*, letter artist, *Buchkünstler*, book artist, *Plakatkünstler*, poster artist and *Reklamekünstler*, advertising artist. While all under the umbrella of 'artist', these various kinds of activity had different roots. Whereas the letter artist had worked for type foundries, originating or revising letterforms for typefaces, since the 15th century, book artists were a more recent development. The term was used to describe someone with responsibility to a printer or publisher for making harmonious arrangements of type, page layout, choice of papers and bindings, as well as illustrations or decorations. Generally, book artists were trained at the art academies. If the emphasis of these first two kinds of designer was towards publication, the next figures in the gradual specialization were poster and advertising artists, who took on work for commercial publicity and exhibitions as well. They, too, would largely come from the art schools. By the 1920s all the assembled activities could be subsumed under the more general heading of commercial graphic design, *Gebrauchsgraphik*.

German Printing as a National Culture

'Germany', it should be remembered, was a term used to define a cultural and linguistic area long before it signified a nation-state. In its former meaning,

Germany or the German-speaking realm (*deutschsprachigen Raum*), was applied at different times from the 15th century onwards to parts of Bohemia, France, Poland, the Netherlands, Austro-Hungary, Luxembourg, Schleswig and Switzerland, as well as that land actually recognized as Germany.[3] In 1871, at the end of the Franco-Prussian War, a group of independent states was unified in the Second German Empire under the King of Prussia which, with some boundary redefinitions caused by war and reparations, lasted until 1945.

In the world of printing, German foundries, printers and publishers could claim a prominent place. Indeed, the invention of printing with moveable types cast from matrices was attributed to a Mainz goldsmith, Johann Gensfleisch zum Gutenberg.[4] Although Gutenberg actually began the experiment while in exile in Strasbourg, the printing press was intimately associated with the German-language tradition in common lore as well as in professionals' eyes. Moreover, its cultural form was distinctive, and the *Fraktur* or broken-letter script, as used for Gutenberg's 42-line Bible, became the tradition within these parts of Central Europe. In the 20th century, a period of political extremes and wilful desire to claim 'national' styles, the association of typeface with a national style was no simple matter.

In the broad scheme of historical development there has been a tendency to regard print culture as a consistently internationalizing process, fulfilled in the late 20th century by techniques and styles of graphic design becoming homogeneous. Commentaries following Marshall McLuhan's influential ideas about the globalization of communications, for example, often stress how a shared and consistent communication is made available through technology.[5] At the turn of the 19th century, however, print and publishing traditions were still strongly regional or national. Cities had particular identities that determined their graphic and typographic cultures. Distinctions could depend on the use of indigenous materials or skills – for instance, local manufacturers' customs – as well as educational and cultural traditions. The original states of Germany retained many of their regional identities with frequent mutual hostility, as was most articulately expressed in the historical antagonism between Bavaria and Prussia, and their respective capital cities Munich and Berlin, for much of the late 19th and 20th centuries.

Eric Hobsbawm has shown how a nation is formed as much by cultural and linguistic tradition as by state political, administrative and economic foundations, an intricate balance between superstructure and infrastructure.[6] The emerging art of graphic design, encompassing both these elements, inhabited a paradoxical situation: its industrial, political-economic basis was its foundries and presses, whereas its manifestation was a form of design. The infrastructure of presses, specialist cutting and folding machinery, inks and papers, spread across Europe, the USA and the rest of the world through emigration and subsidiary companies, often implying a form of German cultural hegemony. At the same time, the graphic language in publication art and design encouraged international exchange. German artists and designers found themselves moving between such centres as Berlin, Leipzig, Dresden, Munich, Frankfurt am Main, Cologne and Düsseldorf, but also beyond national borders to Paris, Prague, Vienna, Zurich, Budapest, Amsterdam, London, New York and Moscow. These movements worked in both directions and increasingly suggested that the artistic language would develop from this cross-fertilization of ideas.

Germany appeared a bastion of strength in print culture but her reputation in the other art industries (the term under which the graphic arts and trades were more broadly placed) revealed considerable need for reform in the last years of the 19th century. Victory over France in the Franco-Prussian War inevitably meant that comparisons were drawn between the respective countries' industrial output, as well as their institutions of arts and science after 1871. Initially this was to Germany's disadvantage, for even if its high-quality craftsmanship and long-standing reputation for tool-making, hand skills and techniques of industrial production were recognized, France was clearly associated with a more distinguished artistic tradition.

1.5 Opening of the essay, *'An die Deutschen Künstler und Kunstfreunde!'*

written by Alexander Koch with an illustration by Bernhard Wenig and published in *Deutsche Kunst und Dekoration*, 1897.

1.6 *Behrens Schriften-Initialen und Schmuck* (Behrens Typeface – initials and ornament)

Designed by Peter Behrens
Page from a typefoundry booklet
1902

1.7 *Österreichische Ausstellung in London, 1906* (Austrian Exhibition in London)

Designed by Koloman Moser
Page from the catalogue
1906

BERNH. WENIG.

AN DIE DEUTSCHEN KÜNSTLER
UND KUNSTFREUNDE!

Mehr denn je erscheint unsere vaterländische Kunstübung wieder vom Auslande, von England, Amerika und Frankreich, abhängig. Nicht allein, dass die kaufkräftigen Gebildeten ausländische Erzeugnisse an Möbeln, Tapeten, Stoffen, Teppichen, Beleuchtungsgeräthen, Edelmetallarbeiten und keramischen Waaren meist den heimischen Arbeiten vorziehen, auch der deutsche Künstler und Kunstgewerbetreibende steht im Banne fremdländischer Formensprache; *das Idiom einer heimischen, individuell deutschen Kunstsprache droht uns verloren zu gehen!*

Immer deutlicher erblicken wir die Ursache dieser beschämenden Erscheinung hauptsächlich darin, dass seit dem Wiederaufleben unserer Kunst-Bestrebungen zu Anfang der sechziger Jahre durch die Einführung des Begriffes »Kunstgewerbe« eine Sondergruppe von Künstlern »zweiter Klasse« geschaffen wurde! Diese falsche Standes-, bezw. Thätigkeits-Scheidung war der schwerste Schlag, der die deutsche Kunst und das deutsche Kunstgewerbe treffen konnte, denn er vernichtete bei Publikum und Künstlern das Bewusstsein der natürlichen Zusammengehörigkeit aller bildenden Künste, der *Nothwendigkeit eines »Ineinander-Aufgehens« sämmtlicher Künstler! Architekten, Bildhauer, Maler und technische Künstler, die sog. Kunstgewerbetreibenden, sie Alle gehören auf das Engste zusammen und auf einen Platz, selbstdenkend, aber doch Hand in Hand schaffend für ein grosses Ganzes!*

Diesem Zusammenschliessen der Künstler verdanken die genannten Länder in erster Linie ihre unbestrittenen Erfolge im internationalen Wettbewerbe der letzten Jahre. Unsere Kunstsprache ist geistig-künstlerisch verarmt durch die Entziehung der Mithülfe fantasievoller und erfindungsreicher Künstler zu Gunsten der hohen Kunst. Denn an sich fehlt es uns nicht an künstlerischen Kräften, nicht an bedeutendem technischen Können in Industrie und Handwerk!

Es gilt also vor Allem, diese beiden Faktoren wieder mit einander in lebendige Verbindung und Wechselwirkung zu bringen. *Wirkliche, grosse Künstler für die — Kleinkunst!* Diese Forderung ist nicht gleichbedeutend mit dem Feldgeschrei: »Fort mit allem Alten!« der radikalen Neuerer; aber eine ganze Reihe neuer Erfindungen und Einrichtungen, neue Rohmaterialien, neue Techniken fordern auch eine neuzeitliche, nur ihnen zukommende Gestaltung und Durchbildung aus wahrhafter Künstlerhand. Wohl ist auch bei uns bereits viel des Vortrefflichen an neuzeitlichen Schöpfungen entstanden, aber es fehlte bisher an einer Sammelstelle, an einer zielbewussten Leitung, wie wir sie in ausländischen Kunstzeitschriften als »The Studio«, »The Artist«, »Art et Décoration« u. s. w. bemerken, wie die »Jugend« sie auf anderem Gebiete anstrebt.

1.5

John Heskett has written that

The most immediate and evident impact of unification on Germany was a period of wild economic boom and speculation known as the Gründerzeit, the founding period, so-called from the number of companies that were founded. The enthusiasm and high expectations generated by military victory were fuelled by the large amounts of capital made available by the French payment of an indemnity of 5 million Francs and the annexation of Alsace and Lorraine with their thriving industries as part of a peace settlement. In the optimistic frenzy that resulted, economic growth, large government orders, a building boom with a demand for domestic comforts, an expanding market for luxury goods and free-spending attitudes, affected all areas of production including the applied arts.[7]

Germany could not make great claims for artistic invention and originality. Whereas a succession of groups and movements in the French decorative arts were challenging artistic conventions, Germany's styles were considered to follow rather than lead. Instead, what was perceived as a derivative historicism in architecture and the decorative arts was favoured, in the belief that it gave greater resonance and stability to a newly established nation.

The most obvious acknowledgment of the need for change came in 1897 in the opening pages of *Deutsche Kunst und Dekoration*, which was to become the leading journal promoting the decorative arts in Germany. This was published by Alexander Koch of Darmstadt, one of a group calling for the reawakening of the applied arts, who launched his appeal by announcing 'The need for complete integration of all artists, architects, sculptors, painters and craftsmen. They all belong intimately together in the same place, each thinking individually yet working together hand-in-hand for a larger whole.'[8]

This call was to be met by a flourishing of Arts and Crafts up to the outbreak of war in 1914. In printing, a response soon came as a generation of artists and designers, as well as some architects, were commissioned to design new typefaces for German foundries, at a time when the cultural meaning and national significance of the revision and invention of type styles was being widely debated. In a number of ways, the problem posed a constant challenge to traditionalist and Modernist alike throughout the first half of the 20th century.

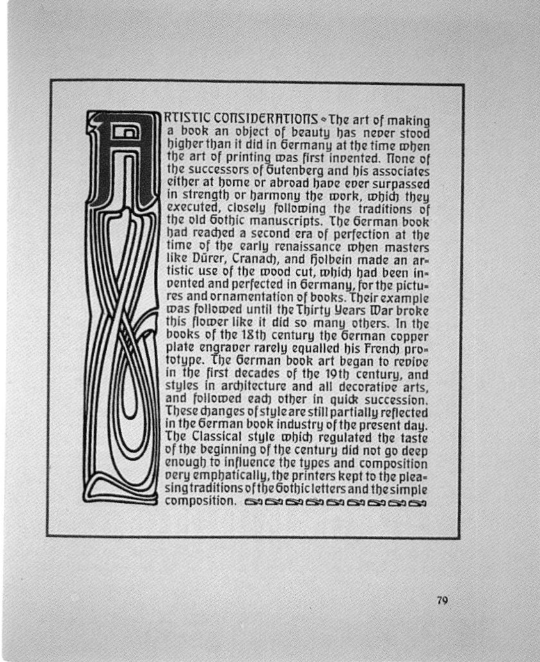

ARTISTIC CONSIDERATIONS ◦ The art of making a book an object of beauty has never stood higher than it did in Germany at the time when the art of printing was first invented. None of the successors of Gutenberg and his associates either at home or abroad have ever surpassed in strength or harmony the work, which they executed, closely following the traditions of the old Gothic manuscripts. The German book had reached a second era of perfection at the time of the early renaissance when masters like Dürer, Cranach, and Holbein made an artistic use of the wood cut, which had been invented and perfected in Germany, for the pictures and ornamentation of books. Their example was followed until the Thirty Years War broke this flower like it did so many others. In the books of the 18th century the German copper plate engraver rarely equalled his French prototype. The German book art began to revive in the first decades of the 19th century, and styles in architecture and all decorative arts, and followed each other in quick succession. These changes of style are still partially reflected in the German book industry of the present day. The Classical style which regulated the taste of the beginning of the century did not go deep enough to influence the types and composition very emphatically, the printers kept to the pleasing traditions of the Gothic letters and the simple composition.

79

1.6

Wandtafeln für Schule und Haus. Original-lithographien. Gedruckt zwei Serien (20 Blatt). Verlag der k.k. Hof- und Staats-druckerei in Wien
1. F. Andri: Pflügender Bauer
2. F. Andri: Kornschneiden
3. Max Kurzweil: Donaufischer
4. K. Ederer: Bauernhaus im Winter
5. O. Barth: Steirisches Bauernhaus im Winter. Motiv aus Altenberg mit Rax
6. M. Lenz: In der Tischlerwerkstätte
Mit diesen Wandtafeln soll für geringe Kosten der Schule ein den modernen Anforderungen entsprechender Unterrichtsbe-

1.7

1.8

1.8 An announcement for the special exhibition of the typefoundry Gebrüder Klingspor at the Arts and Crafts Museum in Frankfurt-am-Main.

Designed by Otto Eckmann. 1907

1.9–1.11 *Behrens-Antiqua und Schmuck* (Behrens Roman typeface and ornament)

Designed by Peter Behrens
Page layout and title page from a typefoundry booklet
1902

At its broadest, design of typefaces for the foundries involved the interpretations of three basic categories. Revisions of 15th- and 16th-century Roman designs were generically called Antiqua. New Blackletter designs under two main kinds, Schwabacher and Fraktur, were collectively known as Gothic in English or Blackletter in American. Thirdly, newly conceived 'germanicized' Roman scripts, a group distinctive to Germany, took the basic Roman letter forms and inflected them with Gothic features.

Whereas the Roman typeface was associated with the Catholic Church and used in the majority of other parts of Europe, Blackletter and the Hybrid Gothic-Roman scripts maintained their significance for Germany. The essential character of Fraktur, the script for book and press typography since the first printed books in the Protestant German-speaking countries, originated in the marks of feather and quill. By contrast, Roman typeforms were based on the inscription of letters according to abstract geometrical proportions. These were considered as an alternative and sometimes 'unGerman' tradition. Questions concerning hand- versus machine-setting, discussed in Arts and Crafts circles across Europe, took on a further complication in Germany. It was implied that Fraktur letterforms,

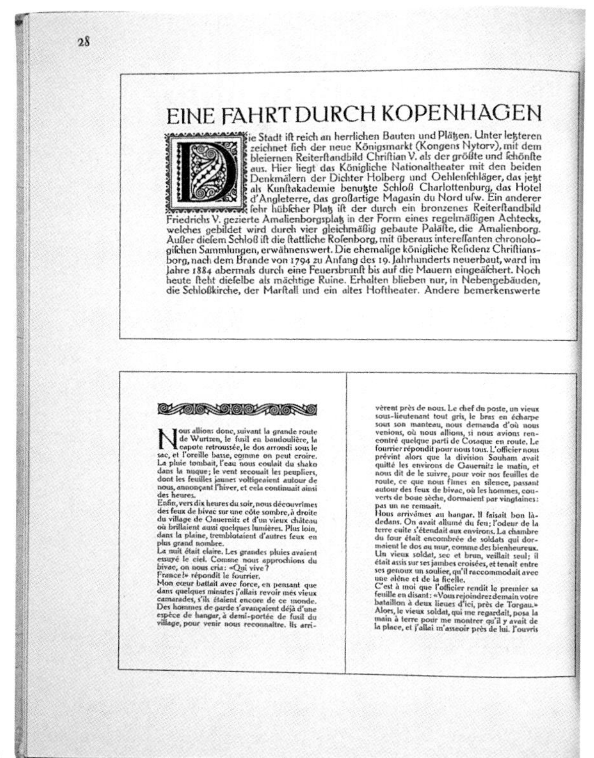

28

EINE FAHRT DURCH KOPENHAGEN

Die Stadt iſt reich an herrlichen Bauten und Plätzen. Unter letzteren zeichnet ſich der neue Königsmarkt (Kongens Nytorv), mit dem bleiernen Reiterſtandbild Chriſtian V. als der größte und ſchönſte aus. Hier liegt das Königliche Nationaltheater mit den beiden Denkmälern der Dichter Holberg und Oehlenſchläger, das jetzt als Kunſtakademie benutzte Schloß Charlottenburg, das Hotel d'Angleterre, das großartige Magasin du Nord uſw. Ein anderer ſehr hübſcher Platz iſt der durch ein bronzenes Reiterſtandbild Friedrichs V. gezierte Amalienborgsplatz in der Form eines regelmäßigen Achtecks, welches gebildet wird durch vier gleichmäßig gebaute Paläſte, die Amalienborg. Außer dieſem Schloß iſt die ſtattliche Roſenborg, mit überaus intereſſanten chronologiſchen Sammlungen, erwähnenswert. Die ehemalige königliche Reſidenz Chriſtiansborg, nach dem Brande von 1794 zu Anfang des 19. Jahrhunderts neuerbaut, ward im Jahre 1884 abermals durch eine Feuersbrunſt bis auf die Mauern eingeäſchert. Noch heute ſteht dieſelbe als mächtige Ruine. Erhalten blieben nur, in Nebengebäuden, die Schloßkirche, der Marſtall und ein altes Hoftheater. Andere bemerkenswerte

Nous allions donc, suivant la grande route de Wurtzen, le fusil en bandoulière, la capote retroussée, le dos arrondi sous le sac, et l'oreille basse, comme on peut croire. La pluie tombait, l'eau nous coulait du shako dans la nuque; le vent secouait les peupliers, dont les feuilles jaunes voltigeaient autour de nous, annonçant l'hiver, et cela continuait ainsi des heures.
Enfin, vers dix heures du soir, nous découvrîmes des feux de bivac sur une côte sombre, à droite du village de Gauernitz et d'un vieux château où brillaient aussi quelques lumières. Plus loin, dans la plaine, tremblotaient d'autres feux en plus grand nombre.
La nuit était claire. Les grandes pluies avaient essuyé le ciel. Comme nous approchions du bivac, on nous cria: «Qui vive?
France!» répondit le fourrier.
Mon cœur battait avec force, en pensant que dans quelques minutes j'allais revoir mes vieux camarades, s'ils étaient encore de ce monde. Des hommes de garde s'avançaient déjà d'une espèce de hangar, à demi-portée de fusil du village, pour venir nous reconnaître. Ils arrivèrent près de nous. Le chef du poste, un vieux sous-lieutenant tout gris, le bras en écharpe sous son manteau, nous demanda d'où nous venions, où nous allions, si nous avions rencontré quelque parti de Cosaque en route. Le fourrier répondit pour nous tous. L'officier nous prévint alors que la division Souham avait quitté les environs de Gauernitz le matin, et nous dit de le suivre, pour voir nos feuilles de route, ce que nous fîmes en silence, passant autour des feux de bivac, où les hommes, couverts de boue sèche, dormaient par vingtaines: pas un ne remuait.
Nous arrivâmes au hangar. Il faisait bon là-dedans. On avait allumé du feu; l'odeur de la terre cuite s'étendait aux environs. La chambre du four était encombrée de soldats qui dormaient le dos au mur, comme des bienheureux. Un vieux soldat, sec et brun, veillait seul; il était assis sur ses jambes croisées, et tenait entre ses genoux un soulier, qu'il raccommodait avec une alêne et de la ficelle.
C'est à moi que l'officier rendit le premier sa feuille en disant: «Vous rejoindrez demain votre bataillon à deux lieues d'ici, près de Torgau.» Alors, le vieux soldat, qui me regardait, posa la main à terre pour me montrer qu'il y avait de la place, et j'allai m'asseoir près de lui. J'ouvris

1.9

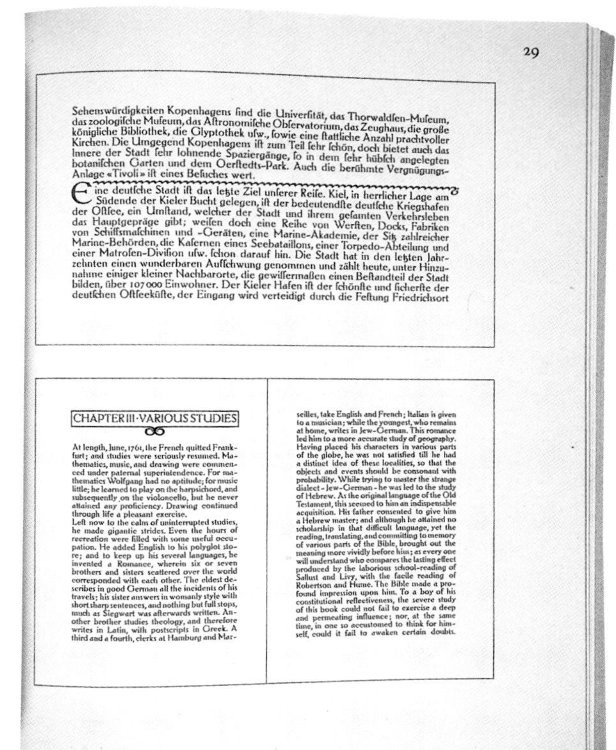

29

Sehenswürdigkeiten Kopenhagens ſind die Univerſität, das Thorwaldſen-Muſeum, das zoologiſche Muſeum, das Aſtronomiſche Obſervatorium, das Zeughaus, die große königliche Bibliothek, die Glyptothek uſw., ſowie eine ſtattliche Anzahl prachtvoller Kirchen. Die Umgegend Kopenhagens iſt zum Teil ſehr ſchön, doch bietet auch das Innere der Stadt ſehr lohnende Spaziergänge, ſo in dem ſehr hübſch angelegten botaniſchen Garten und dem Oerſtedts-Park. Auch die berühmte Vergnügungs-Anlage «Tivoli» iſt eines Beſuches wert.

Eine deutſche Stadt iſt das letzte Ziel unſerer Reiſe. Kiel, in herrlicher Lage am Südende der Kieler Bucht gelegen, iſt der bedeutendſte deutſche Kriegshafen der Oſtſee, ein Umſtand, welcher der Stadt und ihrem geſamten Verkehrsleben das Hauptgepräge gibt; weiſen doch eine Reihe von Werften, Docks, Fabriken von Schiffsmaſchinen und -Geräten, eine Marine-Akademie, der Sitz zahlreicher Marine-Behörden, die Kaſernen eines Seebataillons, einer Torpedo-Abteilung und einer Matroſen-Diviſion uſw. ſchon darauf hin. Die Stadt hat in den letzten Jahrzehnten einen wunderbaren Aufſchwung genommen und zählt heute, unter Hinzunahme einiger kleiner Nachbarorte, die gewiſſermaßen einen Beſtandteil der Stadt bilden, über 107000 Einwohner. Der Kieler Hafen iſt der ſchönſte und ſicherſte der deutſchen Oſtſeeküſte, der Eingang wird verteidigt durch die Feſtung Friedrichsort

CHAPTER III · VARIOUS STUDIES

At length, June, 1761, the French quitted Frankfurt; and studies were seriously resumed. Mathematics, music, and drawing were commenced under paternal superintendence. For mathematics Wolfgang had no aptitude; for music little; he learned to play on the harpsichord, and subsequently on the violoncello, but he never attained any proficiency. Drawing continued through life a pleasant exercise.
Left now to the calm of uninterrupted studies, he made gigantic strides. Even the hours of recreation were filled with some useful occupation. He added English to his polyglot store; and to keep up his several languages, he invented a Romance, wherein six or seven brothers and sisters scattered over the world corresponded with each other. The eldest describes in good German all the incidents of his travels; his sister answers in womanly style with short sharp sentences, and nothing but full stops, much as Siegwart was afterwards written. Another brother studies theology, and therefore writes in Latin, with postscripts in Greek. A third and a fourth, clerks at Hamburg and Marseilles, take English and French; Italian is given to a musician; while the youngest, who remains at home, writes in Jew-German. This romance led him to a more accurate study of geography. Having placed his characters in various parts of the globe, he was not satisfied till he had a distinct idea of these localities, so that the objects and events should be consonant with probability. While trying to master the strange dialect - Jew-German - he was led to the study of Hebrew. As the original language of the Old Testament, this seemed to him an indispensable acquisition. His father consented to give him a Hebrew master; and although he attained no scholarship in that difficult language, yet the reading, translating, and committing to memory of various parts of the Bible, brought out the meaning more vividly before him; as every one will understand who compares the lasting effect produced by the laborious school-reading of Sallust and Livy, with the facile reading of Robertson and Hume. The Bible made a profound impression upon him. To a boy of his constitutional reflectiveness, the severe study of this book could not fail to exercise a deep and permeating influence; nor, at the same time, in one so accustomed to think for himself, could it fail to awaken certain doubts.

1.10

even when mechanized, were closer to their roots in the freehand gesture of scribes, and associations were made between expressive calligraphy and national character.[9]

As in Britain and the USA, the major technical change for type foundries in Germany was the introduction of the autotype system. This allowed type-setting to be carried out by a printer or publisher with a body of type founts operated by a machine-setter at a keyboard, equipped with components for use on site. Previously, a printer had turned to the type foundry to supply suitable amounts of a particular type for hand-setting in a more bespoke way. The first application of Linotype was for the *New York Tribune* in 1886, while Lanston's Monotype was introduced in the USA in 1897. It was not until after 1918 that real inroads in mechanical composition were made in Germany.[10]

The implication of autotype was that the overall demand for complete typefaces could be diminished, as the printer established a collection of representative styles with the aim of using them cost-effectively for a variety of jobs. Economies of scale encouraged holding a restricted number of full families of type. Consequently, competition between type foundries became fierce, with full-page advertisements

BEHRENS-ANTIQUA
UND SCHMUCK VON
PROF. PETER BEHRENS

GEBR·KLINGSPOR IN
OFFENBACH A·MAIN

1.11

frequently appearing in the graphics and printing press in the hope of increasing domestic and foreign markets.

Principal foundries which played their part in the changes in design for publication by commissioning prolific new type designs included Bauer, Klingspor and Stempel clustered together around Frankfurt and Offenbach am Main; Berthold in Berlin; Weber in Stuttgart; Schelter and Giesecke in Leipzig; and Genzsch and Heyse in Hamburg. Among the first designers, a combination of specifically trained typographers and more general architects and designers, were Peter Behrens, Otto Eckmann, F.H. Ehmcke, Rudolf Koch, Paul Renner, F.H. Ernst Schneidler, Walter Tiemann and Emil Rudolf Weiss. Designs were promoted in specimen-type booklets, through which a language of description and evaluation developed. Competition between foundries was usually based on claims for the quality of the type cast, the number of versions in the type family and the possibilities of their application. The assertion of designers' names in the typeface titles reveals that design had become one of the distinguishing features. Fluid boundaries between typefaces intended for setting books and other applications were noticed as a particular German characteristic. As one commentator retrospectively remarked: 'These designers were encouraged to experiment and develop designs for new uses in publicity which were a stimulating and creative influence in typography when there were few fresh letter designs appearing in other European countries, or in America.'[11]

Another reviewer, Rudolf Conrad, pointed out how it was acceptable for graphic artists in Germany to be commissioned to design type to be translated by the type foundry rather than strictly a typographer.[12] Conrad opened his review by considering the typeface 'Eckmann' of 1900, which he dismissed as too personal and inflected with *Jugendstil.* On the other hand, he considered 'Behrens' script of 1902 severe and *sachlich*, a term often used at the time, suitably translated as 'objective'. He also favoured Behrens's 'Antiqua', a Roman typeface of 1908 and Ehmcke's 1910 'Antique'.

1.12 

1.12
Majestic typeface

Designed by Julius Gipkens
Typefoundry booklet
About 1910

1.13

1.14

Conrad's review is typical in its concern to bridge economic, technical and aesthetic questions; but underlying his commentary was something more fundamental. What was a German tradition and how could it be reconciled with international trends?

1.13 'The comparison speaks for the light accuracy of Spectral inks' for the printing company Kast und Ehinger, Stuttgart

Advertisement
1930

1.14 Advertisement for Cröllwitzer paper factory in Halle-Cröllwitz

Designed by Franz Paul Glass
1930

Further Technical Change

As well as holding a prominent position for its foundries and printers, Germany could claim the discovery of lithography, which was the major medium for the colour reproduction of works of art in popular prints and later for posters. The process was invented by Alois Senefelder in Munich between 1796 and 1799, whereas colour techniques were developed in Paris only after 1835. Considerable advances were made in the kinds of lithographic presses available and their output increased enormously in the late 19th century. Initially each colour required a separate stone, making the process expensive and arduous. Replacing the original lithographic stone and flat hand-presses by metal plates and mechanized rotary presses reduced material costs. The new offset presses, which used rubber plates with a reversed image applied to them that rotated while paper received the print at great speed, were the most widespread source of mechanized colour images in the 1920s.

With most of the necessary print technologies in place to provide a swift and effective communications industry, expectations of speed increased in adjacent technologies. Electrification in the 1880s, for instance, led to inventions in lighting, which in turn had an impact on photomechanical reproduction and object photography. Telegraphic communications and air transport became essential for rapid exchange and distribution between advertising and photographic agencies across the continents in the '20s. Paper manufacture, too, was highly developed in Germany and in these years there was an increasing diversification in special treatments of coating, foiling and embossing varieties of paper for prestigious publications and packaging for the display of branded goods in many areas of retail. Accompanying these developments were those in the dyestuff, pigment and ink industries. In the last years of the 19th century, technical experimentation in fixing new chemical dyes made unusual choices of ink colours available to printers and designers, and this resulted in the creation of striking designs.[13]

The spirit of new discoveries is evident in the proliferation of places where work came to be seen. Beyond the more conventional areas of works on paper, this could be in enamel and mirrored signs, decorated light shades, illuminated signage, neon sign-writing, as well as painted advertisements on gable-ends. To these can be added the more extraordinary attempts to claim the public's attention in the form of airborne advertisements, flags, balloons and airships, in addition to fancy-dress processions, decorations and handbills used during the frequent advertising fairs in major cities.

Celebration or Reform?

By the dawn of the 20th century there were two broad responses to this enlarging of the German print industries. The first was to embrace enthusiastically the

Tafel 12

Wir können einem Widerspruch in uns selbst nicht entgehen; wir müssen ihn auszugleichen suchen. Wenn uns andere widersprechen, das geht uns nichts an, das ist ihre Sache.

Wahrheitsliebe zeigt sich darin, dass man überall das Gute zu finden und zu schützen weiss.

Koch, Klassische Schriften. Schrift von William Morris. In Deutschland herausgegeben von Wilhelm Woellmers Schriftgießerei, Berlin. Verlag von Gerhard Kühtmann, Dresden.

1.15

extended possibilities provided by the interplay between design, commerce and technology. Compared with other forms of design, print lent itself to a quickly changing and relatively inexpensive expression of the abundance of goods in the market. Accompanying the growth of the big cities and the market for mass-circulation publications, the foundries expanded the varieties of type and ornament. A demand for novel techniques in print form, whether for illustrations or text in advertisements, magazines and newspapers, was answered by engineers, technicians and designers.

In response to such technical riches, professional associations were formed for the many subdivisions of the industry. An important example was the Deutsche Buchgewerbeverein, an association representing the German book trade, which promoted the range of activities the book trade could offer and regulated standards through its journal, the *Archiv für Buchgewerbe*.

As well as promoting regional meetings and congresses, the specialist trade literature disseminated news about the latest styles or techniques and encouraged international reviews. Like many journals concerned to raise standards of a profession, the *Archiv für Buchgewerbe* published examples of historical and contemporary specimens, and through this selection a canon emerged of what the printing industry recognized as good practice. This in turn had implications for collections and museums. Accompanying such articles were many advertisements testifying to the printers' innovations and their capabilities for larger, faster or more colourful products. It was understandable that such professionalizing bodies erred on the side of caution when it came to aesthetic preference, since they sought to curb the more extreme excesses of commerce. For them, conservative taste, a recognition of skill and respect for hierarchy, were inevitably the way forward.

If the contemporary character of mainstream German print culture derived from a technically driven fascination for special effects, a second broad tendency among articulate reformers was expressed as a concern for an appropriate level of taste and professionalism in industry and a culture of restraint. In contrast to

1.16

1.15 William Morris's Jenson typeface illustrated in *Rudolf Koch, Klassische Schriften nach Zeichnungen von Gutenberg, Dürer, Morris, König, Hupp, Eckmann, Behrens, u.a..* n.d.

1.16 *Deutsche Buchgewerbe Ausstellung, Paris 1900* (Catalogue of the German Book Trades Exhibition)

Designed by Johann Vincenz Cissarz
1900

1.17

1.18

1.17 Opening page of the journal *Pan*

Illustrated by Joseph Sattler
1895 v.1 No.1

1.18 *Ver Sacrum* (Sacred Spring)

Cover
January 1898

1.19 *Archiv für Buchgewerbe* (Archive for Book Trades)

Cover
January 1900

the readiness to embrace new fashions in the print industries, the teaching at the Arts and Crafts schools took the form of a resistance or denial of fashion. William Morris and his followers advocated the renewal of handicrafts and workshop practice, in which printing held an important place, and they formed a common source for this alternative point of view. The medievalizing aesthetic of the British Arts and Crafts reformers ran counter to the tendencies within the technical industries where stylistic illusionism, allegorical representation and highly decorative work were often favoured to allow for virtuoso technique to be shown to the full.[14]

In part a reaction to the perceived superfluity of choice for the book and graphic arts in England, Morris and his contemporary T. J. Cobden Sanderson recommended a return to earlier models of production. This culminated in their founding of the Kelmscott Press in 1891, and the subsequent flurry of private presses established shortly afterwards encouraged small-scale production by

1.19

means of hand-composition, a revival of illumination in capitals and the use of woodcut illustrations. The reform of type, drawing on early Renaissance sources, was one appropriate way to revive what were seen as lost values in printing design. While the writings of Morris were available in the libraries of the Arts and Crafts schools in Europe, the next generation of English designers, including Walter Crane, Anna Simons and Edward Johnston, visited Germany in the 1900s, often meeting their German counterparts, exhibiting works and extending the message of reform.

As a result of this exchange, several workshops run by architects and designers were founded in Germany to promote artistic manufacture along the lines of their English precedents. Among the most significant of these were the Munich-based Vereinigte Werkstätten für Kunst im Handwerk (United Workshops for Art in Handicraft) begun in 1897 and the Dresdner Werkstätten für Handwerkerkunst (Dresden Workshops for the Arts and Crafts) started a year later. Their exhibitions indicate an early interest in the graphic arts. In the International Fine Arts Exhibition at the Glaspalast, the inaugural display of the Munich group, the emphasis was on the decorative arts for the home: furniture, metalwork, ceramics and glass. Graphic arts were included in the designs of programmes, catalogues and posters, as well as illustrated magazines, a mixture of the new aesthetic and graphic satire. The first workshop to address book and graphic design more fully was the Steglitzer Werkstatt in Berlin, led by Fritz Ehmcke.

As Kathryn Hiesinger has suggested, when it came to the transference of Morrisian ideals, German design reformers did not necessarily share Morris's Socialist outlook. Instead, the workshops tried to combine artistic ideals with commercial profitability and a more realistic balance between handicraft and industrial products was apparent.[15] Whereas Morris had criticized large-scale industrial organizations for pursuing novel effects for financial or commercial reward, allowing alienation between the worker and the product, the next generation of designers in Germany perceived less contradiction in addressing hand- and machine-made goods at the same time. For the typographic and graphic arts, this more flexible attitude made it possible to run a private press for limited-edition work and at the same time design typefaces for major foundries. These could be applied to designs in all manner of commercial and industrial contexts beyond the immediate control of designers. This second path led to the opinion that art and commerce were complementary rather than conflicting.

Significant graphic work was carried out in the early years in Munich in the circle around Julius Meier-Graefe, especially by Peter Behrens and Otto Eckmann. It was at this stage that Behrens conceived his relatively free and organic style in response to Art Nouveau. This was consciously a new style, known in German as *Jugendstil* (literally 'the style of youth'), named after the Munich-based journal *Jugend* which ran from 1896 to 1914. *Ver Sacrum* in Vienna, *Pan* and *Simplicissimus* in Berlin were other journals that contributed to the popularity of the style.[16] Graphic artists were responsible for the embellishment of the journals in the form of decorated initials and borders, and from this eventually evolved a desire to create complete typefaces. Woodcuts produced to form illustrations in the periodicals, often with sources in Symbolist poetry, were also sold to private print collectors in portfolios of limited editions.

The Munich United Workshops marked the city's identity as a centre for figurative illustration, which culminated in the poster art of Ludwig Hohlwein. Besides a self-consciously modern style, many illustrators also turned their hands to neo-Renaissance embellishments derived from 16th-century book title pages and behind-glass paintings which were a specifically South German tradition. Such approaches associated Munich with a soft, lyrical and often humorous style which was generally less hard-hitting than the work originating in Berlin.[17]

Recognition for the Graphic Arts

In addition to the independent art workshops, museums and teaching institutes were crucial to the formation of a convincing lobby for reform of the Arts and

1.20

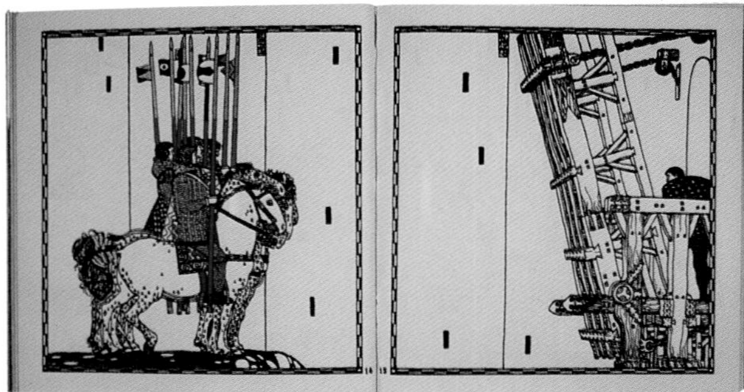

1.21

1.22

Crafts throughout Europe. The leading example, which had great influence on the emergence of similar organizations in many parts of central Europe, was the School of Design in London founded in 1837 and the South Kensington Museum, established by Henry Cole under the encouragement of Prince Albert in 1853.[18] Many of the initial difficulties concerning the balance between teaching principles of design as opposed to the fine arts would linger for the next generations. For example, how should the conventional hierarchy between the fine and decorative arts be challenged? How might designers for industry be taught and drawing skills relate to the wider requirements of industrial manufacture?

Distinct from the academies of fine art, the teaching institutes attached to the museums trained designers and handworkers in the graphic arts and book arts alongside textiles, engraving, glass, ceramics and woodwork. This followed the categorization by material initially recommended by the German architect Gottfried Semper for the organization of the South Kensington Museum. These categories were also used to establish collections which provided a reference in the training of the students of design. The South Kensington emphasis on acquiring near-contemporary objects for instruction was initially followed in Vienna, when in 1864 the Imperial Royal Museum for Art and Industry (Kaiserliches-Königliches Österreichisches Museum für Kunst und Industrie) under Director Eitelberger formed much of its original collection of objects from the 1862 London Great Exhibition and where a School of Applied Arts was established in 1867. In Berlin, the Kunstgewerbemuseum began in 1867 as a private foundation and in 1879 it became the Royal Arts and Crafts Museum (Königliches Kunstgewerbemuseum) and promoted regional museums through the donation of objects. Regional capitals like Hamburg, Dresden, Düsseldorf, Nuremburg and Munich subsequently opened Arts and Crafts museums with the responsibility of collecting and displaying appropriate and exemplary objects for the academies, technical high schools and gymnasia. The purpose of the museums was not restricted just to teaching the next generations; they were also dedicated to

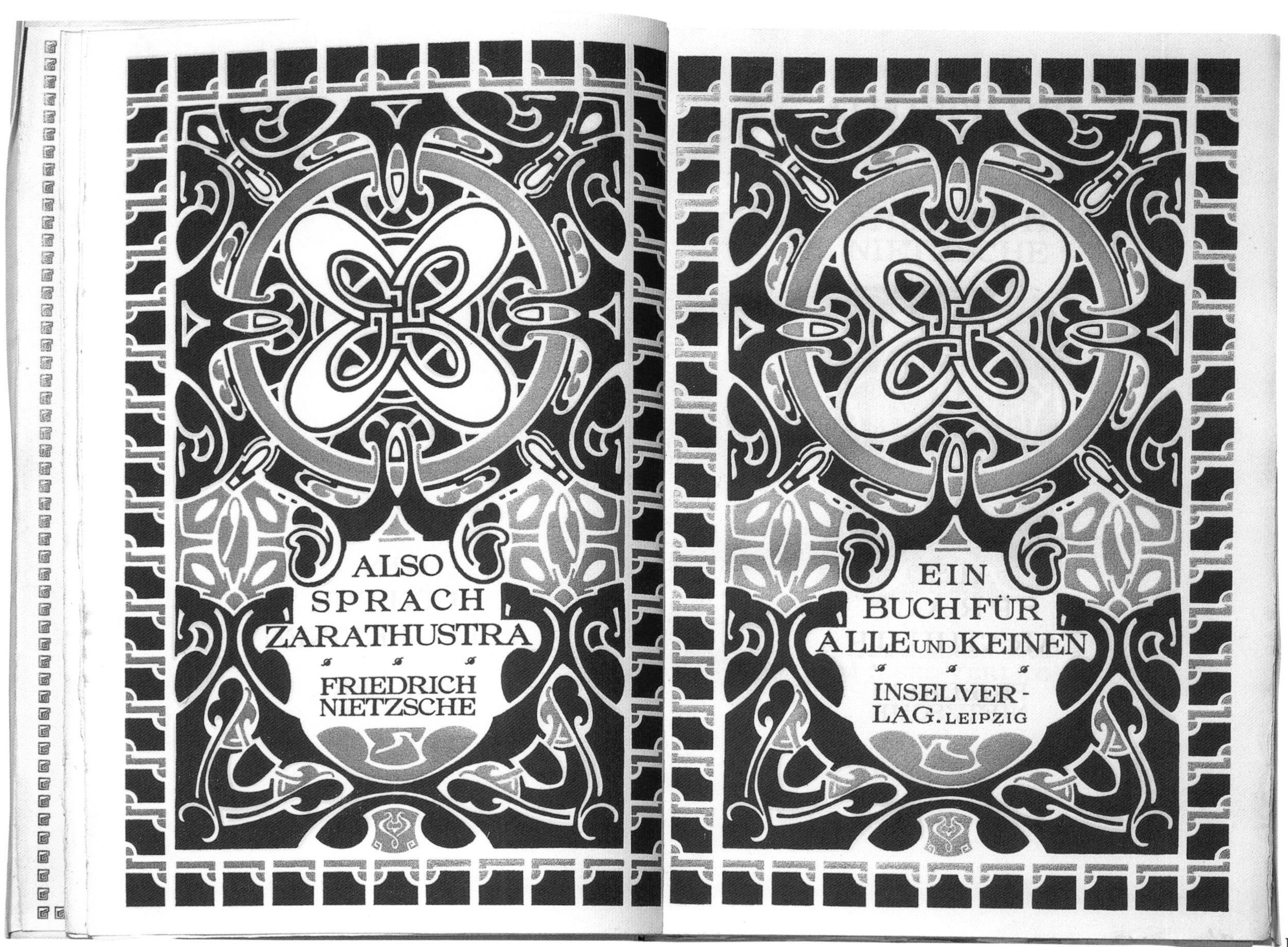

1.23

the encouragement of 'good taste' among the influential owners of industry, although exactly what this was proved a major point of debate.

A fundamental part of the artistic philosophy of that generation stemmed from a belief in the *Gesamtkunstwerk*, the total work of art, in which appropriate formal and stylistic principles were applied across media. This concept was derived from the writings of the philosopher Friedrich Nietzsche, who considered that the aim of the artist and designer should be the complete aesthetic environment. The realization of such a scheme could be operatic in the case of the performing arts – most famously in the case of the composer Richard Wagner. As for interior design and architecture, the villa formed an ideal scale, although more

1.20 *Richard Strauss Woche* (Richard Strauss Week)

Designed by Ludwig Hohlwein
Poster
1910

1.21–1.22 *Die Nibelungen dem deutschen Volke wiedererzählt von Franz Keim* (The Nibelungen retold to the German People by Franz Keim)

Designed by Carl Otto Czeschka
Two double pages
1909

1.23 *Also sprach Zarathustra: ein Buch für Alle und Keinen* (Thus Spoke Zarathustra: a book for all and for none)

Written by Friedrich Nietzsche
Designed by Henry van de Velde
Book
1908

complex plans for garden-city suburbs also evolved. Consequently, these years saw a mounting interest in the aesthetic interior under the heading of 'the house beautiful' (*das schöne Heim*). The equivalent for the graphic arts was the beautiful book (*das schöne Buch*), elevated by its association with all the other arts to an object of contemplation.

This generation of book artists created many prestigious showpieces, destined for bibliophile collections within aesthetic interiors or to be displayed at the universal exhibitions. Among them, the works of Henry van de Velde are distinctive in the attention given to every detail and the recognition they received from contemporaries. A Belgian by birth, van de Velde spent the majority of his time between 1902 and 1917 in Weimar where, as well as being the Professor of the School of Applied Arts, he designed books for Harry Graf Kessler and the Insel Verlag. An example of the book beautiful was the volume *Also Sprach Zarathustra: ein Buch für Alle und Keinen* of 1908. The legend for the book indicates the meticulous stages taken towards its realization: 'For this edition of Zarathustra the script was drawn by G. Lemmen and cut with the collaboration of Harry Graf Kessler. Henry van de Velde designed the heading, half-title, decoration and binding and oversaw it on press.'[19]

As well as such prestigious designs, van de Velde also turned his hand to a variety of graphic projects, most famously the house-style for Tropon, an egg-white cooking preparation, which was celebrated as the first *Jugendstil* commercial commission for an everyday product. The posters and accompanying packaging, stationery and labels employed variations of the same distinctive rhythmic lines defining open and closed forms in characteristic *Jugendstil* fashion.[20]

While it is worth stressing how much of the initial interest in the new aesthetic of *Jugendstil* came from an elegant élite whose concern was largely addressed to the domestic sphere of their own kind (crucially, in the German context), it is also important to recognize how soon this moved to embrace artistic consideration applied to objects of industrial manufacture. As one commentator observed,

'England does not know the notion of the Buchkünstler, of a master who in Germany has the task to make a unity of binding, type, and paper. The influence of the printing craftsman was restrained and the bibliophile book came into fashion. Not only costly editions and private prints, but also average novels decorated graphically.'[21]

The Arts and Crafts museums became the venue for launching principles of letter reform, and several moves were made to interpret the graphic arts and elevate their status. For example, under the inspiration of Alfred Lichtwark, the Director of the Hamburg Arts and Crafts Museum, Justus Brinckmann, held the first German poster exhibition in 1893. Three years later, the Berlin Art Library, attached to the city's Arts and Crafts Museum, began its collection of posters.[22] Also, in an unusual step for its day, Jean-Louis Sponsel, a pupil of Max Lehrs, the Director of the the Print Collection at Dresden Applied Arts Museum, adapted the usual conventions of the historical print archive to the more modern medium of the poster.

It was in the context of these lofty ideas that moves to teach design for publication were also made. Students in the graphic art classes at the Arts and Crafts schools before 1914 were often taught lettering, drawing and ornament. The work followed specific tasks, set by masters, who were often professors. The tradition was to have students copy historical examples of ornament and lettering, and to evolve new designs of composite patterns, whether for packaging, posters, smaller advertisements or trademarks. As well as decorative and commercial design, there was usually a separate class in which students could learn elements of *Buchgewerbe*, which included hand-rendering letterforms, page layout, initial decoration and selecting materials for binding. Once understood, ornament could be applied as surface pattern in what was still very much a paper exercise. At this time, a knowledge of drawing ornament could lead to its application in stamped and pressed metal for radiator-covers, screens or other decorative panels, just as much as in a binding, bookcover or title page.[23]

1.24 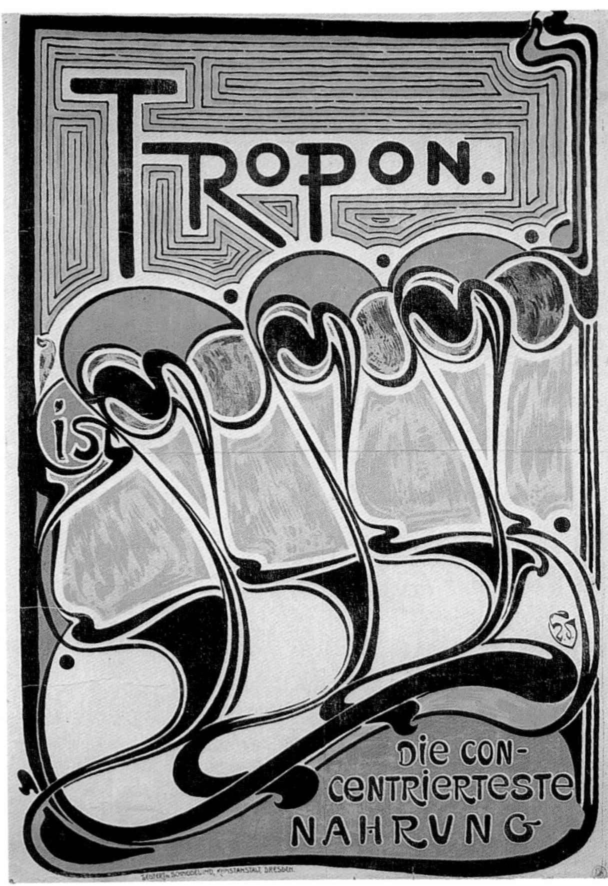

1.25 

1.24 *Tropon, Eiweiss Nährung* (Tropon egg-white preparation)

Designed by Henry van de Velde
Poster
1897

1.25 Photograph of a shop window with a display of Tropon goods about 1900.

Most student work in these classes was on paper, in inks and gouache, and usually would not be taken to the reproduction stage. Access to printing equipment in the schools was rare and this lack was central to the criticism mounted by representatives of the Werkstatt movement during the pre-war years. They argued that students should learn practical as well as drawing skills, on the premise that the style of approach should reflect processes. A major aim was that historicism could be avoided through a knowledge of materials or techniques and a 'style for the age', a modern style, would thus result.

Although this was voiced as an ideal, there was frequently a separation between those trained with highly developed aesthetic skills in the Arts and Crafts schools and the knowledgeable technicians in industry. In practice, the training for apprentices and operators in the printing industry was provided by the technical trade schools (Fachhochschulen) and technical high schools (Technischehochschulen), which consequently separated art from technology. Many working in the book trades, for example, were taught in evening classes and formed the category of the 'art proletariat', as they were known at the time.

The 1880s and 1890s were unsettled decades for the guilds and the hierarchy of training in Germany. The traditional three-tiered system of apprentice, journeyman and master had been disbanded in the 1870s under the change to mechanization and larger units of industry. Responsibility for the future expertise of the work force passed to large employers and the State training system. As Shulamit Volkov has shown, in the crisis of the ensuing 'apprentice question', many small-scale workshops were reluctant to subsidize the training of junior staff.[24] The separation between the skilled craftsman (*Handwerker*) and designer was reinforced with, at worst, risk of an aesthetically uneducated workforce and technically uneducated designers. This was a constant issue that subsequent generations would also address.

1.26

1.26 Cover to the 1916 volume of *Das Plakat*

Designed by Lucian Bernhard

1.27

240 DAS MODERNE PLAKAT

Eckrampe einer hohen Mauer den Genius der Kunst, dessen Fackel vor der dunklen Nacht des Hintergrundes hell leuchtet. Ein Relieffries zeigt ein antikes Wettrennen, wohl als symbolische Andeutung des künstlerischen Wettbewerbs der Ausstellung, die übrige Fläche der Mauer aber ist von der Schrift bedeckt, und zwar von Druckschrift und nicht, wie man als stilgerechter empfunden hätte, von eingemeisselter Schrift. Doch ist immerhin noch an der Schrift zu rühmen, dass sie in deutlich lesbaren lateinischen Lettern gehalten ist, und dass das Wichtigste durch die Grösse der Buchstaben so ausgezeichnet wurde, dass es auch auf einige Entfernung hin noch leicht erkennbar sein musste. Während das Plakat von Gysis in Bild und Schrift doch noch den Charakter der Monumentalität bewahrt, kann das Gleiche von dem Plakat von Rudolph Seitz nicht gesagt werden; doch davon später. Gysis lieferte im Jahre 1892 wiederum einen Plakatentwurf für die Sechste grosse internationale Kunstausstellung in München, der von der Firma Meisenbach, Riffarth & Co. autotypisch vervielfältigt wurde. Um ihn farbig nachzubilden, wurden anfangs hierzu etwa neun Clichésplatten verwendet, in den späteren Jahren wurde dann dasselbe Plakat einfarbig mit nur zwei Clichésplatten angefertigt, ohne dass es dadurch in seiner Wirkung etwas eingebüsst hätte. Das Plakat zeigt dasselbe Kompositionsschema, wie das für Rudolph Ibach Sohn gelieferte: das obere Rundfeld des Hochformates enthält das Bild, darunter wurde für die Verbreitung in den verschiedenen Ländern jedesmal in anderer Sprache die immer noch ziemlich umfangreiche Schrift aufgedruckt. In Deutschland hat sich am längsten die Gewohnheit bei den Künstlern erhalten, Bild und Schrift voneinander zu trennen, man ist darin einerseits von bestimmten Kompositionsgrundsätzen abhängig gewesen, anderseits mag auch eine gewisse Scheu die Künstler davon abgehalten haben, die künstlerische Wirkung des Bildes durch den Aufdruck der Schrift zu stören. Doch lehrt das Beispiel

Nikolaus Gysis

SPONSEL, DAS MODERNE PLAKAT

FRANZ STUCK

VERLAG VON GERHARD KÜHTMANN, DRESDEN
Reprod. C.C. Meinhold & Söhne, Dresden

1.27 Jean Louis Sponsel, *Das Moderne Plakat* (The Modern Poster)

Book
1897

The Poster Movement

In 1896 the art historian Julius Meier-Graefe announced that 'The poster has become fashionable: artists, art-lovers and museums collect them.'[25] In many respects, the poster was the most publicly visible testimony to the increased interest in the graphic arts. However, in the sequence of recognition given to different countries for the visual strength, novelty and vitality of their posters, Germany appeared relatively late. Originally the centre for poster activity was Paris, because to be French at this time meant to be highly fashionable. The French capital was perceived as an artistic Mecca, a place where galleries devoted to the graphic arts were supported by critics who celebrated an avant-garde. It was also the source of a model of specialist art criticism in the *petites revues*, such as *Les Maîtres de l'Affiche*. Attempts were made to adopt such an idea of cultural activity in Germany when Munich, Berlin and Düsseldorf consciously aspired to the status of art cities.

Whereas French posters were characterized in the specialist literature by their imaginative combination of word and image which celebrated the autographic quality of an individual artist's style, German posters were perceived as more matter-of-fact in their approach. Writers on the graphic arts quickly distinguished the work by the new Arts and Crafts reformers from the more prolific eclectic and historicist commercial designs of everyday life. In turn, the new designs attracted the attention of museum curators, and publications followed. The first German book on posters, for example, was *Das Moderne Plakat* by the Dresden curator Jean Louis Sponsel, published in 1897.[26]

1.28

1.28 Photograph of the young Hans Sachs in his 'student den', Berlin 1901.

This book took the form of an international review with the largest section, as might have been expected, devoted to France. Interestingly, it opened with a small section on Japanese graphic arts, acknowledging that many subsequent design developments in the West were indebted to them. Reinforcing the idea that the modern poster was derived from France, German commentaries on posters of the period often began with examples from Jules Chéret and Henri Toulouse-Lautrec. They then turned to the Viennese Secessionists. Many also illustrated works of the Beggarstaff Brothers, as the partnership of James Pryde and William Nicholson was known. Charles Rennie Mackintosh and the Glasgow School, and William H. Bradley of the USA were also invariably included. All artists were assumed to be 'modernizing' the poster by common strategies of reference to Japanese compositional devices, simplification of form and colour, and harmony of lettering and image.

Immediately issues arose in this book which would become constant preoccupations in the justification of graphic design against hostile criticism. Sponsel suggested, for instance, that the modern poster was the most effective means of educating the general public in the new art, the embryo of the idea of the 'art gallery of the public' so often promoted in commentaries. The need for posters

1.29

1.29 *Scholle Muenchen, XXV. Ausstellung der Secession* [The artists' group] Scholle Munich, 25th exhibition of the Secession

Designed by Adolf Münzer
Poster
1905

1.30 *Deutscher Werkbund Ausstellung, Ortsgruppe Crefeld* (German Werkbund Exhibition, Krefeld local branch)

Designed by
Fritz Hellmut Ehmcke
Poster
1911

1.31 *Deutsche Werkbund Ausstellung Coeln, Jos. Feinhals*

Packaging designed by
Fritz Hellmut Ehmcke
Tobacco box
1913–14

to capture the distracted look of the viewer against competing attractions of the urban environment became another constant theme, revealing a fascination with a city's modern qualities and the poster's potential contribution to this.

A Berlin Collector

One of the most prominent promoters of the poster as a new art form was Dr Hans Sachs, a Berlin dentist, who established the Verein der Plakatfreunde (Association of Friends of the Poster) in 1905.[27] He was also a leading figure behind the journal *Das Plakat* which started publication in 1910. The journal encouraged connections with poster societies in other parts of the world and provided thematic surveys of genres of posters, reviews of individual poster artists and guidance on how to collect, store or display them. Initially each issue carried a list of posters available from artist members of the journal, indicating that as well as a public medium for advertising events or goods, the art poster was originally conceived as a collector's item. At this stage, the subject-matter of this group of posters largely concerned theatre, music and literature, more than mainstream commercial manufacture. A much contested issue in *Das Plakat* was whether the poster was a new art form and whether it should be exhibited in galleries like fine art.

Sachs extended an approach learned from Parisian circles to the capital of the German art world, through a programme of exhibitions, lectures and publications from a house equipped with purpose-built storage in the well-to-do Berlin suburb of Nikolassee. The dates of the association's formation and dissolution, 1905 and 1922, indicate the highpoints of the German poster movement. Members were art lovers, collectors, academics and museum directors, as well as designers themselves, including the most prominent of their day, Lucian Bernhard, Julius Klinger and Ludwig Hohlwein. After a slow start, the association became a significant force: by 1906 it had grown to 84 members and by 1914 1,293 were recorded. Sachs was generous with his collection which by 1915 amounted to 3,500 objects. In order to promote 'artistic advertising' he lent works to the two most important exhibitions in 1914, the German Werkbund in Cologne and the International Book Arts exhibition in Leipzig. Sachs's interests did not stop at the level of high-profile posters; instead, he championed the everyday nature of his interests. An indication of his approach was given in an address made to the Association,

> *At best I would like to call my lecture today a chapter from 'The Aesthetic of the Insignificant'... Yes, I would go further. Perhaps cultural and art historians of the later centuries in their investigations into culture and 'unculture', aesthetic sentiment and artistic taste of the Germans in the nineteenth and twentieth centuries, will draw no less on picture postcards; menus and place-cards; New Year greetings and family anniversary cards; notepaper and cartes de visites: in short, the private printed matter of the twentieth century, than on great works of painting and sculpture, architecture and the arts and crafts.*[28]

1.30

1.31

The Werkbund Impulse

By 1910 it was acknowledged that if artistic individuality and experiment had been a French national strength, a more modern model of designer was developing in Germany and parts of the Austro-Hungarian Empire. While Paris championed the *artiste-décorateur*, art historian Nancy Troy has shown that there was increasing concern expressed in certain specialist quarters about the standing of the French decorative arts.[29] It was a message signalled by the German contributions to the universal exhibitions in Paris 1900, Turin 1902, St Louis 1904 and Brussels 1910.

The threat German design posed to other European nations was the way its new aesthetic ideal could be fulfilled more systematically by combining an efficiency of production methods, including machine batch-production and standardization, with an interest in simplification of form. It shunned the attention towards luxury materials and virtuoso technique associated with France. In the graphic arts specifically, this perception was justified by seeing designers who worked for major type foundries moving between élite and popular commissions with ease.

As well as the many specialist organizations of the various book and graphic arts, a more all-encompassing association, the Deutsche Werkbund (literally German League of Work) represented the art industries and included a major interest in typography, advertising and packaging.[30] It was formed in 1907 at a time when many of Germany's industries were experiencing a change in scale. In competition with small-scale specialist businesses, the major concerns, *Grossbetriebe* as they were known, were forming cartels of separate units, partly in response to the large-scale engineering and electrical industries of the USA. These too had resulted from amalgamations and were extending their markets abroad. The German Werkbund was the first national organization of its kind to examine the nature of the connections between manufacturer, designer, consumer and the goods themselves, extending the debate to implications for national trade and world standing. Its founders included twelve designers and twelve manufacturers. Most prominent among them was Hermann Muthesius, architect and adviser to the Prussian government. A contributor to the journal *Dekorative Kunst*, Muthesius was the author of *Das Englische Haus*, a three-volume study of the English tradition of domestic architecture published between 1904 and 1911.

The remit of the Werkbund included manufactured goods made up via complex production routes such as railways, trams and shipping, as well as small-scale consumer goods and items for the home, among them typewriters, irons, kettles, and sewing-machines. Such industrial items were discussed alongside products of the more conventional art industries of the Werkstätte.

A central concern in the Werkbund, as Frederic Schwartz has argued, was the potential alienation between object and worker under the modern division of labour.[31] It was thought that workers were prevented from experiencing the complete object through moves towards standardization and the assembly of ready-made parts in the factory, and that this could have a detrimental impact on quality. Another issue which had direct implications for graphic design was the perceived tension between the inherent properties of goods and their commodity value. It was feared that the modern consumer was at risk of illusion through a form of distancing, often presented with the goods either in the shop window or by their representation in advertising, rather than in their reality.

This in turn led to a broader anxiety about the uncertainty of the modern market,

> *A danger of mass-production consists in the new relationship which it introduces between producers and consumers. Whereas earlier craft manufacture was always carried out according to the specific, precisely formulated wishes of the customer, mass suppliers produce for a large, unknown public, whose desires the manufacturers can only guess at.*[32]

One solution promoted by the Werkbund for negotiating the relationship between manufacturer and consumer was the designer: design could overcome this perceived alienation by reintroducing integrity in an object, conceived in terms of appropriate form, decoration or means of sales. At this stage, the process of designing industrial goods and the rendering of an object for display in trade literature, publicity or advertising were very close. The designer often carried out both, as shown by Peter Behrens's graphic and product designs. The various aspects of graphic design, in the form of trade brochures, publicity, trademarks or logos, advertisements, company stationery and other business printing items, all came into the Werkbund discussion for their part in presenting goods in an appropriate manner, perhaps for the first time in such an explicit way to such a wide audience.

Interestingly, attention turned beyond the manufacturer to how ideas could be communicated to the retailer and consumer. Werkbund members toured the

1.32

1.33

1.34

1.35

1.32–1.35 Drogerie Baass olive oil, Hertels Wanzenmittel, Risslinger wine and Union postcards

Designed by Max Hertwig
Four packaging labels
About 1910

1.36 Julius Klinger
Volume III in the series *Monographien Deutscher Reklamekünstler*

Book
1912

1.37 *Kölner Ausstellung* (Cologne Exhibition)

Designed by
Joseph Maria Olbrich
Poster
1907

country in 1909, speaking on 'The Necessity of Taste Education for the German Businessman' (Muthesius), 'Dwelling and Household Goods' (Erich Haenel), 'Useful and Household Goods' (Schaefer), 'Fashion and Taste' (Else Oppler-Legband), 'Textiles' (Krais) and 'Shopwindow and Interior Decoration' (Osthaus).[33]

This all-embracing debate on the role of the designer in industry reached a head in 1914 at the Cologne Werkbund exhibition. On this occasion, Muthesius argued for an activity that encouraged standardization and the application of scientifically inspired rules to design: 'Architecture, and with it the whole area of the Werkbund's activities is pressing towards standardization [*Typisierung*] and only through standardization can it recover the universal significance which was characteristic of it in times of harmonious culture.'[34] On the opposing side were those who considered that design ought to be an elevated activity separated from the material concerns of ordinary life. Henry van de Velde spoke out for the importance of the creativity of the artist or designer whose responsibility was to individualize an object with decoration and formal originality. He was supported by Peter Behrens, Walter Gropius and Karl Ernst Osthaus, among others. The full impact of the standardization debate was not felt until the 1920s, when under Dr Porstmann and directly inspired by Muthesius, a set of standards for design was introduced.

1.36

The Promotion of Advertising Art

One remarkable individual and prominent Werkbund member, Karl Ernst Osthaus, seemed to be an embodiment of their reform ideals. Through early experiments in the promotion of the applied arts, Osthaus played a significant role in the mounting awareness of graphic design. Son of a banker and in many ways resembling a character from a Thomas Mann novel, Osthaus used his inherited wealth to enrich the culture of his home town.[35] Hagen, on the edge of the Ruhr district, was a prosperous, if unremarkable place, benefitting from the textile and metalwork industries. After a university education in philosophy and art history, Osthaus returned to undertake his mission. His first project was the formation of the Folkwang Museum in 1902, based on an impressive range of fine art, including the first collection in Germany of French post-impressionist works, as well as early Expressionism. Along with contemporary art, Osthaus had a serious interest in Greek, Roman, medieval and non-Western cultures.

As a founder-member of the Werkbund, Osthaus was intensely aware of the art and design debate and it was his ambition to instill the Werkbund's tastes and values initially in Germany then more widely abroad. He cultivated several key architects and designers, turning largely to the Arts and Crafts School in Düsseldorf, where Peter Behrens was Director. Osthaus commissioned van de Velde and Behrens to remodel the Hagen museum and invited several architects

1.37

to design houses to form an artists' colony on the lines of the earlier Darmstadt model. As well as his own house, Am Hohenhof, which was also designed by van de Velde, there were villas by Behrens and Johannes Lauweriks, and nearby a model workers' housing estate by Richard Riemerschmid. He commissioned the new architecture for a town theatre, a crematorium and remodelled railway station, although his final aim, to found an Arts and Crafts school in a building by Bruno Taut to be named the Folkwangschule, was prevented by the outbreak of the First World War.[36]

As if this was not sufficient, Osthaus began in 1901 a larger project which took the form of an imaginary museum, or in his words, 'not a museum, but yet more than a museum'. Under the ambitious title of the German Museum for Art in Trade and Industry (Deutsches Museum für Kunst in Handel und Gewerbe), Osthaus established a structure of interconnecting elements which were aimed to improve the relationship between industrialist and designer, or businessman and artist. The cornerstone of this project was the acquisition of a group of applied and decorative art objects, graphic designs and photographs which were to act as a study collection. Instead of establishing a conventional museum, Osthaus sought to develop temporary travelling displays, using the Werkbund for the majority of his contacts.

He identified graphics as a central focus. As well as the collection of contemporary applied art and design, the project involved a poster-testing station (*Plakatprüfstelle*), which was intended to provide a service to potential clients by advising them on poster designs and their effectiveness. He also commissioned anthropological and architectural photographs to work in the way of a modern picture library, in what he called an illustration centre (*Illustrationszelle*). Photographs of the museum's collections were also assembled in a photograph and slide centre of over 1,600 works.

Osthaus is an intriguing example of an advocate of the *Gesamtkunstwerk*, who took the patronage of modern design to the urban environment and saw his model

1.38 

1.39 

1.38 Photograph of the entrance gallery of the Museum Folkwang, Hagen, remodelled by Henry van de Velde in 1901–2

1.39 Photograph of the exterior of the Salamander shoe shop, Berlin.

Designed by August Endell
About 1910

as the complete town. In this connection, he serves as someone who realized early on how graphic design could be used strategically to connect a total design: posters, catalogues and books were regarded as objects in themselves and worthy of design consideration, but at the same time they were the lubricant for the interface between manufacturer, retailer and consumer.

Specifically in the area of graphic design, aside from the idea of travelling exhibitions, Osthaus promoted a series of six monographs on type, book and graphic artists under the title *Monographien Deutscher Reklamekünstler* (Monographs on German Advertising Artists), which started in 1911.[37] This was the first group of individual publications devoted to German graphic and typographic designs. They included a short catalogue essay on each designer and a list of objects, along the lines of fine-art volumes.

The adviser on the graphic projects at Hagen was Fritz Ehmcke, by this time Professor in the subject at the Düsseldorf Arts and Crafts school. Drawing no distinction between different kinds of object, Ehmcke's suggestion was to 'collect everything that has to do with promoting artistic quality in paper and print', from high-profile prestigious works to small ephemeral items. The first exhibition was shown in the Frankfurt-am-Main Arts and Crafts Museum in 1909 to coincide with the meeting of the Werkbund there. Under the title 'Art at the Service of the Businessman' (*Die Kunst im Dienste des Kaufmanns*), it assembled business stationery, press advertisements and small posters as well as photographic examples of window display. This initial exhibition received extensive coverage and travelled to fifty-five locations until 1915. Perhaps most importantly for the growing awareness of the strengths of German graphic design, selections of work from the Osthaus collection were displayed at the Sonderbund fine art exhibition in Düsseldorf in 1910 and at the world exhibition in Ghent of 1913. The Deutsches Museum für Kunst in Handel und Gewerbe also sent a travelling exhibition 'Deutsches Kunstgewerbe' to spread the message about art and industry to the USA in 1912 and 1913.

1.40 

1.40 The new building of the Leipzig Academy for Graphic Arts and Books Trades in 1890.

By then, like many of the Arts and Crafts museums in the regional capitals of Germany, the Hagen Museum had established a substantial collection of over 800 posters. Aside from prestigious posters, ephemeral printing, sometimes called jobbing printing, was also of great interest and there were over 3,000 objects in the collection ranging in examples from business stationery, trade literature, stamps, trademarks and designs to publishers' marks. In the Cologne Werkbund exhibition, on the encouragement of Osthaus, poster artists and designers contributed a street of shops; examples of window display and signage; mock-up house fronts; an advertising fresco; a selection of enamel signs; a display of posters on walls and a column, as well as examples of smaller packaging designs and graphics in display cases.

Two Centres: Leipzig and Berlin

Leipzig traditions

At the turn of the 19th century Leipzig acted as both a regional centre and a point of international contact. It was already by the 18th century the centre of book production and retailing for Saxony in the eastern part of Germany and increasingly further afield. The city's main point of comparison and competition was Frankfurt- and Offenbach-am-Main in the west, where teaching institutions, exhibitions and a museum were established at parallel stages.[38]

Leipzig's commercial importance was reinforced by trade fairs (the Leipziger Messe), as well as specialist exhibitions of industrial manufacture – such as the annual book fair, where publishers and printers of the city and beyond exhibited their works. In the early stages, the number of books displayed grew from 2,700 in 1750 to 5,000 annually by the beginning of the19th century.[39]

In 1764, the Saxon art academies of Leipzig, Dresden and Meissen were founded by Christian Ludwig von Hagedorn, the Privy Legation Councillor (Geheimen Legationsrat). Although the Leipzig Academy initially taught painting, drawing and architecture, it also gained commissions from the city's publishers to

1.41

provide illustrations in copperplate for books. From this arose the specialization in book arts, which contributed to the identity of the Leipzig school. As well as providing illustrators, the city's artists became skilled in designs for book-bindings, ornament and typefaces, commissioned by the seven prestigious Saxon typefoundries, the printers Offizin Poeschel und Trepte and publisher Klinghardt and Biermann.

1.41 Press advertisement for the Leipzig Advertising Fair

Designed by Georg Baus
1927

After a lull in the 19th century when the conventional artistic hierarchies distracted attention from the 'lesser arts', there was a revival of interest in design for publication with the flourishing of the Arts and Crafts reforms and the awareness of events abroad in this field. Under Director Ludwig Nieper, book arts were reintroduced to the curriculum and workshops were established for woodcut, lithography and etching. In a forward-looking step, the Academy was equipped for photography from 1893. In the same year, a site was allocated for a new building of the Royal Academy of Art and School of Arts and Crafts by the side of the Museum of Fine Arts. By 1900 specialization was further acknowledged in the change of the school's title to Royal Academy of Graphic Arts and Book Trades, where, under the new director Max Seliger, drawing and painting were taught alongside typography, lettering, bookbinding and print techniques.

One of the most important occasions for the representation of Leipzig as a centre for publishing interests was the 1914 International Exhibition for the Book Industry and Graphic Arts (Internationale Ausstellung für Buchgewerbe und Graphik), known by its acronym Bugra.

This substantial exhibition was held partly to mark the 150th anniversary of the Royal Academy of Graphic Arts and Book Trades, but it served more generally to promote German presses, foundries and paper manufacturers.[40] At this time Leipzig saw itself economically and culturally as the fourth city of Germany. Unquestionably, the exhibition contributed to its more general concern for national standing, while acting as a specialist version of the frequent international exhibitions. The founding aim of the exhibition, which opened on 14 May 1914, was to celebrate 'the art of printing, opening up new possibilities of inspiring life in the great masses of men, making accessible to all what formerly had been an exclusive possession of the privileged classes'.[41] It offered an historical overview of the art of printed culture. In its 'Hall of Civilization' a path traced the foundations of script in ethnological and historical sections, beginning with a reconstruction of a ceiling from Altamira in Spain, then passing through Mexican, Mayan and Australasian signs and symbols. This was followed by the early printing of China, Korea and Japan. Passing Egyptian, Hebrew, Graeco-Roman and Celtic examples, the visitor finally came to the history of mechanical reproduction, from the invention of the printing press and moveable type to what were called 'modern technics'. Significantly, a broad history of world civilization led to a specifically German national focus.

The exhibition provided an opportunity for book artists from participating countries to display work alongside publishers and manufacturers for commercial and cultural prestige as well as international recognition. Contemporary issues of the role of artists and designers were addressed in several exhibitions, for example, 'Contemporary Book Arts' selected by Walter Tiemann. As there was also a pavilion concentrating on advertising designs, 'Contemporary Book Arts' concentrated on designs for book jackets, bindings, illustrations, ex-libris, publisher's colophons and items of stationery. It assembled the work of many of the prominent designers from the German Arts and Crafts schools, as well as the works of C.R. Ashbee and Walter Crane from England and Axel Gallén-Kallela from Finland.

The restrained Leipzig tradition is best represented by the figure of Walter Tiemann, Director of the Academy from 1920 to 1933. Initially a painter, his designs epitomized traditionalism in typography and book design. He was also co-founder with Carl Ernst Poeschel in 1907 of Germany's first private press, the Janus Presse. He worked for major publishers and was chosen to design the catalogue of the German exhibition at the St Louis World Fair in 1904.[42] During the 1920s his designs for Insel Verlag, for example, represented a strong sense of restraint during a period when many younger designers advocated an intense engagement with mechanization and employed sans-serif typefaces in modern designs.

The internationalism of Bugra was abruptly interrupted by the outbreak of the First World War when the French, British and Russian pavilions were closed down, many of their exhibits being passed to the Book and Script Museum in Leipzig. Beforehand, visitors were able to see an international street with exhibitions from Austria, a much-praised Italian pavilion, a French display housed in a Louis XVI-style pavilion, British printed books in an imaginary Tudor castle and other contributions from Russia and Japan, along with the German Royal Institutes for Esperanto and Shorthand, both based in Dresden

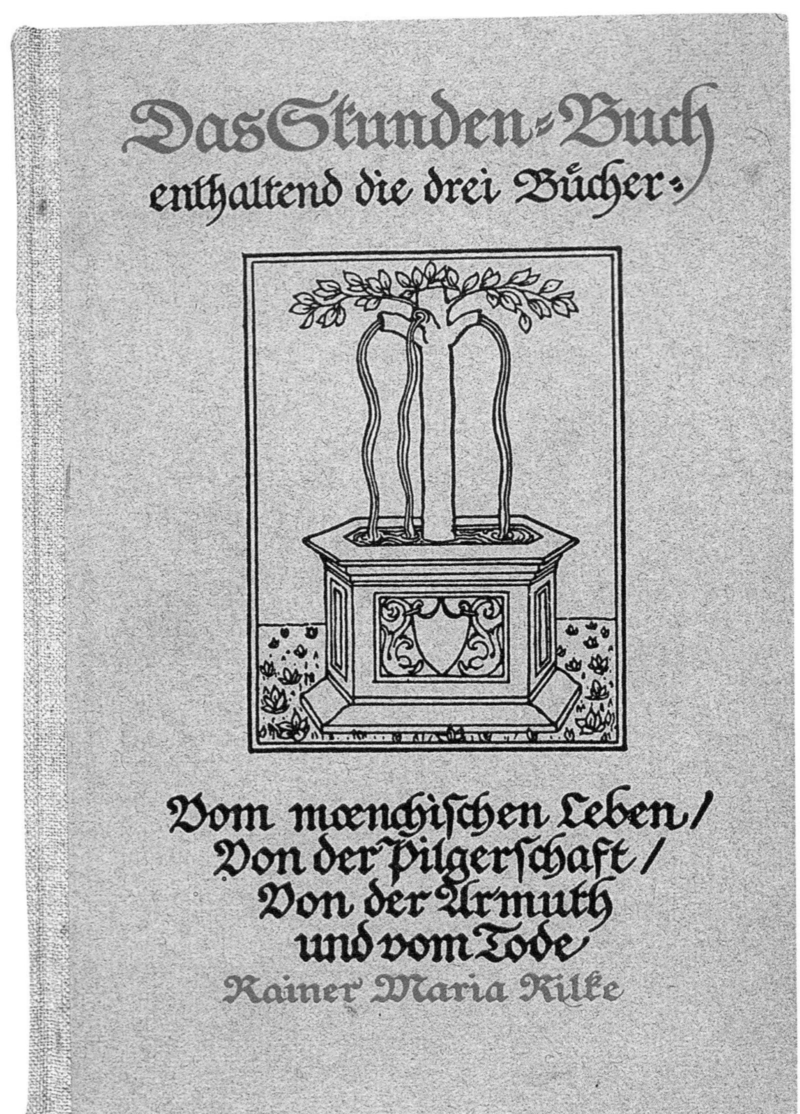

1.42

Da neigt sich die Stunde und rührt mich an
mit klarem, metallenem Schlag:
mir zittern die Sinne. Ich fühle: ich kann —
und ich fasse den plastischen Tag.

Nichts war noch vollendet, eh ich es erschaut,
ein jedes Werden stand still.
Meine Blicke sind reif, und wie eine Braut
kommt jedem das Ding, das er will.

Nichts ist mir zu klein, und ich lieb es trotzdem
und mal' es auf Goldgrund und groß
und halte es hoch, und weiß nicht wem
löst es die Seele los . . .

Ich lebe mein Leben in wachsenden Ringen,
die sich über die Dinge ziehn.
Ich werde den letzten vielleicht nicht vollbringen,
aber versuchen will ich ihn.

Ich kreise um Gott, um den uralten Turm,
und ich kreise jahrtausendelang;
und ich weiß noch nicht: bin ich ein Falke, ein Sturm
oder ein großer Gesang.

7

1.43

1.42–1.43 *Das Stundenbuch*

Poems by Rainer Maria Rilke
Designed by Walter Tiemann
Cover and interior page
1921

at this time. There was also a pavilion dedicated to art and photography, while technical and industrial sections displayed machine halls of various presses in action and a 'paper quarter' with the latest hand- and machine-made papers.

Significantly, at a time of the increasing assertion of women's contribution to many walks of life, the Haus der Frau, designed by Berlin architect Emilie Winckelmann, was dedicated to a broad interpretation of the female cultural sphere.[43] This was organized by an international committee of women, among their ranks princesses, aristocrats, mayoresses and leading women of commerce and culture. For example, the wife of the German art collector, Frau Wallraf of

Cologne and Ellen von Siemens, of the prominent Berlin electrical family, were listed for their assistance.

Echoing the context of the main exhibition, there were displays on the historical contribution made by women in bookbinding and printing since the Middle Ages. Special comment was made on the openings for women in what was perceived as the more flexible field of photographic studios, as well as the more predictable activities of office workers and stenographers. The range of the Haus der Frau was broader than many of the other exhibits at Leipzig and as well as women's professional involvement in graphic design, there were displays on women as leading cultural figures, including authors and composers. An exact indication of the number of women identifying themselves as graphic artists and illustrators was not given in this context, but shortly afterwards, in 1920, the journal *Das Plakat* published a review of German designers, *Unsere Reklamekünstler*, in which, of the sixty individuals selected, only four were women.[44]

Leipzig clearly represented a continuing tradition stemming from Enlightenment principles which were continued in the 20th century. The activities at the Leipzig Academy essentially focussed on the layout, design and embellishment of beautiful or utilitarian books and related printed material. The introduction of newly mechanized techniques for book printing and graphic reproduction presented other challenges, but for Leipzig, this was largely a matter of reform rather than invention, consolidating tradition through style and continuity.

Berlin: a Commercial Art

It has grown dark, and coming from the Zoologischer Garten station, then from behind the Kaiser-Wilhelm memorial church, we stride across Auguste-Viktoria Platz to the promenade along the centre of the broad avenue of Tauentzienstrasse. Floods of light meet us. Right and left are shop windows one after the other, lined with male and female elegance. A spruced crowd

1.44

1.44 *Kronleuchter-Fabrik, Möhring* (Möhring Chandelier Factory)

Designed by Julius Klinger
Poster
1909

1.45 *Oliver, Die Beste Billigste moderne Schreibmaschine* (Oliver, the best and cheapest modern typewriter)

Designed by Paul Scheurich
Poster
1909

1.46 Coffee Tins for Kaffee Hag

Designed by Alfred Runge and Eduard Scotland
About 1910

OLIVER

Die BESTE
und ihrer Vorzüge wegen
BILLIGSTE
moderne
Schreibmaschine

OLIVER

Oliver Schreibmaschinenges. m. b. H.
Berlin. S.W. 68.

1.45

of seers along the street, laughing and flirting, full of life and at leisure. Pedestrians, idlers. Further up at Wittenbergplatz magic illuminations, glittering treasures, silks, gold brocade, bronzes, ostrich feathers, shop windows like jewellery boxes; the new deparment store. We enter, an endless stream, the ruler calls and we gladly follow.'[45]

Characterizing Berlin at the turn of the century, the prominent industrialist and politician Walter Rathenau signalled a new, distinctly modern attitude in the open acknowledgment of the commercial character of its life. 'We do not need to be

1.46

1.47 

1.48 

1.47 Photograph of Friedrichstrasse, Berlin, in 1907 by Max Mischmann.

1.48 Photograph of illuminated advertising on the façade of the department store Kaufhaus des Westens Berlin, during White Week in 1932.

ashamed that Berlin is the parvenu of cities and the city for parvenus', he wrote in the essay 'The Most Beautiful City in the World', 'for parvenu in German means self-made man.'[46]

By implication, in this new urban context, style, fashion and novel techniques became a much more significant element in the expectations of the graphic designer as advertising was consistently required to define newly available goods to propel the market. To many German minds, the epitome of the American experience was this rapidly changing commercial environment, and Berlin became recognized as its symbolic metropolis between 1900 and 1930. Theatre, cabaret, film, café-society, an accelerated living style, more liberal social and sexual attitudes, and a high-profile, articulate, self-conscious avant-garde were all part of this modern cosmopolitan way of life. For commentators on this scene, magazines and journalism, shop fronts and advertisements stood metaphorically as well as literally for this commercialized world. Beyond their obvious functions, they were taken to represent a less direct and more ambivalent mode of interaction, based on economic relations and persuasive strategies. They also presented a moral challenge. For many people, their very nature as mass and popular forms carried negative associations.

Germany's emergence as a world power was particularly strident as the rapid transformation from a rural economy to industrial base took place. The city of Berlin grew on an unprecedented scale at this time. From a population of 774,452 in 1870, by 1910 the inner city had over 2 million inhabitants and Greater Berlin had grown to 3,734,000.[47] The migration to the cities coincided with the impact of new technological developments in manufacturing, sometimes referred to as the second industrial revolution. A pre-eminence in the metalwork, chemical and electrical industries helped to define one central part of the city's commercial identity. Such companies as the large electrical concerns AEG (Allgemeine Elektrizitäts Gesellschaft, General Electrical Company), Siemens and Osram, as well as the related services of transport and publishing were major employers.

Inevitably these firms were aware of their international counterparts and the need to define themselves according to modern approaches in marketing and promotion.

The most significant change in the structure of the graphics industries in the first half of the 20th century, therefore, was the evolution of advertising as a major employer. The situation in Germany was distinctive. While, as we have seen, the print and artistic trades and industries supplying designs for companies were highly developed and perceived as a national strength, from some quarters there was a strong moral resistance to advertising's directing these skills. In turn, print culture had its own hierarchy and the change in scale of modern business practice presented a challenge to its status quo.

In a study of German advertising and marketing, Dirk Reinhardt has outlined an incremental periodization of change from 1850 to 1945.[48] First came the economic and commercial breakthroughs of the 1850s, which provided the necessary infrastructure of manufacturing companies and their increasing requirements to announce products in a widening geographical area. Modern distribution methods of railways and shipping called for a wider network of information based on mechanical reproduction through newspapers and magazines, and by the 1880s posters and packaging supplemented these as alternative forms of message. Then came the economic success which enabled companies to commission new forms of advertising and publicity. Branded goods appeared in the 1890s, in part a response to the growth in size of retail outlets and an increase in mail-order that followed the earlier repeal of postal tariffs. It was from this time that the brand names which feature strongly in the history of German design originated: Leibnitz biscuits in 1892; Odol mouthwash in 1893; Dr Oetker baking provisions in 1899; Tropon egg-white preparation in 1900; Kaffee Hag in 1906, and Persil washing soap in 1909. In the Werkbund context, the especially celebrated campaigns for Pelikan artists' materials and Manoli tobacco also began then.

1.49 *'200 Plakatsaülen'* (200 poster columns for the Düsseldorf Poster Column Company)

Designed by Germain
Poster
1926

1.50 *Plakat Kunst* (Poster Art)

Designed by Fritz Buchholz
Poster
About 1925

1.49

The expansion in commercialization of the public sphere was strictly regulated in Germany and, in contrast with Britain and the USA, the billboard was not used extensively. The most interesting example of poster control was successfully introduced by Ernst Litfass, who invented a poster column which was to become a highly characteristic piece of street furniture in German cities. Following 1848, when political censorship of posters had been withdrawn in the city, the streets of Berlin were the scene of poster chaos. As an entrepreneur, Litfass approached the

PLAKATKUNST
KOJE
NR·71
C·G·NAUMANN
G·M·B·H
REKLAMEMESSE·PETERSSTR·38
LEIPZIG
FRITZ BUCHHOLZ QUASNITZ

1.50

1.51

1.52

1.51 *Garbáty Flaggen gala*
Poster for a tobacco company

Designed by Julius Gipkens
Poster
About 1914

1.52 An advertisement for Verkehrsreklame Hoenicke and Kypke, Hamburg, the company responsible for advertising on the city's transport system, 1931.

1.53 Photograph of a Berlin poster column in 1926

1.54 Photograph of posters on the Berlin underground in 1927.

Prussian government with the suggestion of specially erected columns on street corners to be used for bill-posting. The column was designed so as to accommodate different sizes of poster in an orderly arrangement. Display at other sites was prohibited.[49]

To secure support for his campaign, Litfass arranged balls and firework displays, drawing the attention of significant cultural and court figures. The Litfasss column was announced on July 1851 in the Berlin press and was followed in Dresden in 1856, Stuttgart in 1872, Bremen in 1873, Vienna in 1877 and Leipzig in 1878, all under Litfass's patent. With the advent of electrically run traffic lights and streetlamps, the columns later took on a secondary purpose for housing their controls.

Initially, posters and other designs were handled by space brokers (*Annoncenexpeditionen*), who were responsible for placing advertisements appropriately on behalf of the client company in press or street locations. Berlin had by far the greatest number of these agencies, with 115 companies in 1907, followed by 86 in Hamburg and 53 in Leipzig.[50] By 1900 publicity was considered a necessary fact of life for all companies, and integration between poster and press campaigns was encouraged by design reformers, aware of the American stress on consistency of identity. For instance, Ernst Growald, director of Hollerbaum and Schmidt, the most important art printers in Berlin, recommended that he could take on the responsibility for a client company's complete identity from trademark, logo and stationery, to packaging, press and other forms of advertising. In a typical arrangement at this stage, Hollerbaum and Schmidt would guarantee consistent and effective artistic standards and advise against unnecessary expenditure, for a commission of between 5 and 10 percent. This arrangement presumed that a designer was equipped to tackle all aspects of an identity, while other kinds of marketing specialists and psychologists might be commissioned for specific campaigns.[51]

Even though publicity and marketing requirements were gradually recognized as essential parts of a company's expenditure, advertising agencies employing a range of staff with expertise in analyzing a campaign from product, packaging and publicity only slowly found advocates in Germany before 1914. Their real breakthrough came only in the 1920s: not until 1925 did international advertising agencies, such as Crawfords, J. Walter Thompson, McCann, and Erwin Wasey, establish branches in Berlin. Even then, the economic crash of 1929 and difficulties in persuading clients of the value of their full services and extra costs meant that their success was limited.

By 1925 the Berlin city council arranged for the leasing of the poster columns to be taken over by one company, Berlin Anschlag und Reklamewesen GmBH (known as Berek), which also oversaw illuminated advertising. Clearly, the centralization of public display could be used as a form of censorship and control, and this came to a head in the 1920s, when advertising professionals concerned to maintain aesthetic standards confronted town-planners, conservationists and other lobbyists who were critical of the spread of posters, painted advertisements, enamel signs, mirrors and illuminations which were all perceived as commercial intrusions on the city plan.

1.53

1.54

2.1

2 Behrens, Bernhard and Ehmcke: Three Models of Graphic Designer

Peter Behrens (1869–1940) - Developing a Factory Art

Among the designers who rose to prominence in the first decade of the century, Peter Behrens is most famous for his architecture and the house-style he created for the major Berlin electrical company, AEG. Originally from Hamburg, he studied painting but was self-taught as an architect and designer. He settled in Munich in 1889 at a time when an interest in Arts and Crafts was beginning to flourish. He became a designer with an unusually full range of interests and his architectural practice was one of the most prominent in Germany, attracting fellow architects Mies van der Rohe, Le Corbusier and Walter Gropius to work alongside him in Berlin.

Behrens was a co-founder of the Munich Secession in 1890. This was the first German association of artists to distance themselves from the Academy, along the lines of the French model of the *Salon des Refusés*.[1] In 1895 he carried out his first colour woodcuts under the inspiration of Justus Brinkmann at the Berlin Museum für Kunst und Gewerbe, and in 1897 he was a co-founder of the Munich United Workshops for Arts and Crafts.

His range of work there allows comparisons to be made with his contemporaries Richard Riemerschmid or Bruno Paul, also in Munich, and Josef

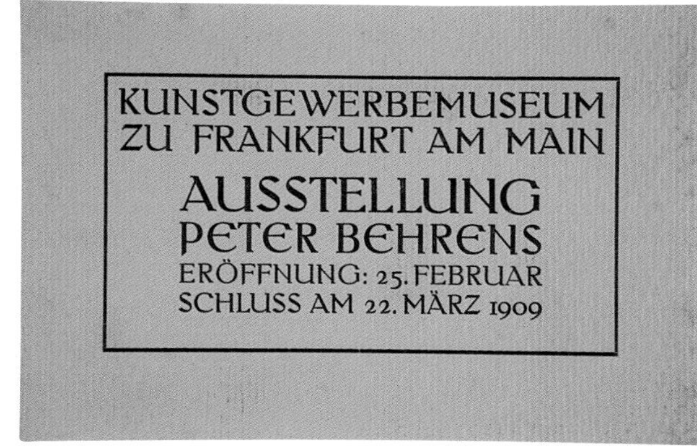

2.2

2.1 *Der Kuss*
(The Kiss)

Peter Behrens
1898

2.2 *Ausstellung Peter Behrens: Kunstgewerbemuseum zu Frankfurt am Main*
(Peter Behrens Exhibition: Arts and Crafts Museum of Frankfurt)

Designed by Peter Behrens
Invitation card
1909

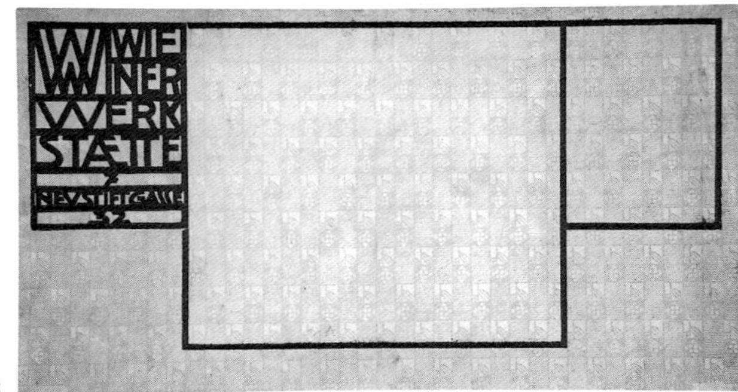

2.3

2.4

2.3–2.4 Envelopes for the Wiener Werkstätte incorporating the monogram for the Neustiftgasse branch

Designed by Josef Hoffmann and Koloman Moser
About 1905

Hoffmann in Vienna. Behrens came to the height of success after 1900 when he was invited to Darmstadt to act as the equivalent of a 'Court Artist' to Ernst Ludwig, Grand Duke of Hesse. There he collaborated with Joseph Maria Olbrich, J.V. Cissarz, Paul Haustein, Daniel Greiner and others. At the artists' colony, Mathildenhöhe, situated on the outskirts of the city, Behrens contributed his own villa, equipped with furnishings he designed.[2]

By that time, an artists' colony was a familiar concept in Germany. At first a rural escape for impoverished painters, this was extended to include the British Arts and Crafts ideal of an art workshop, as in the case of Worpswede in northern Germany.[3] What distinguished Darmstadt from other artists' colonies was its sophisticated cultural output, in which design and the decorative arts held a significant place. The Darmstadt circle was considered the élite of German design at the time, winning, for example, a gold medal at the Paris 1900 Exposition Universelle for its display of interiors. One commentator suggested that, rather than a typical Arts and Crafts ethos, Darmstadt aimed for the higher goal of a symbolic expression of all the arts. This involved a unity of poetry, painting, music and dance, as well as the fine and decorative arts, manifested through the cult of beautiful life. Julius Meier-Graefe thought that the benign court patronage at Darmstadt resembled 'a fairy-tale in the ideal kingdom, with a good king, as opposed to the republic which looks like an old dirty wife'.[4]

The colony was opened to the public for two exhibitions in 1901 and 1904, when the major focus of attention was three houses designed by Olbrich. Although aesthetically a tremendous success in gaining recognition from all parts of Germany, as well as abroad, the practical aim of selling furniture and applied arts was apparently a failure.

Behrens was responsible for organizing the opening ceremony on 15 May 1901 and the accompanying exhibition, 'Ein Dokument Deutscher Kunst', which involved choreographing a pageant and performances in Van de Velde's newly built theatre and overseeing commemorative publications. The design of these

2.5

2.5 Illustration and typographic arrangement for Otto Julius Bierbaum's calendar book, *Der Bunte Vogel* (The Coloured Bird)

Designed by Peter Behrens
1899

2.6 Feste des Lebens und der Kunst: eine Betrachtung des Theaters als höchsten Kultursymbols
(Festival of Life and Art: a consideration of theatre as the highest cultural symbol)

Designed by Peter Behrens
Title page
1900

texts indicates how typographic style reflected the outlook at Darmstadt. For the prestigious publications and posters announcing events, Behrens incorporated stylized figuration, *Jugendstil* ornament and the latest typefaces. For the more modest book of the inaugural address, 'Festival of Life and Art: a consideration of theatre as the highest cultural symbol', he gave equal consideration to typographic composition, letter initials and illustrations, as well as paper quality and binding. Unusual for its time, the publication incorporated single-case, sans-serif typeface in its titling. Its text opened,

> *Therefore we will create a new style in everything. The style of a time does not mean particular forms in one or other special art, every form is only one of many symbols of inner life, every art has a part of style. The style, however, is the symbol of the total discovery, of the whole conception of life and shows itself in the universality of all arts. The harmony of all the arts is the beautiful symbol of a strong nation.*[5]

2.6

2.7 *Kunstausstellung Darmstadt*
(Art exhibition Darmstadt)

Designed by Otto Ubbelohde
Poster
1911

2.8 *Darmstadt, ein Dokument Deutscher Kunst, Die Ausstellung der Künstlerkolonie*
(Darmstadt, a document of German art, the exhibition of the artists' colony)

Designed by Peter Behrens
Poster
1901

2.7

The belief that the arts could find a spiritual and transcendent beauty was often justified among the Darmstadt circle by reference to the importance given to the arts and theatre in the writings of Nietzsche. For example, in *The Birth of Tragedy* of 1872, the German philosopher had examined the nature of Greek tragedy, characterizing the central contrast between Apollonian and Dionysian tendencies in these works. The concern for enchantment, visions and hallucinations found in Nietzsche's writings was echoed in the theatrical performances at Darmstadt. When it came to graphic design, it could be said that Behrens responded to Apollonian ideals of order and self-discipline rather than the emotive abandon of Dionysus.

Behrens moved briefly from Darmstadt to a teaching position at the Gewerbemuseum in Nuremburg, but his more significant position was that of Director of the Kunstgewerbeschule in Düsseldorf which he held between 1903 and 1907. Here he drew around him an impressive group of staff who led a revival in the art industries, substantially raising the profile of north-west Germany. Prior to his appointment, Behrens had developed his interest in typography, first designing the new typeface, 'Behrens', which was cut by the Klingspor foundry of Offenbach am Main in 1901. He described the development of this hybrid Roman-Gothic typeface:

> *A new typeface can only develop organically and almost unnoticeably from a tradition, and only in harmony with the new spiritual and material matter of the epoch. For the precise form of my type I took the technical principle of Gothic script, the stroke of the quill pen. Also, in order to achieve an even more German character, gothic letters were a decisive influence on me for the proportions, the height and width of the letters and the thickness of the strokes. A character that holds together well, in such a way that all superfluities might be eliminated, so that the construction principle of the diagonally-held pen might be clearly expressed was what I sought.*[6]

2.8

2.9

2.10

2.11

Here we find a concern to imbue a modern typeface with German character, a constant *leitmotif* in many commentaries of the time. Shrewdly, this nationalistic concern was incorporated in a wish for greater legibility to non-Germans. The typeface quickly gained in popularity and was used, for example, as the official German typeface for the catalogues of the St Louis 1904 and Brussels 1910 international exhibitions.

The freshness of Behrens's design was immediately recognized. Meyer-Schönbrunn, one of the first serious commentators on graphic design, remarked that Behrens had 'become of upmost importance for the whole of German lettering and advertising. His sharp and steely gothic was, along with "Eckmann", the first thoroughly modern character which could successfully contrast with the tangled mass of the degenerate black-letter and old style.'[7]

The next step in Behrens's career was to guarantee his position in subsequent design histories as an acclaimed pioneer. The *Berliner Tageblatt* of 28 July 1907 announced that he had agreed to take up an appointment in Berlin as artistic adviser to the Allgemeine Elektrizitäts-Gesellschaft.[8] AEG was by this time the world's largest manufacturer of electric cables, generators, motors, arc lamps, light bulbs and transformers. The company was founded by Emil Rathenau

2.12

2.9–2.11 *Behrens Schrift und Zierat*
(Behrens Type and Ornament)

Designed by Peter Behrens
Title page and samples from the typefoundry booklet
About 1902

2.12 *Die Kunst für Alle*
(Art for All)
Special issue on Arnold Böcklin

Designed by Peter Behrens
Magazine cover
1901

when he bought the German rights to Thomas Alva Edison's patented electric light system at the 1881 Paris Internationale de l'Electricité. As described by Tilmann Buddensieg,

> *Behrens's work for the AEG began with the relatively unimportant task of re-designing the company journal. He then turned to the arc-lamp, and from that he went on to establish an all-embracing AEG style that extended to*

the design of factories, transport depots, and model housing estates for the firm's employees. In response to Behrens's work, the AEG's board of directors cautiously extended his contract step by step into what was probably the widest ranging commission of modern times.[9]

2.13 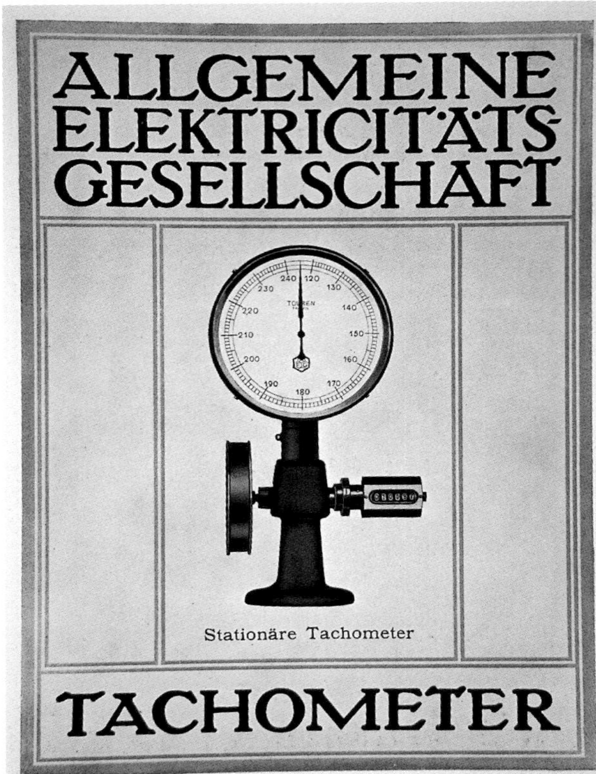

2.14 

2.13 Advertisement for the AEG Tachometer

Designed by Peter Behrens
About 1908

2.14 Advertisement for AEG kettles

Designed by Peter Behrens
About 1908

Behrens oversaw graphic and product design; the former included internal and external publications, advertisements, symbols and trademarks. His arrival coincided with the wider recognition of the commodity character of all elements of modern industrial culture. Accordingly, the aim of letterforms was to fix the product brand-names subconsciously in the mind of the consumer. The most overt example of a typographic house-style was to 'label' the various AEG workshops and assembly-halls in recognition of the publicity value of industrial buildings.

Behrens's work was highly praised. For example, Franz Mannheimer wrote in May 1910:

> *...a factory art* [Fabrikenkunst] *has recently appeared which, like the more-established art industry [Kunstindustrie], no longer has to use the word art as a mere front for barbaric bad taste. That this factory art has developed can be attributed to the nature of contemporary fine and applied art. The dominating principle of objectivity [Sachlichkeit] provided the bridge - the bridge between Peter Behrens and the Allgemeine Elektrizitätsgesellschaft of Berlin.*[10]

Behrens's version of neo-classicism developed in these years with particular reference to 15th-century Florentine architecture; indeed, it was popular at the time to compare Berlin as a thriving commercial and cultural city with Florence under the Medici. Behrens's designs, whether in built form or on the page, depended on a strong contrast in decorative motifs, largely in black and white.

As Alan Windsor has written, 'the words "Greece" and the "Antique" may be taken to mean a curious fusion of ideas regarding archaic simplicity and purity of form. He had acquired them, not so much from Greek art itself, as from his observation of Romanesque architecture in Tuscany... and his study of history and archaeology of classical art in general.'[11]

Behrens was not alone in looking for historical precedent to justify his use of ornament. Various parallels can be made between his style and the ideas of the art historian Alois Riegl, who was working at the Vienna Kunstgewerbemuseum at the time. Riegl contributed to the philosophical foundations for an art movement of greater simplicity and abstraction. In *Stilfragen* (Questions of Style) of 1893 he challenged the idea that increasing ornament necessarily resulted from advances in technical skill. Instead, he argued, there could be internal aesthetic development in design and 'a search for interconnectedness, variation or symmetry' independent of technique.[12] Immediate examples can be found in Behrens's catalogue designs for AEG, where electrical items are arranged on a plain background and only the depicted object is given tonal gradation, enhancing its smooth and modern appearance. Crucially, ornament was derived from abstract motifs rather than organic sources, so familiar in *Jugendstil.*

In a later work, *Spätrömische Kunstindustrie* (The Late Roman Art Industries) of 1901, Riegl extended his theory of ornament with the idea of 'self-containedness', which is helpful in understanding the concept of objectivity as applied to design at the time.[13] He analyzed common properties in objects and works of art. Against the grain of the time, when a great number of theories were exploring subjectivity, Riegl sought an understanding of the individual integrity of objects. He investigated how an object could be isolated from its context, in order to suppress spatial illusion and overcome the subjective reception of the spectator. His search for inherent properties of form also matched the direction modern manufacturing processes were taking. Commentaries on Behrens's work reveal similar preoccupations:

2.15

2.15 Exterior of the AEG showroom, Potsdamer Strasse, Berlin

Designed by Peter Behrens
1910

DEUTSCHE WERKBUND-
AUSSTELLUNG
KUNST IN HANDWERK,
INDUSTRIE UND HANDEL · ARCHITEKTUR
MAI
CÖLN 1914
OCT.
A. MOLLING & COMP. K-G. HANNOVER-BERLIN.

2.16

Behrens's style is particularly suited to this task. In marked contrast to the more popular styles that adapt themselves passively to the object with only a superficial concern for function, the Behrens style seeks to mould the object and is much more responsive to mathematical and constructional ideas. It is a style of exact fantasy, appropriate to a machine artist.[14]

Meyer-Schönbrunn also approved of his designs because they avoided the contemporary excesses of publicity by stressing an article's value and function. His comments again highlighted the concept of objectivity:

With the same objectivity Behrens reformed every organ of modern advertising, which became more important year after year through its ability to affect taste. In the case of Behrens, in contrast to the customary concept of advertising as quackery, the use of shady lures and sensation-mongering exaggeration, his exhibitions, buildings, shop-windows and interiors are based only on the inherent value and function of the respective article.[15]

Although Behrens's career as an architect continued after the First World War, his most instructive years for graphic design were up until 1914. Indeed, in that year his design for the poster for the Cologne Werkbund exhibition was rejected for being too aggressive in the context of an international exhibition and Fritz Ehmcke's more moderate design was preferred. Behrens's model of activity was significant: teaching, writing and working for a leading industrial company. In his architectural and typographic designs he found parallels in style, composition and supporting justification. He had a highly developed understanding of the place of design within industry and made advanced analogies between product and graphic design, or sign and object. In many respects, Behrens's major impact in graphic design was on his contemporaries rather than on subsequent generations.

2.17

2.16 *Deutsche Werkbund Ausstellung Kunst in Handwerk, Industrie und Handel* (German Werkbund Exhibition Art in Handwork, Industry and Trade)

Designed by Peter Behrens
Poster
1914

2.17
Poster for Deutsche Werkbund Ausstellung, Cöln

Designed by
Fritz Hellmut Ehmcke
1914

2.18

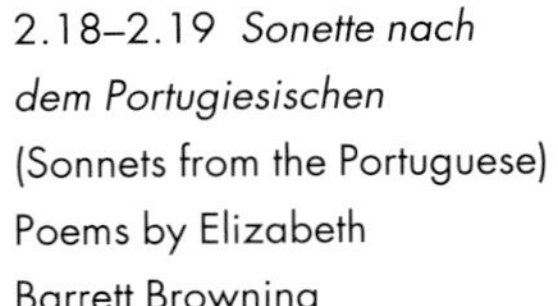

2.19

2.18–2.19 *Sonette nach dem Portugiesischen* (Sonnets from the Portuguese) Poems by Elizabeth Barrett Browning

Designed by Fritz Hellmut Ehmcke
Cover and title page
1903

Fritz Hellmut Ehmcke (1878–1963) - The All-round Designer

Fritz Ehmcke, the second figure of a generation that defined what graphic design could be, came from a practical background. He was a consistent force in promoting graphic design and a significant teacher. His first position was as a lithographer at the luxury paper factory of W. Hagelberg in Berlin in 1893 and in many respects this technical base defined his outlook for years to come. In 1897 he enrolled as a student at the Teaching Institute attached to the Applied Arts Museum in Berlin, under Emil Doepler the younger, an influential teacher who was a rich source of ideas. Doepler taught principles of pattern design and ornament mainly through drawing exercises. In these he developed the students' awareness of positive and negative form, as well as spatial organization of repeated motifs. These were all to become components of Ehmcke's mature style. Ehmcke went on to be an important teacher of design himself, invited by Peter Behrens to Düsseldorf Arts and Crafts School in 1903 and subsequently taking up a similar position at the Munich Arts and Crafts School from 1913 to 1938. He participated in most of the major events in German graphic design, working on the international book arts exhibition in Leipzig and contributing to the Cologne Werkbund exhibition, both in 1914.[16]

In many ways Ehmcke was a major figure in German graphic design, but he has not received as much attention as Modernist designers. He was a prolific commentator on the subject and his largely autobiographical articles give a full picture of his interests and activities. In these, he expressed his immediate dissatisfaction with his early years as a student: '...the facilities at the above-mentioned Teaching Institution at the Royal Arts and Crafts School,... particularly for those times, were extremely wanting. There were no workshops at all and there was a yawning gap between the learning circumstances and the real practical requirements which awaited us in the outside world.'[17]

In October 1900, together with two fellow Doepler students, Georg Belwe and Friedrich Wilhelm Kleukens, he formed the Steglitz Werkstatt, named after a district in Berlin. They were the first Berlin group to form a studio on the lines of the Darmstadt, Dresden and Munich principles, but what distinguished them was the emphasis on the graphic arts. Their accounts of the venture stress its humble beginnings. They started in a hen-shed equipped with a lithographic press and a Boston press for typographic work; later they acquired a mechanized press and several new typefaces, including 'Behrens' and 'König Antiqua'. At first they took on only relatively small jobs such as ex-libris labels, business and visiting cards, postcards, trademarks and publishers' marks.

Even though their early surroundings were rudimentary, their associates included Behrens, Bernhard, Van de Velde, the book artist César Klein and the theatre director Max Reinhardt. As a result of their early local success, they soon began to receive commissions from major firms such as the publisher Eugen Diederichs and Otto Ring's Syndetikon glue factory. For Syndetikon they devised one of the first packaging house-styles based on fashionable *Jugendstil*.[18]

The principles of the Workshop were published in an inaugural statement. The programme's design, set in 'Eckmann' with illuminated capitals, reflected the strong influence of Cobden-Sanderson and Kelmscott. The text ran,

> *Aware of the misunderstanding with which most business people encounter artistic developments of our new times and because we are ourselves artists,*

2.20

we found the occasion about a year ago to form the Steglitz Werkstatt. Here, besides other branches of applied art, print above all will be cultivated in an appropriate manner to produce the most beautiful blooms: then we can speak of a printed book art.[19]

In other areas of the workshop, designs were executed for a range of the applied arts, including furniture, metalwork goods, wallpapers and carpets. After autumn 1901, a school was opened in which Clara Müller-Coburg, later Ehmcke's wife, taught classes in embroidery, tapestry, weaving and drawing.[20] Ehmcke's move to Düsseldorf signalled the end of the richest period of the workshop, but in his later career he would maintain many of the contacts established there.

At Düsseldorf Ehmcke was responsible for establishing the important State lettering course on behalf of the Prussian Ministry of Trade, as requested by Hermann Muthesius. He worked with Anna Simons between 1907 and 1909 and the results were exhibited in the Berlin Art Library. For these courses Simons ran classes on lettering in the Johnston method, Behrens lectured on the history of script and led practical exercises in Roman and German lettering, while Ehmcke taught experiments in illumination and letter forms.[21]

Anna Simons was a crucial link between England and Germany at this time and most contemporary letter reformers of this period acknowledged her as a formative inspiration. Originally from Berlin, she was responsible for taking many of the principal ideas concerning lettering reform and the private press movement from London to Germany. After studying with Edward Johnston at the Central School of Arts and Crafts and at the Royal College of Art from 1902, she travelled to many German cities, including Weimar, Munich, Halle and Düsseldorf, as well as Zurich, delivering lectures on lettering. She also translated Johnston's highly influential book *Writing, Iluminating and Lettering* in 1910.[22]

In the essay, 'Die Wiedererweckung der Schriftkunst' (The Re-awakening of the Art of Lettering), she suggested that lettering could re-emerge as an important daily

2.21

2.20–2.22
Small advertisement, five cut-out dolls and collectors' stamps for Syndetikon glue, Berlin

Designed by Fritz Hellmut Ehmcke
1903

activity, and addressed what she considered to be its lost spiritual aspect.[23] This spiritualization (*Durchgeistigung*) was intended to introduce the fulfillment in daily activity which Simons supposed had existed in crafts before industrialization, a principle based on Morrisian pleasure in work. This she extended by referring to another contemporary, the Viennese Rudolf von Larisch, a major figure in the modern European writing and lettering movement who taught at the Vienna Pedagogical Institute and the Arts and Crafts School.[24] Whereas Johnston was an advocate of penmanship and inscription following the earliest examples of Roman inscriptions, Larisch encouraged a more rhythmic and unfettered approach. He held that the bodily movement involved in lettering was as important as the resulting design, a view he shared with his fellow-Austrian, Rudolf Steiner, who was developing exercises in eurythmy at this time. Larisch's scheme proposed that lettering came from the act of writing, with affinities in music and dance. It was a matter of spacing, weight and overall design, rather than individual detail. He taught lettering with a variety of materials; wood, glass, metal and ceramics. One of his exercises, for example, was to fill the shape of a square with a letterform, a method which led to the distinctive character of much Secessionist book and graphic design.[25]

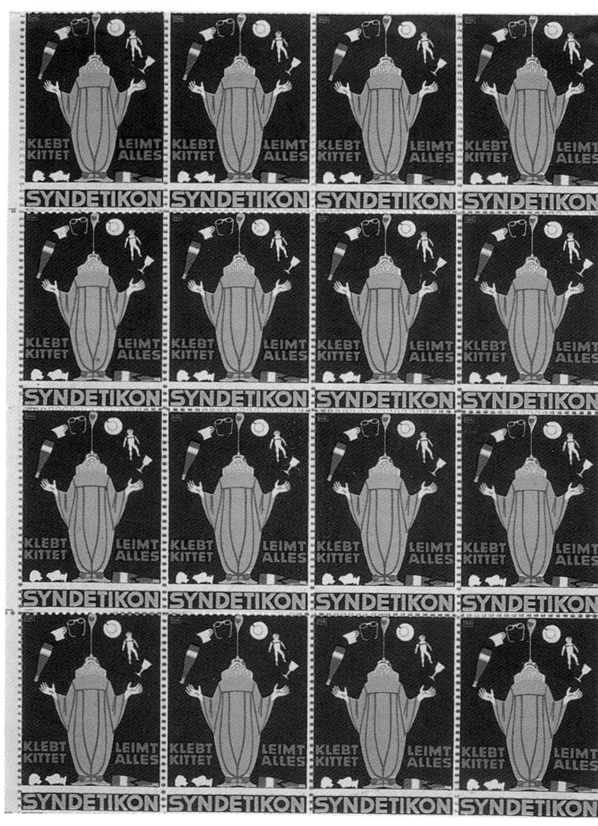

2.22

The group of typefaces Ehmcke designed, 'Antiqua' (1907), 'Kursiv' (1909) and 'Fraktur' (1909–10), revealed a combined understanding of both traditions and were favourably received for their restraint and refinement. The book historian

EX LIBRIS OSWALD DITTRICH

47. Wirkliche Größe. Schriftstudie zu Nr. 30. Materialsprache. Papierschnitt-Schablonen-Abdruck.

dadurch meist bedingte Vereinfachung und Beschränkung auf das Wesentliche gerichtet sein. Ein Beispiel einer solchen äußersten Vereinfachung behufs eindringlicher Materialsprache finden wir in Nr. 28. Die Aufgabe, ein ganzes Büchlein in Holz zu schneiden, hat nach jahrelangen Studien zu dieser scheinbar einfachen Arbeit, bei der aber die Höhe und Breite der Buchstabenschenkel, die Länge jedes Stichelschnittes wohl abgewogen ist, geführt. Man beachte, wie die Buchstaben, nur durch einen Stichelschnitt von einander ge-

102

2.23

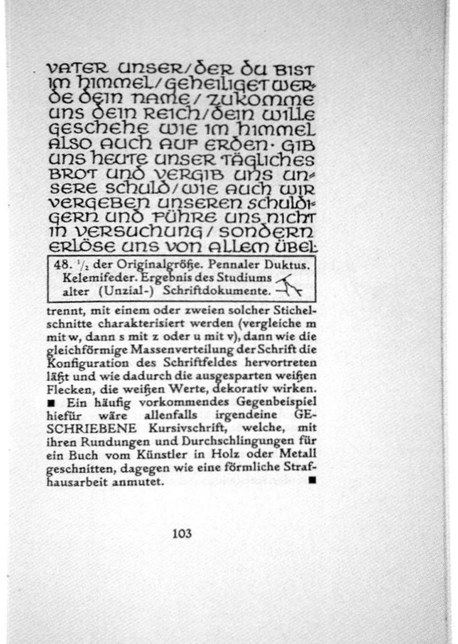

VATER UNSER / DER DU BIST IM HIMMEL / GEHEILIGET WERDE DEIN NAME / ZUKOMME UNS DEIN REICH / DEIN WILLE GESCHEHE WIE IM HIMMEL ALSO AUCH AUF ERDEN · GIB UNS HEUTE UNSER TÄGLICHES BROT UND VERGIB UNS UNSERE SCHULD / WIE AUCH WIR VERGEBEN UNSEREN SCHULDIGERN UND FÜHRE UNS NICHT IN VERSUCHUNG / SONDERN ERLÖSE UNS VON ALLEM ÜBEL:

48. 1/2 der Originalgröße. Pennaler Duktus. Kelemifeder. Ergebnis des Studiums alter (Unzial-) Schriftdokumente.

trennt, mit einem oder zweien solcher Stichelschnitte charakterisiert werden (vergleiche m mit w, dann s mit z oder u mit v), dann wie die gleichförmige Massenverteilung der Schrift die Konfiguration des Schriftfeldes hervortreten läßt und wie dadurch die ausgesparten weißen Flecken, die weißen Werte, dekorativ wirken. ■ Ein häufig vorkommendes Gegenbeispiel hiefür wäre allenfalls irgendeine GESCHRIEBENE Kursivschrift, welche, mit ihren Rundungen und Durchschlingungen für ein Buch vom Künstler in Holz oder Metall geschnitten, dagegen wie eine förmliche Strafhausarbeit anmutet. ■

103

2.24

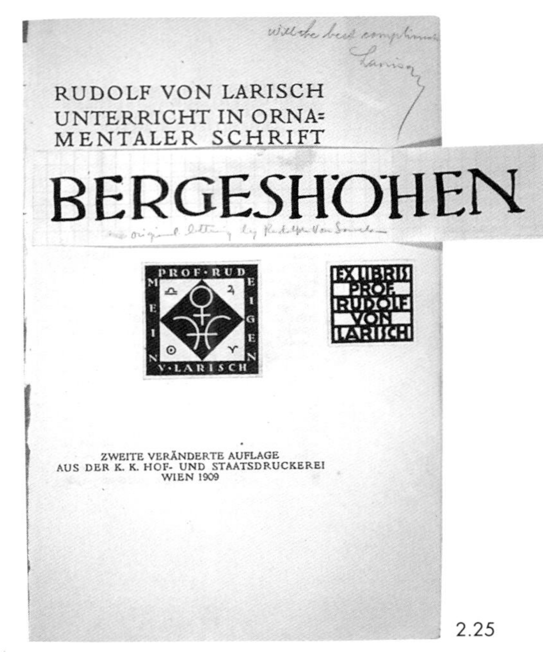

RUDOLF VON LARISCH
UNTERRICHT IN ORNAMENTALER SCHRIFT

BERGESHÖHEN

PROF · RUD
V · LARISCH

EX LIBRIS PROF RUDOLF VON LARISCH

ZWEITE VERÄNDERTE AUFLAGE
AUS DER K. K. HOF- UND STAATSDRUCKEREI
WIEN 1909

2.25

2.23–2.25 *Unterricht in ornamentaler Schrift* (Instruction in ornamental lettering)

Designed by Rudolf von Larisch
Title page and two pages incorporating the designer's handwritten sample, 'Bergeshöhen' and his ex libris. Second edition 1909

Hans Loubier characterized 'Ehmcke' typeface, for example, as suitable for setting poetry, considering it to be 'tender, with fine lines, slender… it has long ascenders… elegant in movement and altogether somewhat precious'.[26]

Like Behrens, Ehmcke turned to 14th- and 15th-century Florence for his compositions, adopting a style based on repeated geometrical motifs, borders and sharp contrasts of tone, often incorporating metallic inks. He was convinced that this was a suitable form for the flowering of German industrial culture. A serious and well-read designer, Ehmcke is best characterized as a traditionalist. This was apparent in his advocacy of the local role of designers. Unusually for his time, Ehmcke recommended that the staff teaching graphics at the Arts and Crafts schools should take work from their communities, to give their particular cultural region (*Kulturkreis*) a firm tradition which, in his view, had been missing for nearly a century. In a list of possible tasks for the designer, which formed his contribution to a study of the Arts and Crafts movement in Germany in 1921, Ehmcke included the design of stamps, stationery for town or city councils, family documents, forms for registry offices and churches, travel guides and postcards of regions, as well as wall-charts of local architectural and geographical features. At a turbulent time of change, this was an unassuming interpretation of design with a distinct sense of everyday purpose, rather than of a more experimental, self-expressive or commercial nature.

DIE FRÜH-
RENAISSANCE DER
ITALIENISCHEN
MALEREI
200
NACHBILDUNGEN
MIT GESCHICHTLICHER
EINFÜHRUNG NEBST
ERLÄUTERUNGEN VON
RICHARD HAMANN

ERSTES BIS VIERTES TAUSEND
VERLEGT BEI EUGEN DIEDERICHS
JENA

2.26

PROLEGOMENA

APOLLODOROS: „O ja, darüber bin ich ziemlich unterrichtet. Erst neulich, da ich von Phaleron nach der Stadt gehe, sieht mich von rückwärts einer meiner Bekannten und ruft mir nach:

„Apollodoros, Apollodoros von Phaleron", er scherzt immer mit meinem Namen, „so warte doch!" Ich bleibe nun stehen und warte auf ihn, und da sagt er mir denn: „Ich habe dich schon unlängst gesucht, ich möchte nämlich so gerne etwas über das Gastmahl des Agathon erfahren, ich meine jenes, an dem Sokrates, Alkibiades und noch viele andere teilgenommen und bei dem sie über Eros gesprochen haben. Was sprachen sie damals alles, weißt du Näheres? Mir hat schon jemand davon erzählt, der es von Phoinix, dem Sohne des Philippos, gehört hatte, und dieser sagte mir, auch du wüßtest Näheres darüber. In der Tat, er konnte mir nicht gerade viel sagen, erzähle du mir nun davon! Denn niemand ist so dafür geschaffen wie du, die Worte unseres großen Freundes zu künden. Zuerst aber sage noch schnell: warst du selbst bei dem Gastmahl zugegen? Ja?"

Darauf erwidere ich ihm gleich: „Dein Freund muß dich wirklich schlecht unterrichtet haben, wenn er meint, das Gastmahl, um das du mich fragst, hätte erst vor kurzem stattgefunden und ich selbst hätte daran teilgenommen!"

„Nicht? Ich dachte!"

„Aber mein lieber Glaukon," fuhr ich fort, „weißt du denn nicht, daß Agathon seit vielen Jahren schon die Stadt verlassen hat? und dann, seitdem ich um Sokrates bin, seitdem ich täglich, ich sage täglich ganz genau weiß, was Sokrates spricht und was Sokrates tut, sind noch nicht drei Jahre vergangen. Früher, ach früher! da lief ich so herum, ohne zu wissen wohin und tat geschäftig und war doch so jämmerlich wie nur irgend jemand, so jämmerlich wie du jetzt, Glaukon, der du noch immer glaubst, man dürfe um keinen Preis denken, nur nicht denken."

2.27

2.26–2.27 *Ehmcke-Mediaeval: Mit Halbfetter Schrift, Kursiv Initialen und Einfassungen* (Ehmcke Medieval: with semi-bold type, italic initials and borders)

Designed by Fritz Hellmut Ehmcke
Typefoundry booklet
About 1926

2.28 *Ehmcke Fraktur*

Designed by Fritz Hellmut Ehmcke
Typefoundry booklet
1912

2.29 *Ehmcke Elzevir*

Designed by F. Hellmut Ehmcke
Typefoundry booklet
1928

Such an essentially conservative view of the role of the designer was compatible with *Heimatschutz* ideology. A popular movement following Ernst Rudorf's ideas, this stressed the preservation of tradition against the tide of Modernity.[27] It considered the big city, a product of late 19th-century industrialization, to be un-German. By contrast, an imaginary ante-1800 Germany was invoked to create the persuasive image of a pre-capitalist idyll. One wing of the *Heimatschutz* following had an antisemitic, racist doctrine which escalated in the 1920s and fed directly into National Socialist ideology. In architecture, this was led by Paul Schultze-Naumburg, who advocated reference to vernacular traditions as a central way to guarantee this identity. However, it would be misleading to cast Ehmcke as a totally backward-looking designer solely concerned with vernacular revival. Although the content and purpose of his design stressed tradition, its form was often distinctively modern.

Ehmcke's career in Munich after 1913 was grounded in his teaching at the Staatsschule für Angewandte Kunst (State School of Applied Art), where his range included all the book arts and commercial graphics. He worked alongside Emil Preetorius, one of Germany's most prominent book illustrators. Ehmcke published a great deal, most notably *Persönliches und Sachliches* in 1928 and *Geordnete und Gültiges* in 1955, collections of essays covering all aspects of graphic design education and practice, as well as the quarterly journal, *Das Zelt*, promoting the

2.28

ALLE Menschen, von welchem Stande sie auch seyen, die etwas Tugendsames oder Tugendähnliches vollbracht haben, sollten, wenn sie sich wahrhaft guter Absichten bewußt sind, eigenhändig ihr Leben aufsetzen, jedoch nicht eher zu einer so schönen Unternehmung schreiten, als bis sie das Alter von vierzig Jahren erreicht haben.
Dieser Gedanke beschäftigt mich gegenwärtig, da ich im achtundfünfzigsten stehe, und mich hier in Florenz mancher vergangenen Widerwärtigkeiten wohl erinnern mag, da mich nicht, wie sonst, böse Schicksale verfolgen, und ich zugleich eine bessere Gesundheit und größere Heiterkeit des Geistes, als wie in meinem ganzen übrigen Leben genieße. Sehr lebhaft ist die Erinnerung manches Angenehmen und Guten, aber auch manchen

DER MYTHUS
VON
ORIENT
UND
OCCIDENT
EINE
METAPHYSIK
DER ALTEN WELT
AUS
DEN WERKEN
VON
J. J. BACHOFEN

2.29

2.30

2.31

2.32

Ehmcke circle.[28] In all of these activities, he reinforced his traditional conception of graphic and typographic design as a practice based on the embellishment of established forms.

Lucian Bernhard (1883–1972) - A 'Master' of German Poster Art

Lucian Bernhard was the most celebrated poster designer in Berlin before 1914 and went on to become one of the first successful European designers in the USA. He was recognized as an important figure during his lifetime and his works featured in most retrospective selections of early German graphic design. He was born in Stuttgart and trained at the Academy in Munich before moving to Berlin, where he established his professional life. As in the case of Behrens and Ehmcke, his early career coincided with the workshop movement and he acted as the artistic director of the Deutsche Werkstätten für Handwerkkunst in Berlin in the early 1900s.

He was also a member of the German Werkbund and artistic adviser to the Verein der Plakatfreunde from 1905 to 1921, a position which took him to the

2.33

2.30 *Reklame Schau* (Advertising exhibition)

Designed by Lucian Bernhard and Fritz Rosen
Poster
1929

2.31 *Deutsche Werkstätten Jetzt* (German Workshops Now)

Designed by Lucian Bernhard
Poster
1912

2.32 Stiller Shoes

Designed by Lucian Bernhard
Poster
1907–08

2.33 Oigee Binoculars

Designed by Lucian Bernhard
Poster
1912

heart of the German poster community. Characteristic of the time, Bernhard also practised as an interior architect, one of his best-known designs being the Café Kurfürstendamm in Berlin's West End. He was clearly ambitious on an international level, and after acting as Professor of Advertising Art at the Berlin Academy, moved to New York in 1925, where he was based for the rest of his life, while continuing an American-German studio with his business partner Fritz Rosen in Berlin.

The most important stage in Bernhard's career was his work for Hollerbaum und Schmidt, the prestigious art printers of Berlin, where he became artistic adviser to its director, Ernst Growald. At the time, the company had in its stable a group of poster artists – among them Edmund Edel, Hans Lindenstadt, Julius Klinger, Julius Gipkens, Hans Rudi Erdt, Paul Scheurich and Karl Schulpig – who formed what was known as the Berlin School.[29]

Bernhard was most closely associated with the tradition of autograph posters, identified by their large format and expert printing, and known generically as the *Sachplakat* (object poster). In this formula a single object was depicted, with the brand name and occasionally a short copyline. This manner of depiction was an interesting mix. Bernhard, like all other poster artists working with Hollerbaum und Schmidt and other similar art printers, used the lithographic stone to achieve saturated colour, with up to sixteen ink colour separations for the most expensive editions.

It has been suggested that Bernhard's stark portrayal of objects was influenced by the English Beggarstaff Brothers. His posters also shared the aesthetic qualities of contemporary retail catalogues and small press advertisements in which objects were highly lit for studio photography. The goods gained the character of commodities: shining, new and coded for sale. Within this formula, Bernhard's work stood out for its striking colours and use of lettering. New inks were developed at the time to prevent fading or running, as the posters were billed around the cities. Out of this came a distinctive range of colours, initially bright with strong contrasts, but later works were realised in sophisticated combinations of tertiary colours, cool greys and greens. Bernhard frequently incorporated his own type design, Bernhard Antiqua, a Roman typeface with Gothic inflections. His designs, characterized by simplicity of subject, monumentality of form and strongly individualized colours, were praised for eradicating the superfluous.

Prior to this increased interest in original designs for posters, printers would hold blanks which could be adapted with copyline to suit the customer. On occasion, the same lithographic design could be used to suit different purposes for a single client, with only the wording in letterpress altered.[30] Whereas in the USA advertising agencies acted as buyers of space in newspapers or magazines and advised clients in their advertising strategy, the usual relationship in Germany until 1914 was between printer and the retailer or industrialist. Artistic variety was used to attract the client, and artists' and printers' names were featured for the first time as a form of self-advertisement. Branded goods were still a novelty in many areas of the market and an iconic approach which asserted the company brand and distilled the message into a strong visual equivalent was considered most effective. Nevertheless, when the First World War set new demands for the poster to persuade people in matters of patriotism, the *Sachplakat* was deemed to have become formulaic and exhausted.

Bernhard's career, more than that of any of his contemporaries, raises the question of the early exchange between American and German strategies. He emigrated in the 1920s, but already before the War he and Growald were clearly fascinated with the transatlantic activity. For instance, Growald contributed several chapters to the most comprehensive study of advertising, the two volumes edited by Paul Ruben under the title *Die Reklame: ihre Kunst und Wissenschaft* and published in 1913.[31] The title revealed a fascination with understanding the American 'scientific' methods of advertising; but Growald's comparison between German and American approaches tended towards stereotypes and generality. Advertising, he contended, suited the national character of the Americans; its clearest message was to the businessman. The German made the mistake of

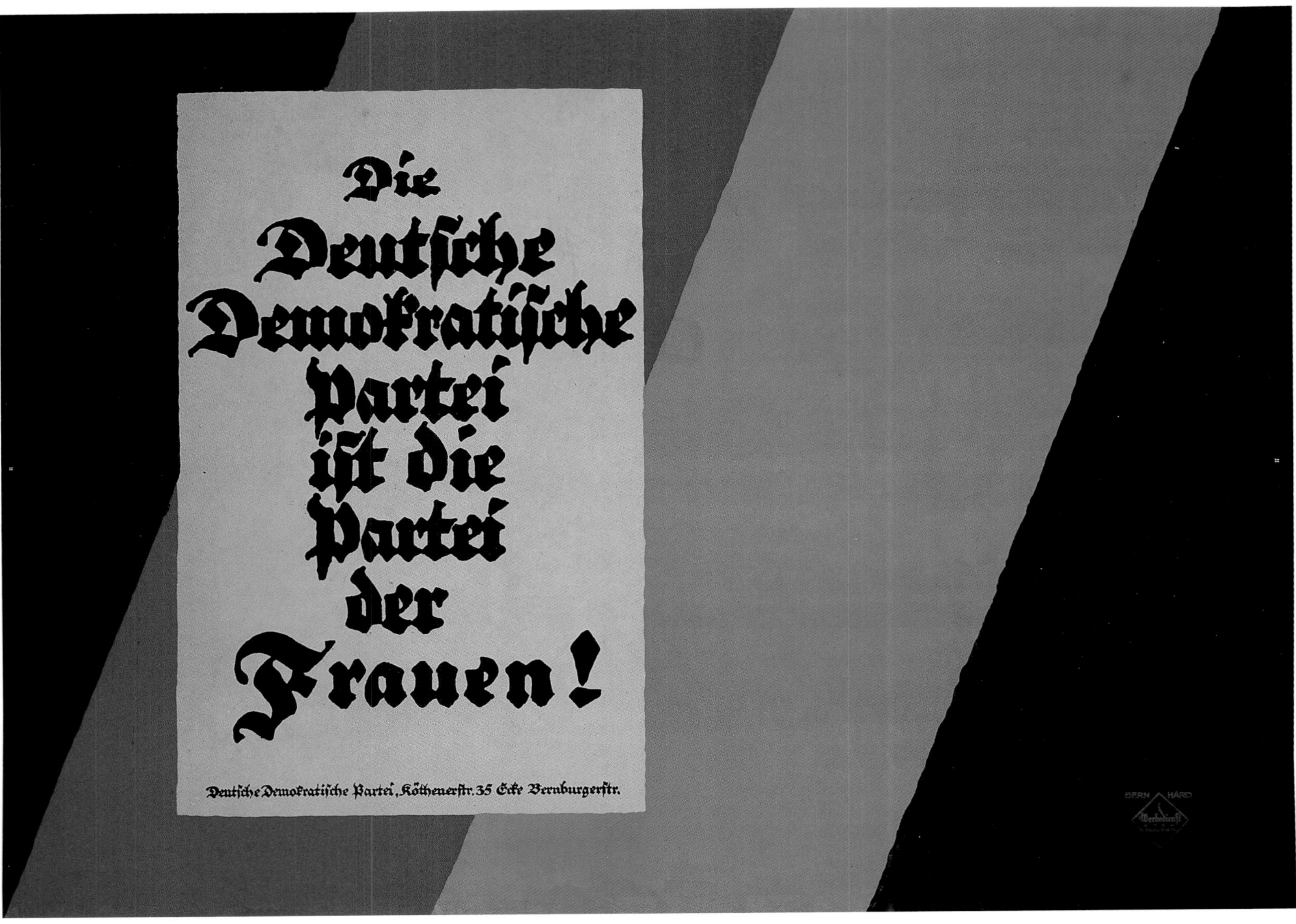

2.34

2.34 *Die Deutsche Demokratische Partei ist die Partei der Frauen!* (The German Democratic Party is the party for women!)

Designed by Lucian Bernhard
Poster
1920

commissioning what he liked for his money, whereas the Americans placed the specialist at his service, paid for his work and received his expertise. In describing what he called the fundamental difference, he wrote that 'the American public loves and treasures adverts, a successful advertising idea impresses them; it rewards the proficiency of the businessman and reflects well on the goods.'[32]

One contention was that Germans were not interested in strategy, preferring to follow their own taste rather than informed advice. Growald wrote, 'The American succeeds in making the advertisement work, so that it fulfils its purpose.
The German succeeds in making it please him. The American confronts the advertisement objectively – the German subjectively.'

Manoli and Advertising Strategy

In 1919, Manoli, a major German cigarette manufacturer, published a celebratory book designed by Bernhard, to mark the company's first twenty-five years in business. Concerned to promote smoking and to stress the rise in popularity of German as opposed to imported cigarettes, the book explained attitudes towards publicity.[33] Self-congratulatory in tone, the book nevertheless gave an interesting indication of a major company's attitude.

Manoli's policy was based on assertions of quality. Accordingly, campaigns established associations with luxury. Customers were depicted as mature, of sporting or officer background, or otherwise elegant women. The principle was 'to show people how to smoke', as well as to indicate the aspirational character of the product. The company was an inaugural member of the Deutscher Werkbund and its advertising chief, E.E.H. Schmidt, recruited some of the leading Berlin poster artists for its campaigns. Julius Klinger oversaw the lettering for packaging and press advertisements, for example, while Hans Rudi Erdt designed several major posters. In turn, Bernhard was responsible for posters during the war which turned advertising strategies on their head with images such as servicemen sharing cigarettes.

In an analysis of their success, supported by sales statistics, three central themes emerged. Firstly, there were the eye-catching press advertisements, often with single sentences intended to have subconscious appeal. Secondly, effective lettering on posters was considered essential to establish the brand in the public's mind. Thirdly, silhouetted figures were praised for the visual impact they made in attracting attention on poster columns. In characteristic fashion for a member of the Werkbund, Manoli concluded that it should maintain its task of 'educating the public', a role it clearly felt it had fulfilled.

A study of 1923, Kurt Friedländer's *Der Weg zum Käufer, eine Theorie der praktischen Reklame*, indicated how similar marketing strategies were being introduced to German design education. Friedländer divided his book

2.35 

2.35 Manoli Kardash Cigarettes

Designed by Lucian Bernhard
Poster
1912

into the various stages he believed the observer passed through in the act of looking; from noticing (*Bemerken*), reading (*Lesen*), remembering (*Erinnern*), and finally to transacting (*Handel*). He offered an explanation of advertising's impact through association of ideas, repetition, intensity of word or image, verse, alliteration and humour. Much of the evidence in this work was drawn from earlier studies, such as Walter Dill Scott's *The Theory and Practice of Advertising* (1903) and *The Psychology of Advertising* (1908), and examples of successful American press advertising were illustrated.[34] Compositional devices such as intensity, size, repetition, opposites, location and movement were all examined. As for subject-matter, novelty, humour and ugliness were

2.36

2.37

all considered possible strategies. The crucial step was the application of behavioural psychology to understand consumer motivation. Significantly, such advice manuals opened up the questions of difference between the individual and collective or national and social. Bernhard would experience an intense version of this when he settled as a European in the USA.

2.36 *Blende nicht – leuchte mit Bosch-Licht!* (Illuminate with Bosch lights – to avoid blinding)

Designed by Bernhard-Rosen
Poster
1927

2.37 *Lärme nicht – warne mit Bosch-Horn* (Sound with Bosch horns – to avoid deafening)

Designed by Bernhard-Rosen
Poster
1927

2.38

2.39

2.38 *Gebrauchsgraphik*, February 1927

Designed by Lucian Bernhard and Fritz Rosen
Depicting the Bernhard-Rosen design studios based in New York and Berlin
Magazine cover

2.39 Photograph of Lucian Bernhard (right) with Hans Sachs in New York 1956

Bernhard in America

Bernhard was among the first German designers to be shown in New York, and together with Ludwig Hohlwein he had the reputation of leading 'the German style'. From an office in the New York Times building in Times Square, offered to him by the proprietor Adolph Ochs, Bernhard produced designs for the American public. In an interview with Oskar Hahn in February 1926, he explained how he adjusted to his new context as a foreign designer, in a period following a world war when to be German was not popular. Maintaining his commitment to his personal style was not easy in a visually more conservative context.

> *The exhibition of my German work has brought me whole-hearted recognition from the American advertising experts. And yet, when commissions are given, a distinct departure from this work is always demanded. This is due, firstly, to the fact, even though this is not mentioned, that I am regarded as one of the most pronounced exponents of German poster art, and one is afraid that an unadulterated German poster style might unfortunately arouse political offence among a great part of the American public. Then again one must deal with the fact that public taste has been vitiated and misdirected for so many years through the one-sided use of posters based merely upon the enlarged photograph, that nobody has enough courage to come forward with a strong, simple and actual style of poster.*
>
> *I am glad to see that Hohlwein of Munich is now represented on the New York billboards by a number of his own posters. He is the European artist who is best able to fulfill the demands which the American public makes upon the realistic, illustrated poster, and he thus represents a bridge between American and European conceptions in this field.*
>
> *The American wants a 'picture', an 'idea'. A purely optical idea is no idea at all for him. He demands what he calls 'human interest'. If he can get*

this, and get it intensified by strong and piquant colour effects and good composition, so much the better, and it is these factors which the Americans so justly admire in the work of Ludwig Hohlwein.[35]

The change in Bernhard's work from the object poster to his mature style indicates his adaptation to the 'American' approaches stressed in the interview. If his visual identity remained similar, with the continued interest in depicting a single motif or logo, he added to this in the '20s an increased attention to copyline and the need for a concept by which the customer would be drawn to read further and notice the work.

Bernhard's future lay in the USA and although he kept the Berlin office up to 1933, he eventually emigrated. In 1929 he and Rosen held a large retrospective exhibition in Berlin, signalling their continued prominence in the field. In the same year Rosen was invited to design the publications and poster for the international advertising congress in Berlin. However, when Bruno Paul failed to secure his recommendation of Bernhard as Professor of Graphics at the Berlin United State Art Schools in the face of antisemitic resistance, Bernhard took up his position at Harvard University instead.

Bernhard was the most commercial in character of the three designers considered here, a figure who adapted to the American business culture and major advertising agencies. Arguably, it was Bernhard who most successfully translated ideas from the Arts and Crafts debates of 1914 to the modern commercial world which was increasingly the context of the '20s. All three designers, Behrens, Ehmcke and Bernhard, reached stylistic maturity before the First World War. Working on the threshold of Modernism, they did not substantially transform their approaches after the War. Instead, while they embraced modern business organization and employed the latest techniques of reproduction, they stopped short of Modernist design.

2.40

2.40 Amoco Gas

Designed by Lucian Bernhard
Poster
1946

»FARBE UND FORM«
EIN BILDPROSPEKT DER

PREIS: RM 1.–

SCHULE REIMANN

PRIVATE KUNST- UND KUNSTGEWERBESCHULE

An illustrated prospectus of the

REIMANN SCHOOL BERLIN

3.1

3.1 *››Farbe und Form‹‹ Ein Bildprospekt der Schule Reimann Monatsschrift für Kunst und Gewerbe Reimannschule, Berlin* (Monthly Review of Arts and Crafts at the Reimann School, Berlin)

Edited by Albert Reimann
1927

3.2 *Staatliches Bauhaus Weimar 1919–1923*

Cover designed by Herbert Bayer
Written by Walter Gropius and Laszlo Moholy-Nagy
Book
1923

3

Modernism and Graphic Art Education: The Bauhaus and the Reimann School, 1919–1938

The designs created by the pre-1914 generation of artists and architects often interpreted a search for modernity as being allied to causes for national economic well-being. By contrast, the preoccupation with the 'national' question of German culture seemed anachronistic to the next generation. The War was inevitably followed in Germany by a period of social and political upheaval. In the face of a massive housing shortage, an influenza epidemic and rapid currency inflation (by 1923 one million German Reichsmark were valued at one US dollar), the focus turned to the means of enhancing international communication. The years of the Weimar Republic, founded when the seat of government was moved from politically volatile Berlin to historically stable Weimar in February 1919 and ended when Adolf Hitler was appointed Chancellor of Germany on 30 January 1933, coincided neatly with the first fulfilment of experimental Modernism in design.

3.2

Sometimes known retrospectively as 'high' or 'heroic' Modernism, this movement was characterized by a shared belief among a vocal and talented group, representing all genres in the arts, that a new start could be made which addressed modernity, internationalism and the machine. In this sense, the destruction of war led to a *tabula rasa*, a blank page for artists, designers and writers to fill. An event such as The Congress of International Progressive Artists, held in Düsseldorf in 1922, and attended by many artists and designers interested in moving from painting to graphic design, paralleled such events in the wider political and social sphere as the foundation of the Third International of the Communist Party in 1919 and the League of Nations in 1920.

While machines were widely associated with the effects of war, they were also increasingly invoked as the most appropriate means to realize the modern world. One of the longest standing and significant debates over the meaning of manual and mechanized production was renewed in the '20s by a call to work with the machine, even if in many cases it was more rhetorical than real. Paul Renner, who became an important figure in this period as a writer on typography and as the designer of Futura, the most successful sans-serif typeface of the time, summarized the shift in artistic sensibility when he wrote in 1927:

> *We forty-eight year olds received our first impressions in a fin-de-siecle atmosphere. We found ourselves immersed in an artistic world which was somehow almost unconnected with real existence. The spiritual person found himself at that time disgusted by every form of politics, machines, factories, economics or progress: he left those to the bourgeois. He lived as a bohemian in cafés, as a hermit or in esoteric circles. Then, already before the turn of the century, a change was afoot in this world-abstaining attitude. Whether Nietzsche was the symptom or the cause, we do not wish to investigate here. A political activism, in part nationalist, in part of revolutionary complexion, went through Europe. The intellectual burst in to this world which up until then had been avoided.*
>
> *He became a jockey, a diplomat, an organiser of grand styles, or just a confidence trickster. The intellectual preached scorn for intellectualism... the conceptions of art were devalued. Instead, people valued the music-hall,*

the skill of the circus performer, the comedian and the dancer. And the engineer was more valued than the architect. Only then was it time to understand the machine and to master it. After the war and the revolution the intellectual had to jump into the vacuum created by the end of the old world order. In between, however, the new sense of Form had become a strength which demanded to belong to the building of the new world.[1]

This description finds echoes in the activities of many leading cultural figures of the Weimar period, whose Modernity was defined by an engagement with the everyday. Perhaps not surprisingly in the context of the journal of the German Werkbund, Renner attributed to design, and specifically form-giving, a significant place in shaping the new world, and there were many designers' statements which shared his prophetic tone.

The Weimar Social Context

The War had created a hiatus, a chance to take stock, but also a break to allow contrasts between 'before' and 'after' and a justification for change. This was often expressed in terms of generations, but class allegiance was also to feature strongly in the diverse responses to industrial change. A radicalized visual culture increasingly challenged the status quo and conservatism of the German middle classes.

Many artists and designers aligned themselves with revolutionary politics. Instead of bohemians at the margins, alluded to by Renner, they became activists organized in political groups, and produced posters and pamphlets to announce political demonstrations and support for social causes. For example, the Arbeitsrat für Kunst (Working Council for Art) and the Novembergruppe (named after the unsuccessful Communist revolution of November 1918 in Germany) were led by architects, among them Walter Gropius. Expressionism became a political style, transformed from a search for individual redemption

3.3 *Arbeiter! Bannt die Gefahr von Rechts! Wählt Sozialisten!* (Workers! Avert the danger from the Right! Vote Socialist!)

Designed by Josef Schwingen, Schlegl and Kötter
Poster
1920

3.4 *Das Politische Plakat* (The Political Poster)

Cover by César Klein
Periodical
1919

3.5 *Schafft Rote Hilfe! Fünf Jahre IRH* (Create Red Help! Fifth anniversary of International Red Help)

Designed by Heinrich Vogeler
Poster
1928

3.6 *Nie Wieder Krieg* (Never Again War)

Designed by Käthe Kollwitz
Poster
1923

3.3

characteristic of pre-1914 years to a broader-based wish for class redemption. Concern was expressed especially for the clearest victims of the war, the underclass of the industrial proletariat and wives of returning or killed soldiers, and children.[2]

The situation, furthermore, was complicated by changes in the class structure of Germany in these years, with the continuing shift of populations to the cities and new forms of employment. One constituency or public remained unchanged, the conservative middle classes whose cultural outlook has been described by Jeffrey Herf,

3.4

3.5

The German Mittelstand encompassed small- and middle-sized families, artisans and shopkeepers, white-collar workers in big industry and civil-service, and the professional middle class – lawyers, doctors, professors, higher civil servants, and engineers. These diverse groups were bound together by common reactions to the rapid development of industrial capitalism in Germany. Anxious and afraid of large capital on the one hand, and the organised working-class on the other, they viewed the nation as a redemptive unity. Right-wing nationalist spokesmen claimed that the nation-state alone was above narrow class-interests.[3]

3.6

By 1920, however, with the growing number of salaried employees in office jobs, in banks, insurance offices, government offices and retailing, a new urban class was identified which stood in a different relation to both the property-owning middle classes and the skilled and unskilled industrial workers.

> *Who would seriously deny that the life-style of white-collar employees was superior to that of the workers! White-collar employees dressed better, lived in nicer homes, possessed higher quality goods, pursued educational opportunities, attended lectures, concerts, or theatrical performances, and read good books. Their standard of living approximated that of the propertied class, not perhaps in range and freedom but in type.*[4]

These better-off white-collar workers were described as generally more experimental in outlook and lifestyle. If a new design evolved, it was likely to have its greatest impact on them. Artistically, this new class were defined as the subjects of photographers and painters, or became the topic of articles in the proliferating photojournals. They were singled out for their 'new look' and their reactions to the changing patterns of workday and leisure time. In 1924, representations of this new style in painting and photography were grouped together for their overt, matter-of-fact character by the curator Gustav Hartlaub under the term *Neue Sachlichkeit* (New Objectivity) in an exhibition in Mannheim.[5]

To many Germans, this new class's political position posed a threat, as it remained ambiguous and liable to swing to extremes. To this was added the troubling uncertainty about its morals. Obviously not all of this generation subscribed to the same set of cultural interests, but there was sufficient common ground for the movement to be identified as *die neue Wohnkultur* (new living culture). Interests in fashion, design, sport, new sexual politics, film and photography were all subsumed within a modern, collective ideal.

Most interesting in the context of graphic design are the comments made by Siegfried Kracauer, the literary and film critic, who was also a contributor to the illustrated weeklies. One of his overriding themes was the impact of mass entertainment on culture, and in an intriguing way he connected the new class's eagerness for entertainment with a different conception of ornament, developed in the book, *The Mass Ornament*. Having witnessed the popularity in Germany

3.7

3.8

3.9

3.7 – 3.9 Three covers from *Das Illustrierte Blatt* (The Frankfurt Illustrated Newspaper)

'The Jackson Boarding House'
5 May 1928
Photograph by Sasha Stone

'In the Swing'
8 September 1928

'Louise Brooks in Pandora's Box, *currently showing in Berlin'*
14 November 1928

of Anglo-American mass-formation dance groups such as the Tiller Girls in the mid-1920s, he linked their form of entertainment with the division of labour and anonymity in modern capitalism.

> *In the domain of body culture, which also covers the illustrated papers, tastes have quietly been changing. The process began with the Tiller Girls. These products of American distraction factories are no longer individual girls, but indissoluble girl clusters whose movements are demonstrations of mathematics. As they condense into figures in the revues, performances of the same geometric precision are taking place in what is always the same packed stadium, be it in Australia or India, not to mention America. The bearer of the ornament is the mass.*[6]

In another article, 'Shelter for the Homeless', he described the commodity world of this new class and commented on what he saw as their spiritual homelessness.

> *The mass of white-collar employees distinguishes itself from the working-class proletariat by being intellectually homeless. For the moment they are incapable of finding their way to their comrades, and the house of*

3.10

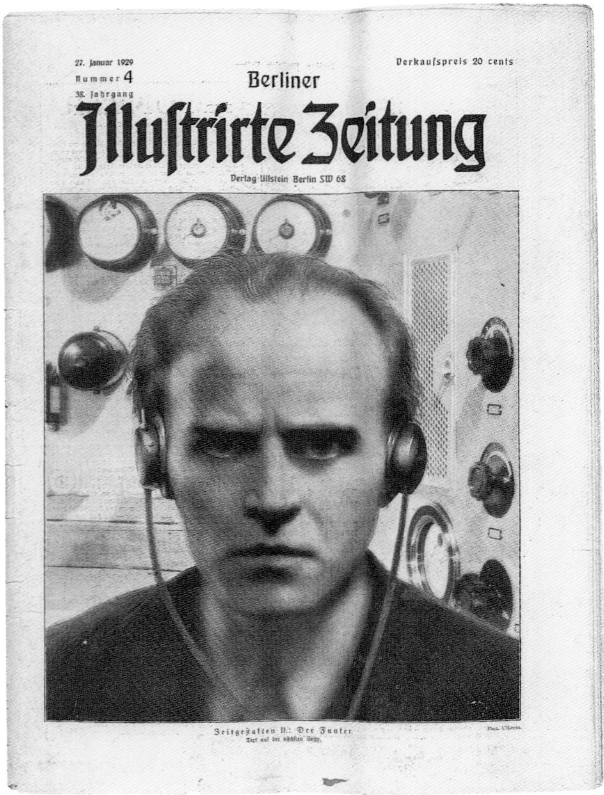

3.11

bourgeois ideas and feelings in which they previously lived has collapsed due to the erosion of it foundations, brought on by economic development. They are living at present without a doctrine to which they can look up, without a goal to guide them...

It is to be understood, incidentally, that 'at home' encompasses daily as well as residential life, as charted by advertisements in magazines for white-collar employees. They concern, in the main: pens; Kohinoor pencils; haemorrhoids; hair loss; beds; crepe soles; white teeth; rejuvenation treatments; coffee consumption habits; dictaphones; writer's cramp; trembling, particularly in the presence of others; quality pianos on weekly installments; etc.[7]

Though pessimistic in tone, Kracauer recognized the role of advertisements in the construction of identity. Characterizing such concerns as diversions, he identified the new commodity culture of Weimar as feminine and, in its nature, less authentic than what had preceded it. Inevitably the role of contemporary design education, specifically that directed towards graphic design and advertising, was increasingly implicated in these debates as the next generation of modern designers took a position on mass reproduction, the availability of goods in the market, and the social responsibility of the designer.

The Bauhaus

In 1919, Walter Gropius, already a well-established architect, was invited to transform the School of Arts and Crafts in Weimar for the new era. The school had previously been one of the most prominent under the direction of Henry van de Velde, who had been forced to leave on the outbreak of war and return to his native Belgium. The Bauhaus that resulted from Gropius's scheme was an educational experiment intended to produce architects and is looked on now as the 20th century's most formative school for the education of designers.

3.12

3.13

NHALTSVERZEICHNIS

DAS STAATLICHE BAUHAUS — SEITE
Walter Gropius: Idee und Aufbau des Staatlichen Bauhauses 6 7

I. DIE SCHULE
Gertrud Grunow: Der Aufbau der lebendigen Form durch Farbe, Form, Ton 20
Paul Klee: Wege des Naturstudiums 24
Wassily Kandinsky: Die Grundelemente der Form 26
Wassily Kandinsky: Farbkurs und Seminar 27

ABBILDUNGEN und FARBTAFELN
FORMLEHRE: Naturstudium, Raumlehre, Farbenlehre, Konstruktionslehre, Kompositionslehre

Abb. 1 **Aus der Vorlehre:** Darstellung der Grundform einer Materie. Übungsaufgabe. Zeichnung. W. Menzel 30
2 Naturstudie. Farbige Zeichnung. J. Pap 31
3 Naturstudie. Darstellung verschiedener Materien. H. Hoffmann 32
4 Aufgaben zur Übung in der Darstellung charakteristischer Eigenschaften verschiedener Materien 33
5 Zeichnerische Darstellung der charakteristischen Eigenschaften einer Materie (Holz). Übungsaufgabe zur Entwicklung des Auges als des rezeptiven Sinnes und des Tastsinnes als des produktiven Sinnes. L. Leudersdorff-Engstfeld 34
6 **Aktzeichnen:** Akt. Statischer Aufbau der oberen Hälfte. G. Schunke 35
7 Akt. Bewegung nach oben I. Kerkovius 36
8 **Aus der Vorlehre:** Materiestudie. Übungsaufgabe: Gestaltung verschiedener Materien zu gegenständlicher Wirkung. Maske. W. Willers 37
9 Plastische Materiestudie. Übungsaufgabe: Gestaltung verschiedener Materien zu gegenständlicher Wirkung. K. Auböck 38
10 Materiestudie. Kombinierte Kontrastwirkung. Materiekontrast (Glas, Holz, Eisen). Kontrast der Ausdrucksformen (zackig glatt): rhythmischer Kontrast. Übungsaufgabe zur Beobachtung der Ähnlichkeit im Ausdruck bei gleichzeitiger Anwendung verschiedener Darstellungsmittel. M. Mirkin 39
11 Materiestudie. Komposition aus verschiedenen Stoffen, gebunden durch rhythmische Formen. Übungsaufgabe: Beobachtung der komplementären Wirkung verschiedener Stoffe zur Untersuchung. M. Bronstein 40
12 Materiestudie. Gestaltung einfachster Materien zu geschlossener Wirkung. Übungsaufgabe. W. Herzger 41
13 Materiestudie. Kombination einfachster Materien. Übungsaufgabe: Entwicklung des Tastsinnes und Beobachtung des subjektiven Materialgefühls. W. Dieckmann 42
14 Materiestudie. Kombination aus einfachsten plastischen und rhythmischen Formen. N. Wassiljeff 43
15 Hell-dunkel. Proportionen (helldunkel = optische Tiefenbewegung). Übungsaufgabe 44
16 Zeichnung. Rhythmische Ausdrucksform durch Variation des Helldunkels. Übungsaufgabe zur Entwicklung des subjektiven rhythmischen Empfindens und zur objektiven Erforschung der Helldunkel- und Proportionsgesetze 45
17 Rhythmische Kontrastformen. Zeichnung. Übungsaufgabe 46
18 Horizontal-vertikal Komposition, entwickelt aus dem Helldunkel (optische Tiefenbewegung). Übungsaufgabe. G. Teltscher. 47
19 Aus dem Unterricht Itten in Wien: Ausdrucksform. M. Téry-Adler 48
20 Aus dem Unterricht Itten in Wien: Rhythmische Übung. M. Téry-Adler 49
21 Helldunkel Verwerfung. F. Dicker 50
22 Plastische Darstellung. Räumliche horizontale-vertikale Komposition. Übungsaufgabe zur Entwicklung des Proportionsgefühls und des statischen Empfindens. G. Schunke 51
23 Plastische Darstellung. Helldunkel Proportionen. (Helldunkel räumliche Tiefenbewegung.) Übungsaufgabe. H. Müller 52
24 Plastische Darstellung. Würfelkomposition. Übungsaufgabe zur Beobachtung der statisch-dynamischen Beziehungen. E. Mögelin 53
25 Aus dem Unterricht Itten in Wien: Proportionen-Analyse nach Giotto. M. Téry-Adler 54
26 Aus dem Unterricht Itten in Wien: Materie. Ausdrucksform-Analyse nach Greco. M. Téry-Adler 55
27 **Analytisches Naturzeichnen:** Charakteristik der Gegenstände. G. Schunke 56
28 Konstruktive Analyse. M. Rasch 57
29 Geometrische Zusammenhänge. M. Rasch 58
30 Lineare Analyse. I. Kerkovius 59

FARBTAFEL I Originallithographie. L. Hirschfeld-Mack 61
II Originallithographie. L. Hirschfeld-Mack 63
III Vierfarbendruck. L. Hirschfeld-Mack 65
IV Originallithographie. R. Paris 67
V Lithographie: „Grundelemente“ (zu Kandinskys Artikel) 69

II. DER BAU: A. Die Werkstätten
B. Der Raum
A. Werkstätten

Abb. 31 **Tischlerei:** Die Werkstatt 73
32 Schwarzpolierter Tisch: Form und Ausführung M. Breuer. Lehrlingsarbeit 74
33 Bücherschrank. Vogelahorn und schwarzpolierte Birne. Form und Ausführung M. Breuer. Lehrlingsarbeit 75

Its example was followed internationally and the teaching and writings of its staff have been made available through extensive research and publications.[8]

The history of the Bauhaus is well-documented. The school's links with the wider field of Constructivist designers in the Soviet Union and Hungary were testimony to its international ambitions, as were the interventions of Theo van Doesburg, an advocate of De Stijl principles, and the appointment of Paul Klee, a Swiss, and Wassily Kandinsky, a Russian, as teachers ('Masters of Form'). The school syllabus was revised on several occasions to accommodate the growing need to produce successful designs for industrial production, and after 1923 there was a move away from the use of luxury or craft materials under the slogan, 'Art and technics a new unity'.[9]

In 1925 Gropius oversaw the transfer of the school to purpose-built accommodation according to his designs in Dessau, a city where it was believed more industrial commissions could be won. A statement made around the time stressed the new resolve to address the design of everyday industrial goods and defined attributes most frequently associated with the Bauhaus.

3.10–3.11 Two covers from the series *'Figures of the Time'* in the *Berliner Illustrirte Zeitung*

'The Sports Teacher'
Photograph by Riebicke
10 March 1929

'The Radio Enthusiast'
Photograph credit Ullstein
27 January 1929

3.12–3.13 *Staatliches Bauhaus Weimar 1919-1923*

Designed by Laszlo Moholy-Nagy
Title page and table of contents
1923

3.14 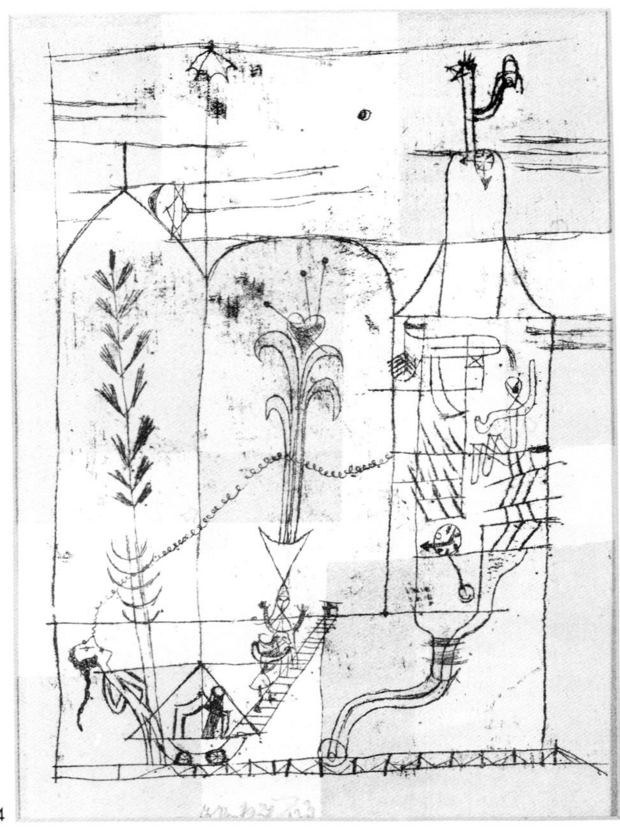

3.14 Scene from Hoffmann

Paul Klee
Print
1921

It is only through constant contact with newly evolving techniques, with the discovery of new materials and with new ways of putting things together, that the creative individual can learn to bring the design of objects into a living relationship with tradition and from that point to develop a new attitude toward design, which is:

- *A resolute affirmation of the living environment of machines and vehicles.*
- *The organic design of things based on their own present-day laws, without romantic gloss and wasteful frivolity.*
- *The limitation to characterize, primary forms and colours, readily accessible to everyone.*
- *Simplicity in multiplicity, economical utilization of space, material, time, and money.*
- *The creation of standard types for all practical commodities of everyday use is a social necessity.*[10]

Another fundamental reorganization of the school took place when Gropius left in 1928 to set up an architectural practice in Berlin. Among his colleagues who also left were Herbert Bayer, to work for the Dorland advertising agency, Marcel Breuer to work for various furniture companies and Laszlo Moholy-Nagy, who continued to promote the new typography and work as a designer. With a new faculty, the second director, Hannes Meyer, took the school further in the direction of standardization in design and engineering in built form.

The Bauhaus was closed in April 1932 by the city of Dessau, by then controlled by a National Socialist majority; afterwards it had short-lived revivals in Berlin under Mies van der Rohe and Chicago under Moholy-Nagy, where it was first called the New Bauhaus and subsequently the Institute of Design.[11]

30

FORMLEHRE

NATURSTUDIUM
RAUMLEHRE
FARBENLEHRE
KONSTRUKTIONSLEHRE
KOMPOSITIONSLEHRE

Abb. 1. Aus der Vorlehre:
Darstellung der Grundform einer Materie
Übungsaufgabe. Zeichnung
W. MENZEL

3.15

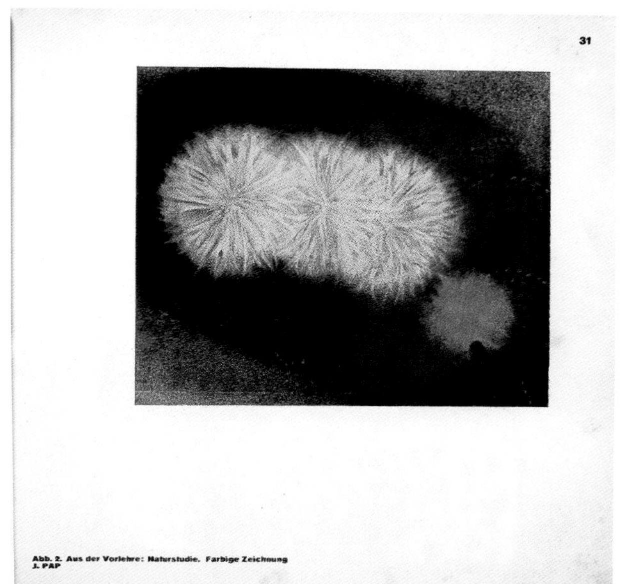
31

Abb. 2. Aus der Vorlehre: Naturstudie. Farbige Zeichnung
J. PAP

3.16

The Curriculum

From the outset of the Bauhaus, studios were organized according to materials. The most important feature in determining the school's design methodology was the *Vorkurs*, a foundation course which all students were required to take. Its aim was to examine the basic vocabulary of design; to abstract principles of composition from nature; to understand materials irrespective of their application to any practical purpose; and to find general laws in lines, structure, tension, composition, colour and light. It was a consequence of such thinking that furniture was made from cantilevered aluminium, steel and glass, for example, and experimental yarns in synthetic materials were developed for fabrics. In graphics, these exercises led to an increasing abstraction. In all departments of the school, basic geometrical forms and primary colours were considered the rudiments of a design language, more elemental and therefore more suitable for communication than figuration and natural colour.

In April 1919, in the first programme of the 'Staatliches Bauhaus Weimar', graphic techniques were listed under training in the crafts or '*Handwerk*' (etching, woodcut, lithography, and engraving), while lettering was taught in the drawing and painting section.[12] The more advanced printing equipment at Weimar had been closed down on the departure of Van de Velde in 1914 and the Bauhaus printed work between 1919 and 1923 was largely typeset by outside printers. Later on, the Dessau Bauhaus was equipped with a composing

139

DRUCKEREI
Abb. 93. Die Werkstatt
Formmeister: L. FEININGER
Technischer Meister: K. ZAUBITZER
1923

3.17

3.15 – 3.17 Pages from *Staatliches Bauhaus Weimar 1919–1923* depicting the Teaching of Form and the Printing Workshops.

3.18 *Jealousy*

Laszlo Moholy-Nagy
Photomontage
1927

3.19–3.20 *Kasimir Malevich, Die gegenstandslose Welt* (The Non-Objective World)

Designed by
Laszlo Moholy-Nagy
Book cover and double page
1927

room in its basement for more advanced work. During the first years, graphic work consisted largely of the printing of postcard series and portfolios of artists' prints – in other words, graphic art rather than design. Additional posters, leaflets and manifestos all indicate that there was not a systematic approach to typography but a mixture of Expressionist and Dadaist tendencies, symptomatic of the flux in the fine art world more generally at that time.

On the arrival of Moholy-Nagy as a member of staff in April 1923, typography and letterpress design became a distinct subject, coinciding with a renewed emphasis on design for the machine. This was partly in response to a need for well-designed information and publicity about the school and partly because typography was considered essential to the new approach to a total art, design and architecture. Increasingly, during the middle '20s, the new typography and the new photography were used in Bauhaus publicity and also as a source of income for the company Bauhaus GmbH from commercial practice.

Moholy arrived from Budapest and Berlin with a background in abstract painting. His design philosophy was a curious mixture of technological determinism, a belief in the social role of design and a mystical preoccupation with properties of light as an aesthetic organizing principle. Many of his boldest experiments embraced the theme of the city and modernity. As a member of the international Constructivist avant-garde he was a prolific polemicist in journals such as *MA* as well as a designer, photographer and film-maker.[13] From his statements we gain a sense of the direction in which he was to steer not only the metal workshop (under his leadership), but also to communications in the school more generally. A statement on Constructivism in 1922 indicates his most extreme utopianism:

> *Before the machine, everyone is equal – I can use it, so can you. There is no tradition in technology, no consciousness of class or standing. Everybody can be the machine's slave or master.*

...Words are heavy, obscure. Their meaning is evasive to the untrained mind. Past traditions hang on their meaning. But there is art. Art expresses the spirit of the times; it is art that crystallises the emotional drive of an age. The art of our century, its mirror and its voice is Constructivism.

Constructivism is neither proletarian nor capitalist. Constructivism is primordial, without class and without ancestor. It expresses the pure form of nature, the direct colour, the spatial element not distorted by utilitarian motifs.

The new world of the proletariat needs Constructivism; it needs fundamentals that are without deceit. Only the natural element accessible to all eyes is revolutionary.[14]

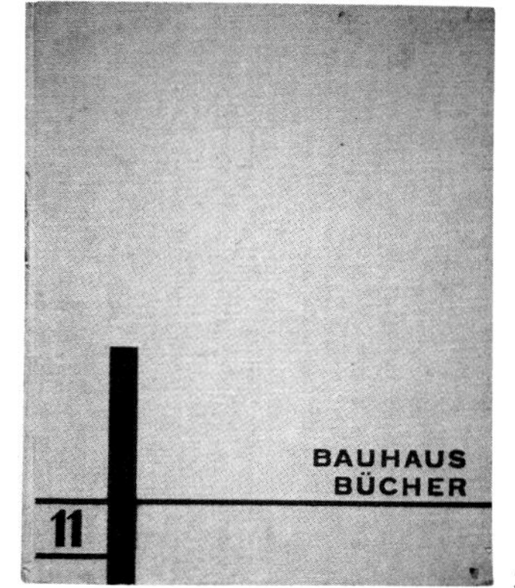

3.19

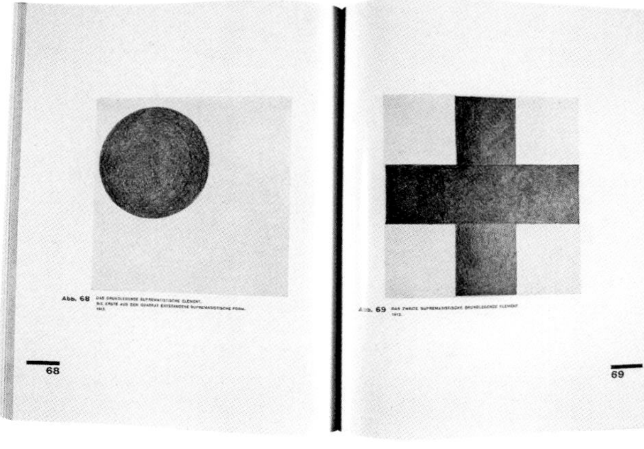

3.20

While international in aim, many of the foundations of Constructivism were derived from artists and designers working in the Soviet Union. The hope that technology would transcend class boundaries in areas of cultural production was grounded more on the way previous hierarchies had removed art from the wider population than any evidence that the mechanized image was more democratic *per se*. Indeed, any assertion that mechanization equalled democracy in visual language could be seen as evidence of utopian naivety. Moholy was writing with the knowledge of the experiments in abstract typography by El Lissitzky, for example, in the poster '*Beat the White with the Red Wedge*' (1919) and his early publications, such as *The Story of Two Squares* (1922).[15] These used advanced aesthetic ideas for popular purposes, namely a political poster and a children's story-book, in the belief that abstraction could provide a universal language that avoided the problem of illiteracy.

In his first book, *Malerei Photographie Film* (Painting Photography Film) of 1925, Moholy's general argument was by then the familiar one of the move 'from the easel to the machine': he predicted a transition from static visual art to a form of synoptic communication created by editing film or photographs.

3.21

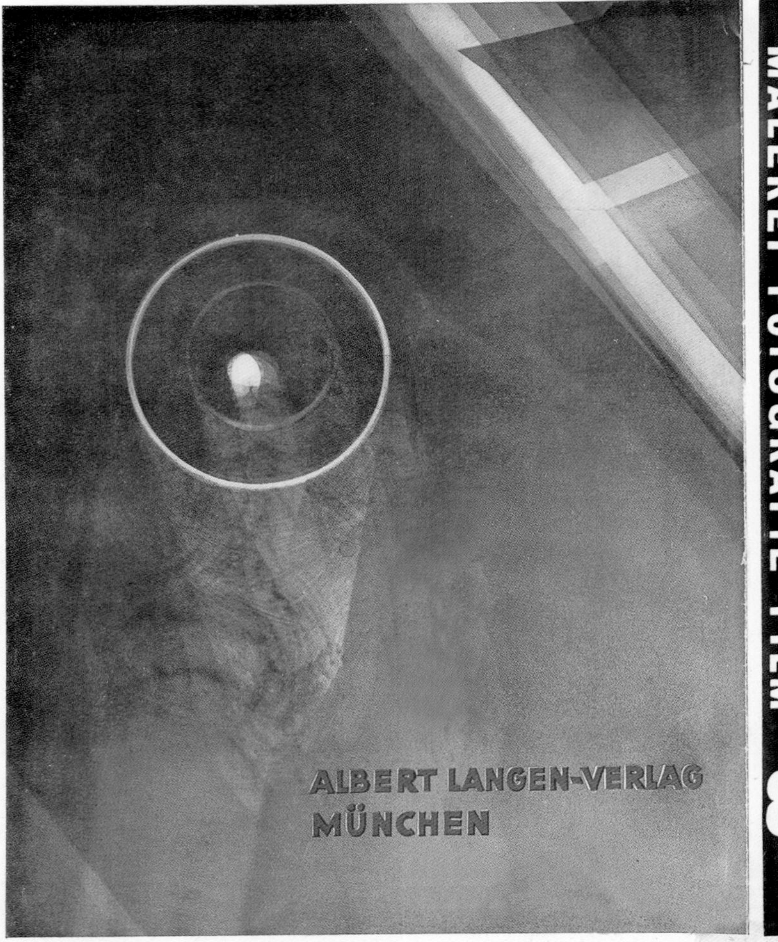

3.21 *Malerei Photografie Film* (Painting Photography Film)

Designed by
Laszlo Moholy-Nagy
Book jacket
1927

'The form, the rendering is constructed out of the optical and associative relationships: into a visual, associative, conceptual, synthetic continuity: into the typophoto as an unambiguous rendering in an *optically* valid form.'[16]

The summation of the book was a sketch for a film, 'Dynamic of the Metropolis': 'In this book I seek to identify the present ambiguities of present-day optical creation. The means afforded by photography play an important part in this, though it is one which people still fail to recognize today: extending the use of light as a creative agent: chiaroscuro in place of pigment.'[17]

Here was Moholy's commitment to the spiritual quality of light. Further on in the book, he laid down what was to become a seminal statement for graphic designers concerning the combination of word and image. In this he distanced himself from the creator of fine art, acknowledged the role of technology and indicated that visual communication had fundamental implications for society.

He called this combination of word and image produced by mechanical means 'Typophoto':

> *The technician has his machine at hand: satisfaction of the needs of the moment. But basically much more: he is the pioneer of the new social stratification, he paves the way for the future.*
>
> *The printer's work, for example, to which we still pay too little attention has just such a long-term effect: international understanding and its consequences.*
>
> *The printer's work is part of the foundation on which the new world will be built....*
>
> *The hygiene of the optical, the health of the visible is slowly filtering through.*
>
> *What is Typophoto?*
>
> - *Typography is communication composed of type.*
> - *Photography is the visual representation of what can be optically apprehended.*
> - *Typophoto is the visually most exact rendering of communication.*[18]

In the phrase 'hygiene of the optical' Moholy managed to encapsulate several concerns of Modernist design. Just as Bauhaus interiors sought to achieve a space where light was an active component, defining planes and drawing attention to undecorated surfaces, both literally and metaphorically suggesting hygiene, so Moholy's photographs and photograms were made from light and shade, the material from the immaterial. The primacy of the eye and the need to cleanse the senses could be understood as a reaction to the social and political events of the previous years, the war, disease and starvation. Its utopianism at this stage

3.22

3.23

3.22 Albert Gleizes, *Kubismus* (On Cubism)

Designed by Laszlo Moholy-Nagy
Book cover
1928

3.23 *14 Bauhausbücher*

Designed by Laszlo Moholy-Nagy
Leaflet
1929

helped to re-energize visual communication with a radically altered style. Later, however, such an abstract belief in a single set of guiding universal principles would find its critics among others also fighting for a new social world.

By 1925 the Bauhaus was advertising in the *Dessauer Zeitung* and in the list of workshops were included 'Letterpress typography, advertising and artists' prints'.[19] This marked the stage when members of the staff, especially Moholy-Nagy, Herbert Bayer and Joost Schmidt, began to define their typographic ideals. The move was from innovative typography to integrated photography and photomontage, first with existing typefaces, then with the new range of sans-serifs. By 1929 the Bauhaus magazine announced that the printing and publicity workshop was taking on 'printing orders, printed items in modern typography, advice in new advertising design and publicity, design and production (or overseeing production) of publicity material, catalogues, trade-marks, pamphlets, press advertisements, posters, etc, and window displays and exhibitions.'[20]

In other words, a fully integrated notion of graphic design was being taught. More details about the photographic work carried out in the publicity department were given in the 1929 prospectus, showing that it taught 'advertising and printing, photography, modes of publicity and their application as advertisements, posters and shop-windows, the most important typesetting, printing, reproduction and light techniques, lettering, drawing, photography, publicity strategy, cost analysis, standards, knowledge of materials and machines.'[21]

Finally, in the syllabus of the Berlin Bauhaus, a detailed outline of the path students would take was given,

> *Lettering is a subject in the general level 1 for all studios in the first semester. In level 2 (2nd and 3rd semester) there is a subject area in advertising, practical and experimental typography, printing and reproduction skills. Level 3 (4–7 semesters) focusses nearly completely on publicity, with theoretical education in publicity, free and experimental work in all*

kinds of publicity, printed, and exhibition stands, etc. Also in this subject area the Photography course under Walter Peterhans concentrates on publicity: moving from free technical experiment to work carried out to develop advertisements, object photography and reportage.[22]

Standardization and Scientism at the Bauhaus and Beyond

The standardizing of typographic and graphic design was carried out in such a concentrated way that it can be taken as a case-study of how the wish to standardize became synonymous with Modernism in design.

It would be misleading to suggest that standardization was an exclusively twentieth-century principle. Certain typefaces had been measured according to an agreed standard since at least the early 18th century.

Standardization in type design meant, first of all, using a certain restricted group of typefaces and setting in one-case only, usually the lower-case for publications and upper-case for more applied graphic design. A movement for *Kleinschreibung* (literally, writing small) was promoted by Dr Porstmann, a government specialist in measurement systems from 1917 onwards, originally for the Association of German Engineers (Verein Deutscher Ingenieure), and summarized in his book, *Sprache und Schrift*.[23] For the German language, this recommendation was doubly challenging: not only was there a tradition of capitalizing all nouns, but also the dominant typeface category in books, magazines and newspapers was Gothic. While defenders of *Kleinschreibung* argued that it would lead to world understanding and increased legibility, its opponents saw it as un-German. As Robin Kinross has argued, the movement may have arisen from a wish to update business practice and bring Germany into the modern, international world, but it also carried an ideological challenge as a further attack on the hierarchy of the pre-war establishment.

The preferred typefaces among Modernists were Egyptian sans-serifs, known as Grotesk in German. These were advocated on the grounds that they had

3.24

3.24 *Bauhaus*

Designed by Herbert Bayer
Magazine cover
1928

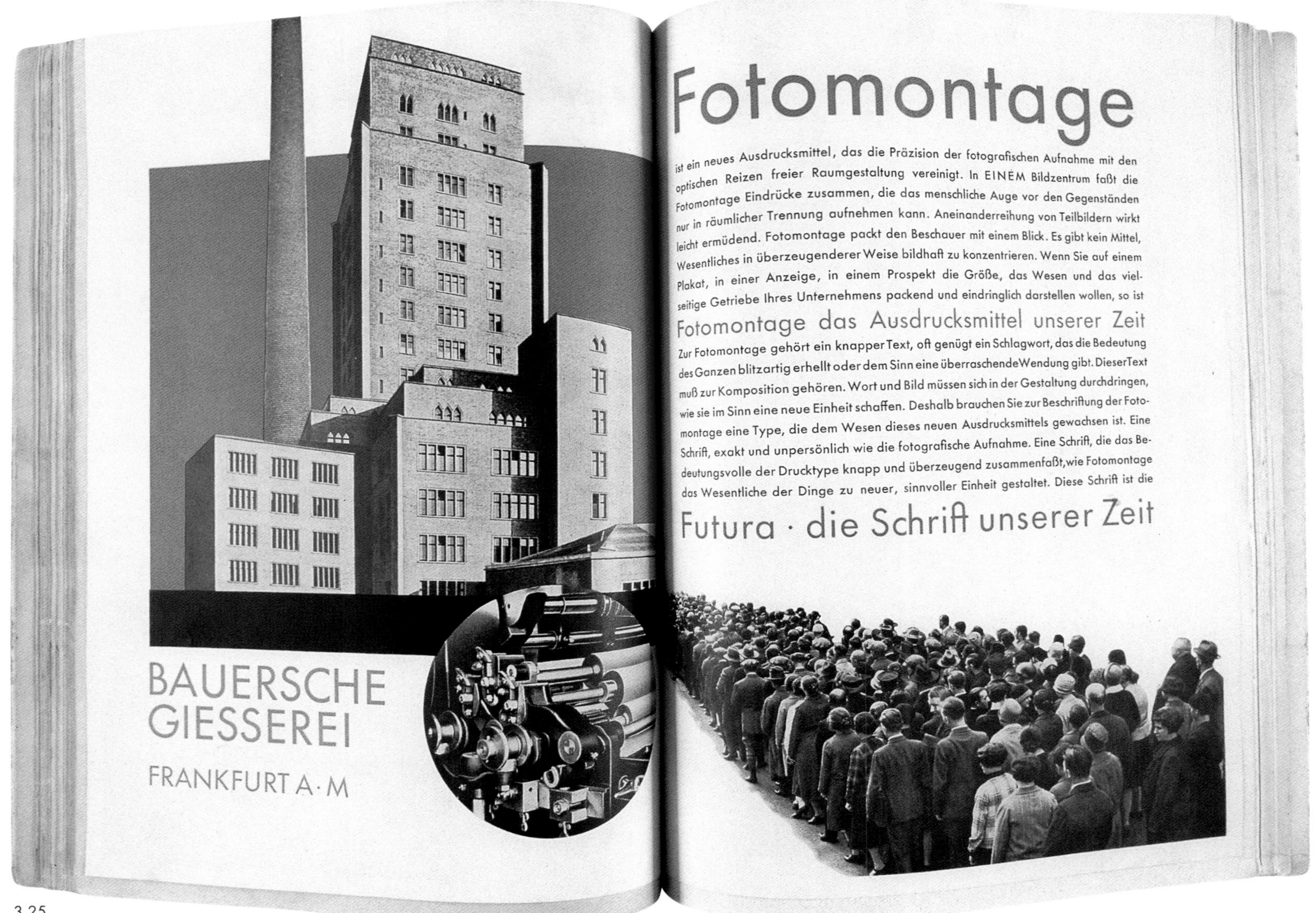

3.25

3.25 – 3.27 Announcements for Futura typeface *'Die Schrift unserer Zeit'* (The type of our time) and *'Futura für Fotomontage'* (Futura for photomontage)

Designed by Paul Renner
1930

evolved from their roots in Roman letterforms, 'unnecessary' ornament had been removed and abstract principles of harmonic composition could often be found in their support. Social Darwinism and German idealism were therefore combined in justification of the script. A range of Grotesk typefaces had been cast by German foundries before 1914 and, in fact, the first examples of the new typography used these, rather than the commissioned typefaces of the later '20s. For example, the early letterpress and offset printing at the Bauhaus was determined by what was held by the local printer. After an initial stage of using Behrens's Mediaeval, the first house style was made up from an anonymous sans-serif cast by J. G. Schelter and Giesecke of Leipzig, *Breite Magere* (wide thin) of 1870, *Breite Halbfette*

3.26

3.27

(wide half-bold) of 1890 and *Breite Fette* (wide bold) of 1902.[24] Along with these, Venus Grotesk by Bauersche Giesserei of Frankfurt am Main, cast between 1907 and 1911, was well-used in the early designs but, strictly speaking, the novelty was in the sense of composition rather than in the typeface used.

Among the German foundries announcing new sans-serif typefaces was Ludwig and Mayer of Frankfurt am Main, who in 1926 produced Erbar, a design by Jakob Erbar, then teaching at the Cologne Werkschulen.[25] In 1928, Paul Renner's Futura, cast in a family of variants by Bauersche Giesserei, was released to considerable interest. It was advertised as *'die Schrift unser Zeit'* (the typeface of our time) and promoted as compatible with photomontage.[26]

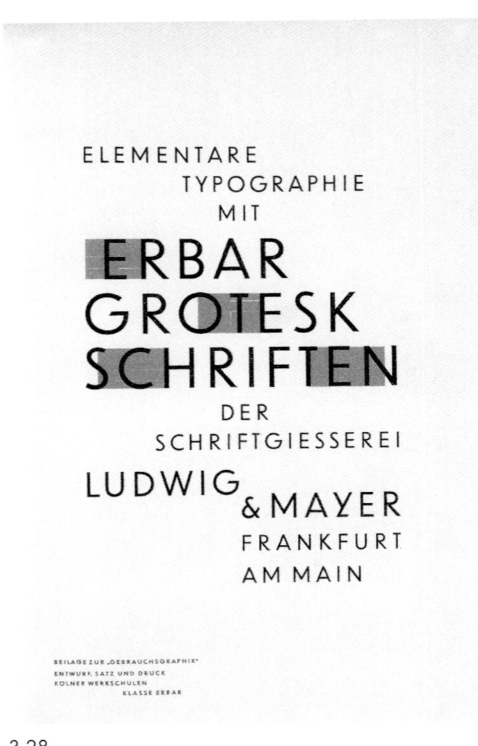

3.28

3.29

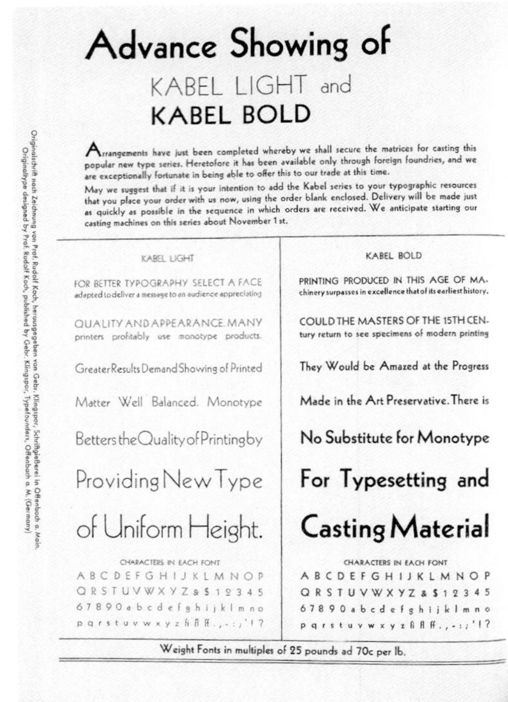

3.30

3.28 *Elementare Typographie mit Erbar Grotesk* (Elementarist Typography with Erbar Sans-serif)

Typeface designed by Jakob Erbar
Advertisement
1927

3.29 *Berthold Grotesk* (Berthold Sans-serif)

Typeface designed by Georg Trump
Advertisement
1930

3.30 Kabel Light and Kabel Bold

Typeface designed by Rudolf Koch
Advertisement
1929

A competing foundry, Gebrüder Klingspor, commissioned Rudolf Koch, best known for his calligraphy and interest in historical letterforms, to design a sans-serif Kabel.[27] And Georg Trump, typographic adviser to Berthold in Berlin, was responsible for Berthold Grotesk. Trump, having trained under Ernst Schneidler at Stuttgart, was employed by Berthold while also working at the Munich Meisterschule für Deutschlands Buchdrucker as a colleague to Jan Tschichold and Paul Renner.[28]

As well as these pure sans-serifs, alternatives with possibilities for more commercial application in advertising and publicity design were Radio by Professor Behrmann (1930), City by Georg Trump (1931) and Beton (Concrete) by Heinrich Jost (1930). Although these were also Egyptian typefaces, they carried associations in their names and forms that distinguished them from the more rigidly geometric and functionalist designs.

The general movement for standardization lay outside the immediate community of artists and designers. Porstmann, besides recommending single-case lettering, introduced the idea of regular sheet sizing for business stationery, technical drawings, publicity, magazines and newspapers. He was concerned to show how the artist must accept the restrictions of standardization if the business life of Germany was to succeed:

> *With the invasion of artistic works into the daily work environment – which is the major goal of contemporary art – artistic freedom must be strongly confined. For everyday work, business life and economy definitely promote further adherence to a known form, just as everyday people must observe an exact external appearance if they want to live in harmony with their fellow citizens.*[29]

And later he wrote, 'It is the concern of the graphic designer [*Graphiker*], in spite of standardization, or better still, in adhering to the standards, to create a varied impression, and a new area of work, which is not without its attractions, is opened up.'

In 1926, *Gebrauchsgraphik* published the official 'Principles for the Standardization of Formats for the Graphic Industry'. This was issued by the Standards Committee (Normenausschuss) for the Graphic Trades, who, as an indication of their thoroughness, had consulted with the Reich Savings Commissioner, the Committee for German Industrial Standards (Normenausschuss der deutschen Industrie), the Association of German Paper Manufacturers and the Association of German Wholesalers. The committee discussed rules for the standardization of paper. Sizes ran according to the A system, with the largest, A0, equalling one square meter, although not in square proportion. It was the standard unit by which all subsequent subdivisions were taken, from an envelope to a poster. Following this announcement, German printing machines and associated equipment were required to match these measurements. Portsmann argued that greater efficiency would result if in letterheads, for instance, all correspondence was designed following a set pattern for the place of address, telephone number and bank account number. Filing and office procedures would thus be smoother. The dimensions of storage and arrangement of offices were affected, as well as all aspects of office, postal and transport systems.

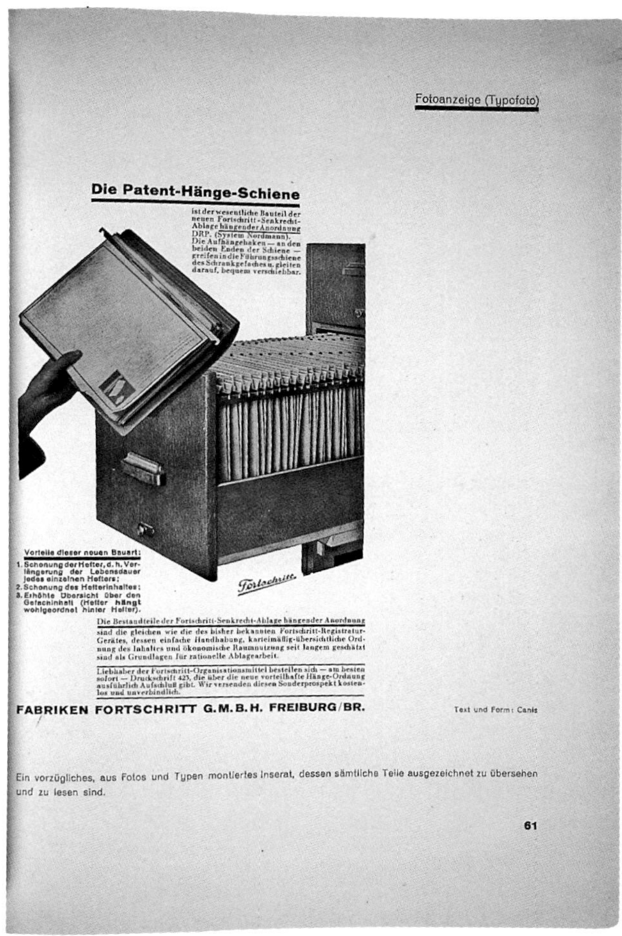

3.31

3.31 *Fabriken Fortschritt* for Filing Cabinets

Designed by Johannes Canis
Advertisement
1928

3.32

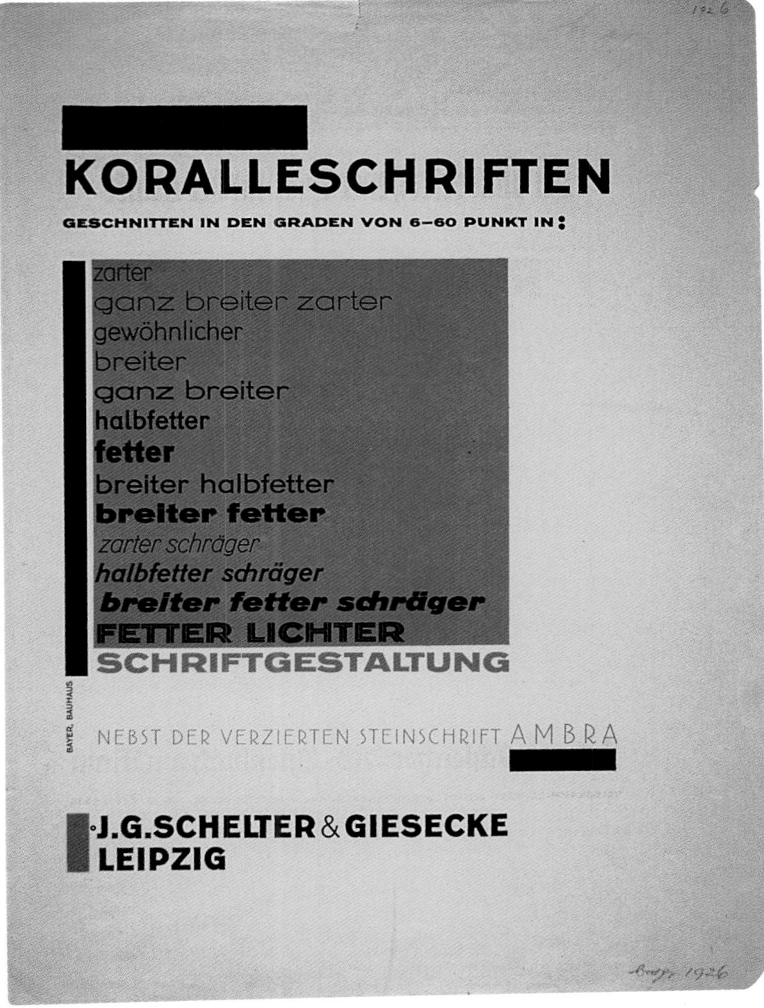

3.33

3.32 Announcement for *Die Monotype*, Universal setting machine

Designed by Herbert Bayer
Printer's sample
1926

3.33 *Koralleschriften* (The Koralle type family)

Designed by Herbert Bayer
Printer's sample
1926

Colour, arguably much more liable to personal taste and artistic temperament, was nevertheless also subjected to a system of notation for job specifications. Dr Wilhelm Ostwald, a professor of chemistry in Leipzig, devised a system by which the descriptive and evocative names of colours could be replaced by a scientifically 'infallible' system. In a country with a highly advanced chemical colour industry producing dyes for a variety of textile, graphic and metal work, such a system, with its international code, was a huge benefit. The system was a modern version of a colour circle created by the Romantic artist Philip Otto Runge, whose interest in natural philosophy and the arts led him to study the composition of colour.[30] Following Runge's scheme, Ostwald arranged the eight pure colours in a circle and the hues in subdivisions within the circle. Each division was labelled with a letter and number according to its position. There were twenty-four hues and twelve greys, with all possible combinations resulting in 680 colour gradations which were used to give print specifications. The Ostwald system appealed to the new typographers as yet another sign that art could be exact and scientific when appropriately applied to industry.

3.34

3.34 *Signal*

Designed by Herbert Bayer
Typefoundry booklet
1929

Herbert Bayer's Teaching

Exercises set by Herbert Bayer for students in devising geometrical alphabets seem less extraordinary and gather more meaning if seen in the context of this enormous interest in sans-serif typefaces and the contemporary movement for standardization. Indeed, Bayer adopted the language of rationalism when he set out 'An experiment for a simplified system of writing' to explain his version of a single-case alphabet, Universal, in 1926. He quoted Porstmann directly:

> *'There is no large and small alphabet. It is not necessary for* one *sound to have a large and small sign. The simultaneous use of two characters of completely different alphabets is illogical and unharmonious. We would recommend that the restriction to* one *alphabet would mean a saving of time and materials (one thinks of the typewriter).'* [31]

The principles of composition adopted by the new typographers were initially derived from Neo-Plastic and early Constructivist paintings. These included the use of the entire page for an active, asymmetrical layout with parts of the text emphasized by blocks and underlining. As in the case of Moholy's designs for the Bauhaus book series, circle, line and plane were used for compositional coherence with the circle to stand for asterisks, planes for emphasis and lines to direct the reader to certain parts of the page. These artistic and philosophical justifications were increasingly supplemented by more matter-of-fact considerations

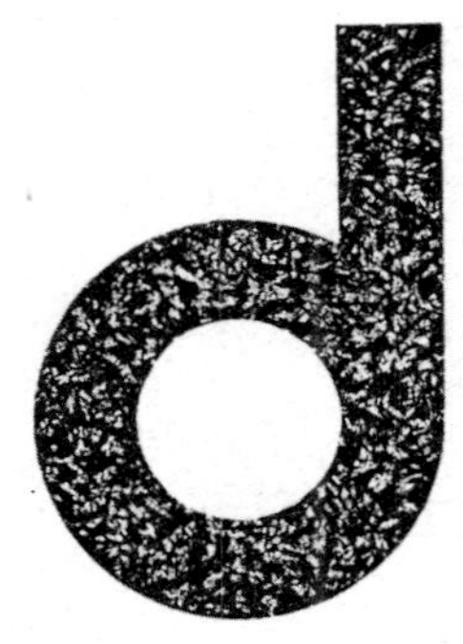

3.35

3.35 Proof of the Universal alphabet

Designed by Herbert Bayer
1926

in line with Taylorism and scientific management. Arguments for the new typography on the basis of functionalism stressed its cost-effectiveness, as it reduced the variety of typefaces, and in many instances only one size of type was used. Claims were also made that it saved space, reduced expenditure on paper and was more legible to a wider public, as it avoided the difficulties of German scripts for an international readership.

By 1928, however, Bayer realized that these ingredients formed an easily plagiarized formula:

> *A quick adoption of nothing but external appearance was the result. An example of the proliferation of the 'Bauhaus style' is seen in the order book of a Frankfurt printer; nearly half of all printing orders received in one year called for work to be done 'in the Bauhaus style'. What remained were merely heavy dots and bold lines or even ornaments and imitations of nature carried out with the typographical material.*[32]

As staff at the Bauhaus were sensitive to the charge that the school was merely promoting a style rather than a more fundamental set of design principles, the proliferation of elements of Bayer's graphic approach hit a raw nerve. His reaction was to introduce a lighter and more eclectic range of typeface styles in his designs around this time and to become interested in the possibilities of Surrealism. 'To "design advertising"', he wrote, 'implies not only designing in good taste;... a truly "objective" approach is only one that can prove the outward appearance to have deeper causes, that is to say, that the essential aspects of the problem are understood before and during the design process.' Yet again, this was the wish expressed by a designer to be more than dependent on form-giving, to find a deeper analysis which somehow guaranteed aesthetic beliefs in a scientific grounding.

Die Schule Reimann – Berlin

The case of the Reimann school in Berlin is interesting as a comparison with other art and design schools in the years preceding and immediately following the First World War. It grew out of a Sunday art school under the direction of Albert and Klara Reimann, a professional, educated Jewish couple. In 1902 it was extended as the Schülerwerkstätten für Kleinplastik (Training Workshops for Decorative Sculpture) with fourteen students. Gradually the school defined its identity and distinguished itself from the established, subsidized Arts and Crafts schools by teaching the most recent and fashionable subjects, as well as those well-rooted in German education.[33]

Unlike the Bauhaus, where the model of activity was architectural, the emphasis at the Reimann school was on areas which might be considered traditionally to be more feminine. At first the school provided classes in drawing from nature and from the nude, as well as small-scale modelling (*Kleinplastik*), woodcutting, chiselling and turning. This range of subjects reflected Arts and Crafts thinking about materials and acknowledged the activities of women in the domestic sphere

3.36

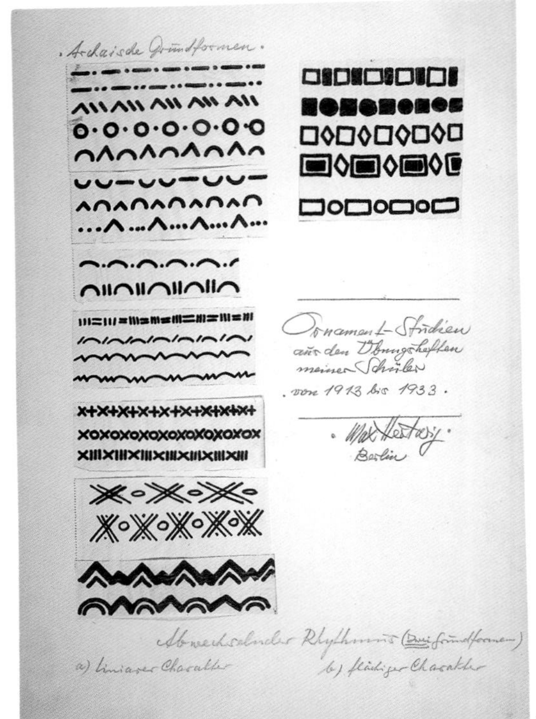

3.38

3.37

by offering a range of subjects which might enhance their accomplishments. As the school grew, new subjects were added, such as ivory carving in 1906, batik in 1908 and painting in 1909. In 1911 it was awarded the status of a Higher Trade School for the Art of Decoration, and offered courses acknowledged by the Association of Berlin Specialist Shops, the German Werkbund and the German Association of Salesmanship Teaching.

The changes in the syllabus echoed the move of the applied arts from the domestic to the commercial field occurring elsewhere, most notably in the Wiener Werkstätte and in Paul Poiret's Atelier in Paris. Reimann later explained that when he established the school there had been nothing in the Berlin fashion world equivalent to Poiret's classes for training designers, and that he was consequently anxious to establish courses where cutting was taught prior to drawing, in his case, under the designer Kenan.[34] This came at the end of a decade when the Berlin department stores had been modelling themselves on the Paris model and had established *couture* lines. Matching the intentions of Berlin's forward-looking companies, including the department stores Wertheim and Kaufhaus des Westens (Ka De We), the Reimann school emphasized areas of the curriculum which equipped students for employment in the areas of design mediating between production and consumption. These included shop-window display, stage-, exhibition- and poster-design as well as packaging and commercial illustration. The school also offered specialized courses in all matters of tailoring and costume-making, textile design, fashion presentation and illustration. It grew rapidly, and was represented in many exhibitions in Berlin, as well as the International Exhibition for the Book Industry and Graphic Arts in 1914 in Leipzig, where it was awarded a Diploma of Honour.

3.36 – 3.38 Studies of ornament by Max Hertwig, Berlin, between 1913 and 1933.

Another of the Reimann school's attractions was its window-display courses under Georg Fischer. Exercises included covering cubes in grey and black fabric with invisible stitching, dressing mannequins, imitating clothes in paper or fabric-paint on dummies, and executing background scenes or sign-writing for display. An exhibition was held at the town hall of the Schöneberg district of Berlin in 1926 with 30 shop-windows covering 70 metres, all with functioning electrical equipment.[35]

Mainstream Berlin companies, such as AGB textiles, the Berlin electricity board, Lesser shoe shops, Ka De We and Wertheim, all turned to Reimann staff and students for commissions. During the 1920s many evening and part-time courses were developed, taking the number of enrolled students to nearly 1,000 a year, by contrast with the 200 matriculated students at the Bauhaus.[36] In its own publications the school presented the idea that it was flexible and well-equipped, with well-trained staff all with commercial experience and 'modern' in outlook. A forum for the display of these fashionable capabilities was the costume balls (*Gauklerfeste*) held at the Zoological Garden and Kroll Opera House, which were featured in the illustrated press during the '20s and became a celebrated element of the Berlin social season.

In 1927, aware of the power of publicity, the Director Albert Reimann published a special issue of the school magazine, *Farbe und Form,* to commemorate its first twenty-five years, in conjunction with an exhibition at the Berlin Arts and Crafts Museum. In this anniversary publication, the school stated its aims:

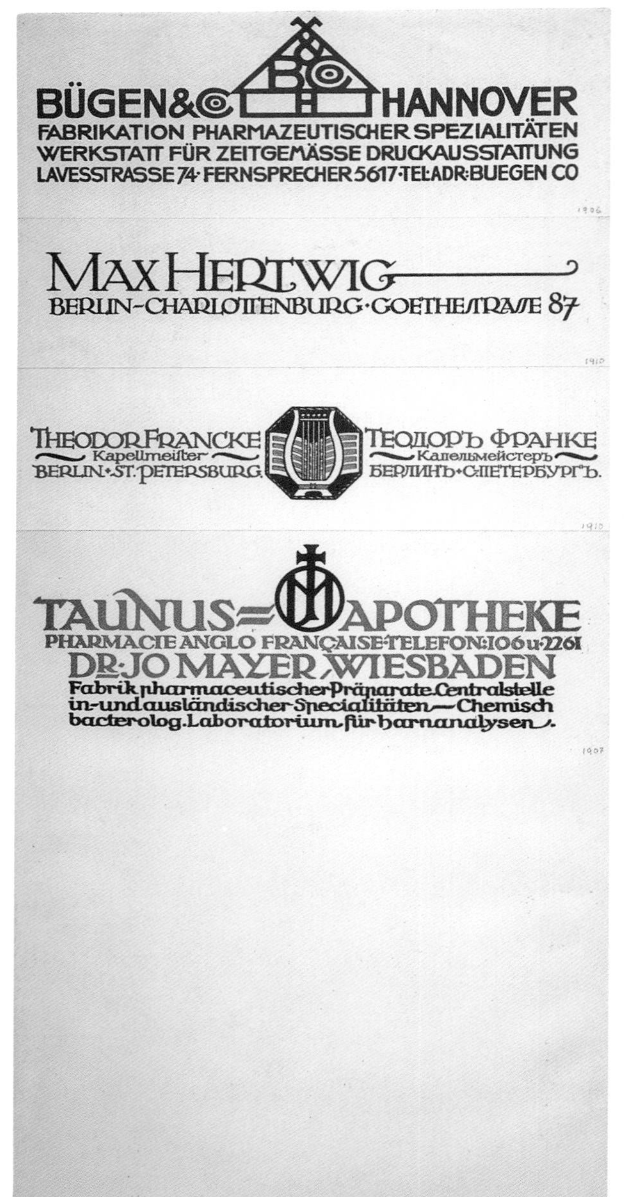

3.39

3.39 Four letterheads

Designed by Max Hertwig
About 1913

3.40 *Farbe und Form Monatsschrift für Kunst und Kunstgewerbe*

Designed by Max Hertwig
Cover
1927

'... to serve craft, by creating minds for the thought process of design and hands for its execution... to serve Industry, by achieving its strengths and raising the level of taste of its products... to serve Commerce, by training artistic strengths in its publicity, shop windows and interior design.'[37]

In the area of graphic design, a class for 'Poster Art' was formed in 1911 under the well-known poster artist Julius Klinger; then in 1913 Max Hertwig formed the Commercial Graphics (Gebrauchsgraphik) class.This distinction was still present in 1927 when there was a class for 'Gebrauchsgraphik' combined with 'typography', and separate classes for poster design. Also in the graphic field was the class for bookbinding, a residue of the craft training originally part of the school's curriculum.

An important element in Hertwig's teaching was the study of ornament. He had studied with Fritz Ehmcke in Düsseldorf and is thus an example of continuity from before the First World War. Starting with basic archaic forms, the students worked through exercises as part of the class, moving on then to linear and planar illusion, form and counter-form and finally to repeated single motifs and organic free forms. The exercises ended with the practical application of these principles in book title pages and other full designs for frontispiece borders and book jackets.

According to Hertwig's description in *Farbe und Form* of the class for 'Lettering, Commercial Graphics and Surface Art', all students were first taught calligraphy as the basis of composition, 'just as a tailor would be taught to sew'. This led to the composition of small press advertisements and announcements, packaging and business printing, including labels, signets and trademarks. 'Until then, all these things were a matter of the printer's taste. A primitive procedure, waiting for the hands of the expert.'[38]

The course equipped the students in layout and lettering, but mainly in black and white for small-scale press-work or jobbing typography. The companion class, 'Poster and Advertising Graphics', was under the direction of Carl Gadau. It would seem from the comment by Gadau that there was an overlap between the two

FARBE UND FORM

12·JAHRGANG
HEFT: 2
1927: FEBRUAR

MONATSSCHRIFT FÜR KUNST
UND KUNSTGEWERBE

MIT DER BEILAGE „MITTEILUNGEN
DER SCHULE REIMANN"

VERLAG „FARBE UND FORM"
BERLIN W30 REIMANNHAUS

HERTWIG

3.40

classes, partly reflecting personal interests of the two teachers: 'When I took over the class seven years ago, it was only a poster class, but thanks to my experience as a commercial designer for twenty years, I am persuaded that Commercial Graphics has less to do with poster exercises than with the creation of black and white works, press advertisements, letterheadings, etc. as in practice these things are much more needed.'[39]

Against the grain of the Modernists, Gadau considered it was important for a student to become competent in '*Handwerk*', rather than to develop 'big ideas'. Although most work was carried out in ink on paper, Gadau also mentioned that the students were encouraged to think of printing processes and to choose colours according to eventual printing techniques. It is significant that he chose the term '*Gebrauchsgraphik*' to denote this activity, restricted and commercial as it was.

A third member of the staff, Elsa Taterka, also taught graphic design, specializing in evening classes on caricature and grotesque drawing. In her statement in the 1927 commemorative volume, she suggested that clean objective form was not enough for modern consumers, whose speed of life and emotions needed something akin to the fantasy of film or novels to capture their attention.[40]

Much later, an indication of the forward-looking nature of Reimann's directorship was the appointment of Werner Graeff as Professor of Photography in 1930. A leading exponent of the new photography and a member of the Circle of New Advertising Designers (ring neuer werbegestalter), Graeff had also published an important manifesto for the styles and functions of photography in the preceding year, *Es kommt der neue Fotograf!*. Under him there were classes in technique as well as the aesthetics of film and photography; by 1934 there was a range of seven classes.[41]

German art and design education in the Weimar years succeeded in keeping up to the demands for more practical training and at the same time teaching principles of form and composition. Although syllabuses from American university courses in advertising were published in the German design press, the emphasis was still on the activity of design, with an increasing sensitivity to modern typography. Formalist experiment in typography and lettering underpinned many of the more progressive designs which were to develop, rather than the behavioural psychology and marketing analyses sometimes alluded to in sample curricula. This wish for a more 'scientific' approach was also apparent in the graphics press, where analyses of markets started to appear in the last years of the '20s. Arguably, just at the point when this transition was to take place at the Bauhaus, two crucial figures, Bayer and Moholy-Nagy, left. This, combined with the rapidly challenging political situation, meant that a fuller realization of a scientific approach which went beyond aesthetics was delayed in Germany until the 1950s, when visual communication was taught alongside semiotics and time-based media (for instance at Ulm Hochschule für Gestaltung). The later careers of Herbert Bayer and Laszlo Moholy-Nagy in the USA indicate a continued wish to address this issue.

The Bauhaus teaching of typography and photography echoed general tendencies in the wider graphic field, with the emergence of new categories matched by increased specialization and new technologies, especially among typographers. Their work was characterized by a search for a basic graphic vocabulary, which paralleled studies in other media at the school. Perhaps stylistically more coherent and modern than most, the school was promoted internationally through the series of Bauhaus magazines and books, in a way which distinguished it from other Arts and Crafts schools. The wider question was whether this Constructivist-inspired language, essentially reductive in tendency, could be adjusted successfully to suit advertising and systems of communication which depended on levels of associative and symbolic meanings. It was here that perhaps a training at the Reimann school introduced a level of practicality and business awareness that led to the application of design in a wider range of contexts than has usually been recognized. It was in this world that the interests, tastes and aspirations of Kracauer's 'little shopgirls' and, more generally, the modern consumer, would be fulfilled.

WERKSTATT PRESSA KÖLN F·H·EHMCKE
KÖLN
MAI BIS
OKTOBER
WELTSCHAU AM RHEIN
1928
PRESSA
OFFSETDRUCK: KÖLNER-GÖRRES-HAUS, G·M·B·H

4.1

4.1 *Pressa Köln, Mai bis Oktober, Weltschau am Rhein,* (Pressa Cologne, May to October – world show on the Rhine)

Designed by Ehmcke workshop, René Binder and Max Eichheim
Poster
1928

4.2 *Das Internationale Plakat*

Designed by Franz Paul Glass
Exhibition catalogue
1929

4 Forces of Persuasion: Magazines, Exhibitions and Associations

The success of German design in the 20th century resulted from the high seriousness with which it was promoted. Frequent exhibitions drew attention to the country's pre-eminence in publication and graphic design before 1914, and in the post-war Weimar years there was a renewed interest in such events. In the broad field of advertising design, Berlin was home to the 1925 Advertising Fair (Reichsreklamemesse) and the 1929 International Advertising Congress (Reklameschau). In 1927, Leipzig was again the venue for the important International Book Exhibition, while a rash of photographic, typographic and poster exhibitions took place in other centres up to the National Socialist takeover in 1933. Specifically in the area of Modernism, it was the late Weimar years when the success of the new typography and new photography came to the fore, as in the celebrated international exhibition *Film und Foto* (Fifo) which was first held in Stuttgart in 1929.[1]

Among the cultural forums instrumental in promoting graphic design, the most notable were the magazine *Gebrauchsgraphik*, the Cologne exhibition Pressa, and an association of avant-garde designers called *ring neuer werbegestalter* (Circle of New Advertising Designers).

4.2

4.3 

4.3 Photograph of H. K. Frenzel, the editor of *Gebrauchsgraphik* from 1924 to1937.

4.4 A characteristic title page from *Gebrauchsgraphik*, January 1930, set in Futura typeface.

Gebrauchsgraphik - A Modern Graphic Design Journal

> *I should like to say that German publications devoted to advertising art are read and studied here with the greatest interest by the experts (the Gebrauchsgraphik is a particular favourite and is to be found in every studio) and that German achievements are greatly respected.*[2]

Although there had previously been magazines devoted to specialist areas of graphic and typographic art, it was only when *Gebrauchsgraphik* began publication in 1924 that an all-embracing coverage began. In many ways it formed an international model for other graphic design magazines for much of the century.

A natural successor to the journal *Das Plakat, Gebrauchsgraphik* was by no means alone in addressing the subject of graphic design. By the late '20s the estimated number of journals in this field was twenty-two in Berlin and sixteen in Leipzig.[3] The magazine's title was the generic term that encompassed design for publication, advertising and typography, rather than the more specialist interest of some similar journals. In other contexts, the prefix *Gebrauch* was used to signify a non-élitist, politically radical and often Marxist approach, as in Hanns Eisler's *Gebrauchsmusik*.[4] Eisler, the composer, and Bertolt Brecht, the dramatist, applied the concept of 'functional transformation' to their work. Through this, elements drawn from everyday life were incorporated into compositions to establish a sense of dislocation. In music, distinctions between classical and jazz instruments were intentionally collapsed, while in poetry, ordinary speech and the language of business were used to destroy illusionism and help to challenge directly conventional notions of entertainment. By contrast with performance media, *Gebrauchsgraphik*, whether as a magazine title or a generic category, carried an underlying acceptance of the capitalist application of design for improved economic growth. Politically more radical graphic practice was represented

SIEBENTER JAHRGANG

HEFT 1
NUMBER

SEVENTH VOLUME

MONATSSCHRIFT ZUR FÖRDERUNG
KÜNSTLERISCHER REKLAME

GEBRAUCHSGRAPHIK
INTERNATIONAL ADVERTISING ART

MONTHLY MAGAZINE FOR PROMOTING ART IN ADVERTISING

HERAUSGEBER PROF. H. K. FRENZEL, EDITOR

OFFIZIELLES ORGAN DES BUNDES DEUTSCHER GEBRAUCHSGRAPHIKER

OFFIZ. ORGAN DES REICHSVERBANDES DEUTSCHE REKLAME-MESSE E. V.

SOLE REPRESENTATIVES FOR
THE UNITED STATES OF AMERICA AND CANADA:
THE BOOK SERVICE COMPANY
15 EAST 40TH STREET NEW YORK CITY U. S. A.

PHÖNIX ILLUSTRATIONSDRUCK UND VERLAG GMBH. BERLIN SW61

4.4

JAHRG. 1
HEFT 8
GEBRAUCHSGRAPHIK
MONATSSCHRIFT
ZUR FÖRDERUNG
KÜNSTLERISCHER
REKLAME
MODE UND TEXTIL
VERLAG: PHÖNIX ILLUSTRATIONSDRUCK U. VERLAG GMBH. BERLIN SW68

GEBRAUCHSGRAPHIK
RHEIN=RUHR

JAHRGANG 3/HEFT 12
GEBRAUCHS-
GRAPHIK
MONATSCHRIFT Z. FÖRDERUNG
KÜNSTLERISCHER REKLAME
LEIPZIGER
HEFT
PHÖNIX JLLUSTRATIONSDRUCK et
VERLAG G·M·B·H· BERLIN SW 68
HERAUSGEGEBEN VON PROF. H. K. FRENZEL

OKTOBER
1928
OCTOBER
GEBRAUCHSGRAPHIK
INTERNATIONAL ADVERTISING
ART
HERAUSGEBER • PROF. H. K. FRENZEL • EDITOR
PHÖNIX ILLUSTRATIONSDRUCK UND VERLAG GMBH., BERLIN SW 61, BELLE-ALLIANCE-PLATZ 7-8
Alleinvertreter für die Vereinigten Staaten von Nordamerika und Kanada
THE BOOK SERVICE COMPANY
15 East 40th Street, New York City U.S.A.
Sole Representative for the United States of North-America and Canada

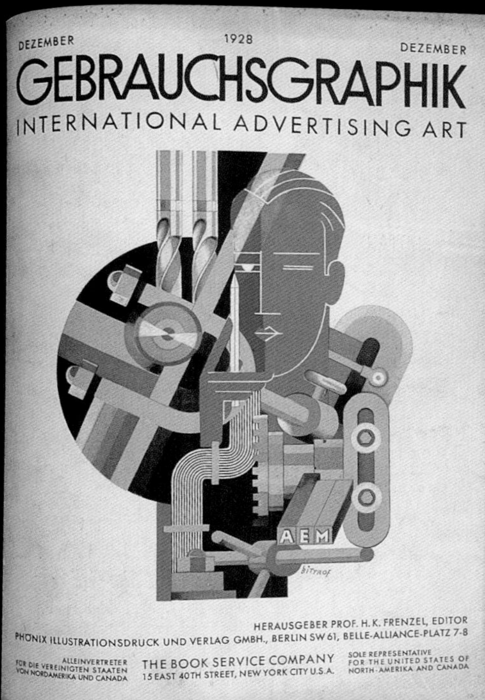
DEZEMBER
1928
DEZEMBER
GEBRAUCHSGRAPHIK
INTERNATIONAL ADVERTISING ART
AEM
HERAUSGEBER PROF. H. K. FRENZEL, EDITOR
PHÖNIX ILLUSTRATIONSDRUCK UND VERLAG GMBH., BERLIN SW 61, BELLE-ALLIANCE-PLATZ 7-8
ALLEINVERTRETER FÜR DIE VEREINIGTEN STAATEN VON NORDAMERIKA UND CANADA
THE BOOK SERVICE COMPANY
15 EAST 40TH STREET, NEW YORK CITY U.S.A.
SOLE REPRESENTATIVE FOR THE UNITED STATES OF NORTH-AMERIKA AND CANADA

JUNI 1930
HERAUSGEBER PROF. H. K. FRENZEL EDITOR • PHÖNIX ILLUSTRATIONSDRUCK UND VERLAG GMBH • BERLIN SW 61 • BELLE-ALLIANCE-PLATZ 7-8
GEBRAUCHSGRAPHIK
GRIT KALLIN
INTERNATIONAL ADVERTISING ART

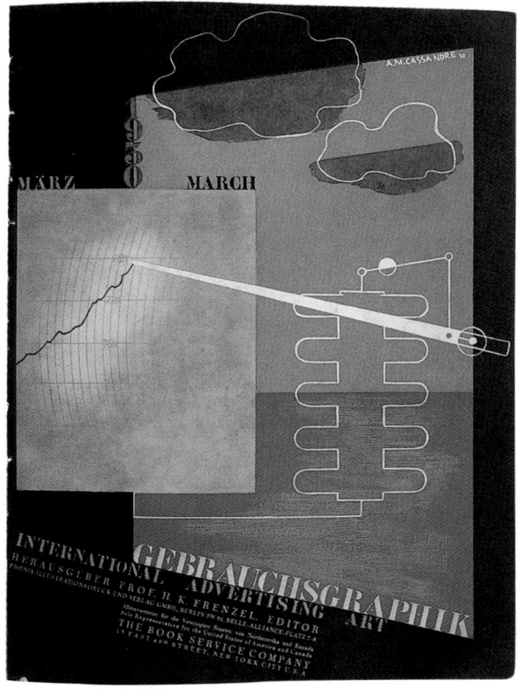

4.11

4.12

4.13

by those artists or designers who advocated *Tendenzkunst* (tendentious art) and propaganda, among them John Heartfield, George Grosz, Heinrich Vogeler and, for a time, Jan Tschichold. They turned to their own publications and contexts for a more extensive polemical intervention. Among the avant-garde a synthesis of diverse media was more likely and was part of a broader advocacy of *die neue Wohnkultur*. No doubt, a magazine such as *Gebrauchsgraphik* represented for them a pragmatic trade concern.

The Magazine's Background

Gebrauchsgraphik started publication in Berlin in July 1924, and two years later it became a regular monthly journal. Until his death in 1937, the editor, Professor H.K. Frenzel, was a significant force in defining the newly emergent role of designers for industry and contributed to major advertising events in Germany as well as Europe and the USA. Born in Silesia, he had trained in scientific draughtsmanship, painting and graphic art at the Leipzig Academy of Graphic Arts. He then worked for a newspaper press in Berlin. A founder member of the Bund Deutscher Gebrauchsgraphiker (BDG; Association of German Commercial
4.5 – 4.10 Graphic Designers), which was established in 1920, he went on to organize

4.5 – 4.10 A range of *Gebrauchsgraphik* covers showing the stylistic variety employed in the magazine.

4.5 Kreuscher, *Mode und Textil* issue, August 1925
4.6 Werbebau (Max Burchartz and Johannes Canis), *Rhein Ruhr* issue, August 1926
4.7 Hans Möhring, Leipzig issue, December 1926
4.8 Uli Huber, October 1928
4.9 Max Bittrof, December 1928
4.10 Grit Kallin, June 1930
4.11 A.M. Cassandre, March 1930
4.12 Joseph Binder, June 1931
4.13 Stephan Schwarz, July 1931

exhibitions on its behalf and, as a result of the perceived success of the German contribution to the Gothenburg 1923 exhibition, his contemporaries conferred on him the title of Professor.[5]

A major emphasis in Frenzel's prolific writing was on the improvement of German advertising. After speaking out against the poor level of design and displays of bad taste at the Berlin 1925 Advertising Fair, he was appointed to head the Reich Association of German Advertising Fairs. This involvement culminated in the International Advertising Congress held in Berlin in 1929, an event which was particularly welcomed for bringing experts in the field to Germany. Frenzel had links with several art directors in the USA, whom he visited in 1924 and 1926 to carry out interviews for the magazine. His contact with Sir William Crawford, a prominent figure in British poster and advertising design, resulted in the opening of a branch of his progressive London advertising agency 'Crawfords' in Berlin around 1926. Frenzel acted as German adviser to the agency and through this exchange the designer Ashley Havinden, who was especially noted for the Chrysler automobile advertising campaign, was introduced to the German public.[6]

A further indication of Frenzel's internationalism was his appointment as German representative at the Milan International Advertising Congress of 1933 – by then on behalf of the National Socialist Professional Subject Division of the Chamber of Fine Arts (Fachgruppe Reichskammer der bildenden Künste). He also continued as an occasional contributor to the British magazines *Penrose Annual* and *Modern Publicity*.[7]

Frenzel was clearly a person of international significance who used *Gebrauchsgraphik* as his mouthpiece for ideas about graphic design. After one year of publishing, an indication of his main objectives for the magazine was given in the editorial of July 1925: 'Strong endorsements from all parts of the world should goad us on to even greater achievements. As previously, it will be our aim to further the value in work of commercial graphic design. We hope we shall succeed in giving our specialist area a particular place of attention and thereby be useful to the salesman and the whole of economic life.'[8]

Frenzel's driving theme was the quality of work:

> *The works reproduced by me in Gebrauchsgraphik are entirely in accordance with the idea which I have adopted as the policy of my periodical. I wish to circumscribe a field covering what can be regarded as good present day graphic art. If I were to take to publishing only what satisfies me completely I should have to adapt a certain policy, and the periodical would no longer reflect the actual present state of graphic art.*[9]

The same issue announced a formal relationship with the BDG, the national professional association for graphic designers, which was interested in improving codes of practice and links between German industry and designers of advertising and publicity. According to the terms of the agreement, Frenzel would maintain overall editorial control while the BDG published a supplement in each issue reporting on its events, exhibitions and meetings. This relationship guaranteed a readership for *Gebrauchsgraphik* and also reinforced the identity of the magazine as a significant professionalizing agency for new graphic design in Germany.

Gebrauchsgraphik's Coverage

The magazine began its career with a series of special issues. Its aim at that stage was to promote the role of the advertising designer, typographer or illustrator to industrial patrons. Consequently, introductory thematic issues were devoted to 'The Poster', 'Illustrators', 'The Office', 'German Typefoundries' and 'Official Graphic Design', either as areas of practice or aspects of business and commercial life in which a designer might be used.[10] Links were highlighted between the patronage of good design and economic well-being, and the general optimism in editorial approach reflected the recuperation of Germany's industrial base between 1924 and 1930.

HUT AB VOR D

CHRYSL

ENTWURF: CRAWFORDS REKLAME-AGENTUR G.M.B.H.
BERLIN W.35, POTSDAMERSTR. 111.

4.15

4.14

4.14 *Hut ab vor dem neuen Chrysler 65* (Hats Off to the New Chrysler 65)

Designed by Ashley Havinden
Poster
1929

4.15 Advertisement for Crawfords Agency in Berlin 1928.

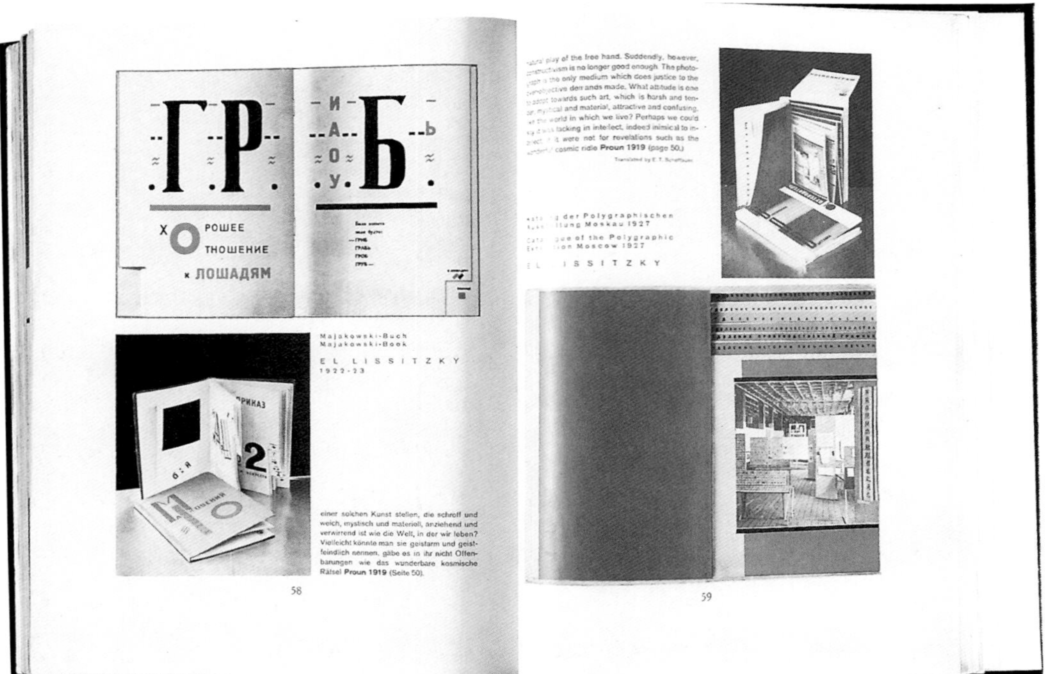

Majakowski-Buch
Majakowski-Book

EL LISSITZKY
1922-23

einer solchen Kunst stellen, die schroff und weich, mystisch und materiell, anziehend und verwirrend ist wie die Welt, in der wir leben? Vielleicht könnte man sie geistarm und geistfeindlich nennen, gäbe es in ihr nicht Offenbarungen wie das wunderbare kosmische Rätsel **Proun 1919** (Seite 50).

58

play of the free hand. Suddenly, however, constructivism is no longer good enough. The photograph is the only medium which does justice to the … demands made. What attitude is one … towards such art, which is harsh and ten… mystical and material, attractive and confusing … world in which we live? Perhaps we could … lacking in intellect, indeed inimical to in… it were not for revelations such as the … cosmic riddle **Proun 1919** (page 50.)

… der Polygraphischen … Moskau 1927

… of the Polygraphic … Moscow 1927

EL … ISSITZKY

59

4.16

TRAUGOTT SCHALCHER

el LISSITZKY, MOSKAU

Das Land der Russen mit der Seele suchend — so tastet man sich vorsichtig und genießerisch durch das Werk dieses Künstlers. Lenin spricht. Vor dem Kreml stauen sich unabsehbar die Massen des Proletariats. Eine Karte von Rußland wird ausgebreitet. Sie verliert sich hinter statistischen Tabellen. Der 25. Oktober 1917 wird uns als „Großer Tag der Sowjets" eingehämmert. Noch und noch und noch. Dort ist ein Plakat für die Rote Armee, aber nicht weit davon wirbt der Künstler für Pelikantinte. So ist in Lissitzky Russisches und Deutsches, Merkantiles und Kommunistisches seltsam gemischt. Bei aller

"Seeking the land of Russians with the soul —" to adapt the poet's words, cautiously and enjoying every step, one feels one's way through the work of this artist. Lenin is speaking. The proletarian masses stand in dense throngs before the Kreml. A map of Russia lies spread before us. It is almost concealed behind tables of statistics. October 25, 1917 is being celebrated as the "Great Day of the Soviets." Here is another striking effect, here another and another. Here is a poster for the Red Army and cheek by jowl with it the artist calls our attention to Pelikan inks. Such is the singular mixture of Russian and

49

4.17

4.16–4.17 Two layouts from an article on El Lissitzky from *Gebrauchsgraphik*, December 1928.

The regional character of German printing, book and newspaper publishing and wider industrial organization was signalled early on in *Gebrauchsgraphik*. Some of the early special issues focussed on established centres of printing and regional capitals of industry, Dresden, Berlin, Munich, Hanover, Cologne and Leipzig among them. The usual pattern was for a feature article to be on a designer or design school of the region who contributed a cover design and back-page advertisement in conjunction with a local, high-profile printer. Such was the case, for instance, with 'Werbebau', the association of Max Burchartz and Johannes Canis, when the first photomontaged cover was used on the magazine.

The special issue on Berlin featured a main article on prospectuses and brochures produced by the city's major electrical companies as well as graphic and information design for its transport systems, all stressing the commercial character of the city and its patrons. A city such as Leipzig, by contrast, was focussed on as a centre for typographic design and book publishing with a strong tradition of specialist production.

The critical or discursive language of the magazine can be described as pluralist; it did not express a dominant or preferred aesthetic. Evaluations were often made in terms of stylistic resolution, professionalism, novelty or formal coherence. The scale of work and its impact were taken into account, while skill and technique, especially regarding kinds of illustration, intaglio printing and bibliophile work, were also recognized. A move towards providing international coverage was made from 1927 when the editorial announced:

> *Beginning with volume four, Gebrauchsgraphik is to carry the subtitle 'International Advertising Art'. In adopting this we feel that we are following the line of natural development which has hitherto taken place in its achievement in the service of art in advertising. The great attention which has been paid to Gebrauchsgraphik in every part of the world has confirmed us in our conviction that the size of today's commerce transcends all national boundaries and is assuming the character of world economics. Thus it requires an international understanding of advertising, its most valuable means of expression. We assume this concept consciously and it is our aim and desire to mirror the face and features of international trade propaganda.*[11]

4.18

4.18 Otto Arpke, a prominent Berlin graphic designer featured in *Gebrauchsgraphik*.

Photograph by Martin Höhlig, 1930.

The three issues which followed were devoted to a range of poster design, advertising and typography in Germany, the USA, Belgium, England, Holland and Switzerland. The definition of 'international', at that time, was in fact North America and Western Europe, although later in the same year an article on Japanese advertising appeared. Little interest, however, was shown in the pages of *Gebrauchsgraphik* in the Soviet Union at a time of great graphic experiment, with the exception of the work of El Lissitzky, who lived throughout most of the Weimar period in Germany, where he was responsible for the designs of Soviet contributions to German exhibitions.

By 1930 the ripples from the Wall Street crash of the previous autumn were discussed and more overt details were included on the economy and its implications for design. Frenzel opened the year with 'Where is Advertising Going?', a plea for German industries to use advertising and publicity designers.

4.19 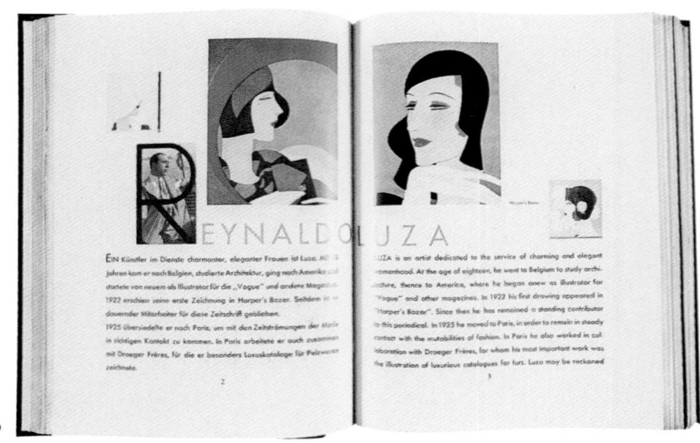

4.20 

4.19 An article on the Italian designer Reynaldo Luza from *Gebrauchsgraphik*, February 1930.

4.20 An article on the illustrator Dora Mönkemeyer-Corty from *Gebrauchsgraphik*, March 1930.

4.21 *Adler Turf Cigarettes*

Designed by
Dora Mönkemeyer-Corty
Poster
1921

A direct response to the critical economic situation came with the introduction of a regular section called '*Wirtschaft und Werbung*' (The Economy and Publicity), which provided statistical and demographic analyses of German markets under such headings as 'Income and Consumption', 'The Automobile Market in Germany' and 'Growth of Unemployment in Germany'.[12]

By then, graphic design was interpreted as affecting all aspects of life. In one issue, for example, 'El Lissitzky Moskau' by Traugott Schalcher was followed by '50 Years of Ullstein 1877–1927', which looked at the design record of the most prolific German publishing house. '30 Years of Typography' presented a qualified attack on the new typography, while 'The Window Display as Educator' stressed the familiar argument that retail design might infiltrate the public's awareness of good design and Rudolf Gabrie reviewed German contemporary book covers from a French standpoint. Such a list illustrates the journal's range in a single issue.[13]

Although there was a move throughout the period from national to international in its coverage of graphic designers, there was not an evolutionary progress from traditionalist to Modernist. The journalist Eberhard Hölscher wrote of Frenzel's editorial approach:

> *But very few can imagine how much inventiveness and gift for composition he had to expend in making his periodical always fresh and animated. He had an unusually versatile technical talent for this, and anyone privileged to watch him doing his work was directly infected by the indefatigable and almost childlike delight he displayed in experimenting with the arrangement of his pages, testing different plans, pasting and building them up, till everything had been arranged to his satisfaction.*[14]

Although this implies that the design of the magazine was subject to the same personal intuition as the editorial process, there are sufficient significant

ADLER-COMPAGNIE A.G. ZIGARETTENFABRIK, DRESDEN
Cortý 21
ADLER-
TURF
ZIGARETTE
KUNSTANSTALT JRIS, DRESDEN

4.21

4.22

4.22 Advertisements for printers and artistic studios from the back pages of *Gebrauchsgraphik*, February 1931.

parallels in the changes when *Gebrauchsgraphik* is compared with other publication design of the time to suggest that it was an informed as well as subjective approach.

Advertisements were printed as a supplement of each issue and often reflected the subject-matter of the particular number. Lists of contributors and contact addresses became a regular feature, aimed at promoting work from German and foreign clients. The balance between the editorial pages became a problem early on. The tendency for advertisers to submit overstated designs which could hinder the overall visual integrity of the magazine was noticed in one of its first reviews. In 1924 the competing printers' journal, *Offset,* commented on the tension between advertising and editorial content:

> Gebrauchsgraphik *sets out to present a survey of newly appearing advertising art and to contribute to the development of exemplary advertisements. Such a programme is a good one. So, too, does the magazine appear to be.*
>
> *Overcome by the extensive range of machine advertisements that appeared in Number 1, as well as by their quality, the publisher and his colleagues have managed to persuade the pretentious advertising agent in Number 2 - a special issue on Drink and Tobacco - with wise restrictions on artistic and high-class workmanship.*[15]

Inevitably, it was tempting for advertisers in the journal to provide their best in terms of new printing techniques, colour photography, lacquered and other specially finished papers, cutting and folding, pull-outs and embossing. Clearly *Gebrauchsgraphik* was funded by advertising revenue from interested printers, foundries and paper manufacturers, and the editor needed to act carefully in order not to detract potential advertisers' revenue for the sake of editorial finesse.

The Wider Context

Coverage of North America was a consistent leitmotif in *Gebrauchsgraphik*. In addition to a special issue on 'Amerika' in October 1926, the journal often published commentaries on American education in advertising design, records of German designers working in the USA and reports of successful graphic design projects by American companies.[16]

The launch of the Art Directors' Club of New York in 1922 and its annual anthology of selected layout design, magazines and publications indicated that a more advanced stage in the division and specialization of design processes had been reached there than in Europe.[17] American business science had already addressed the question of advertising and marketing, and university courses were taught in the new subjects. For *Gebrauchsgraphik* readers, much of this information was summarized by B.W. Randolph in February 1926 in a significant article, 'American University Education in Advertising and Marketing', which presented a characteristic syllabus from New York University.[18]

The special issue on America, a result of Frenzel's visits, concentrated on the history of the union as well as addressing the value of looking towards contemporary American design practice. The editorial was illustrated with a portrait of Benjamin Franklin, 'father of American advertising'. Frenzel had attended the 22nd congress of the World Advertisers' Club in Philadelphia and on his return contributed an article to *Gebrauchsgraphik* on printing traditions from the time of American independence . However, the main thrust of his argument soon emerged:

> *America is the land of the 'record'; not only in sport are the highest achievements longed for. The whole economic system is oriented this way.... Advertising is the literature of the Americans. The advertisement section of a newspaper is more interesting to him than the editorial, for he finds there the things that brought him to his position and status.*

> *Big magazines like the* Saturday Evening Post *have to thank their excellent advertising for their enormous growth, and it means a great deal when a university professor can say to a visiting stranger, 'If you want to read good English, then please read our advertisements!'*[19]

In the same issue Frenzel provided a survey of press advertisements and significant advertisers' copylines. American practice was presented as concentrating on the function of an advertisement's message, the study of its intended market and analysis of its text. American practice also favoured the use of figurative illustration. In turn, American commentaries stressed the abstract nature of the visual solutions in German and other European designs.

An interview between Frenzel and Frederic Suhr of New York in 1928 on German designers selling work in the USA reveals many of the contrasts between the German and American systems.

> *Frederic Suhr:... Professor Ludwig Hohlwein in Munich is universally conceded to be one of the greatest poster artists. He has been admired in America for more than 20 years and has had great influence in the poster field. Recently there appeared in America some posters of Prof. Hohlwein for an American concern. From an artistic point of view they were beautiful; from an advertising point of view, to my mind, they were a failure. This was not the fault of Mr Hohlwein, who sat in Munich and made these posters which had to be put up in America; it was the fault of the American firm that engaged him to do the posters. An art director should have been sent to Prof. Hohlwein, if he could not come to America, to prevent him from making the mistakes he made. First of all, no art director in America would have a man with so strong a personality as Hohlwein on competitive accounts. Secondly the people in his posters were not American or cosmopolitan types, they were distinctly local types, peculiar to Germany,*

4.23

4.23 *Ausstellung, Die Elektrizität im Haushalt* (Exhibition, Electricity in the Household)

Designed by Ludwig Hohlwein
Poster
1924

4.24

PHOTOGRAPHIE
VISION DU
MONDE

GENÈSE DE LA PHOTOGRAPHIE

COMME toutes les inventions, l'invention de la photographie est la conséquence, le résultat d'un vœu, lisez : d'une volonté d'expression préalable. Le mécanisme de la photographie permet de fixer, de transmettre des images. Mais ce mécanisme est la mise en pratique d'une idée, d'une conception du monde.

Une civilisation purement matérialiste, devait donner naissance à un art dont l'objet initial était de capter les impressions visuelles. Le XIXe siècle ne pouvait engendrer qu'un mode de transcription de l'univers externe, réputé en tous points conforme aux lois de l'optique.

Si la daguerréotypie naquit il y a cent ans, si elle connut une vogue instantanée, si elle fit la conquête des deux mondes, c'est qu'elle correspondait, avant même de tomber dans le domaine public, à un besoin affectif et intellectuel.

Tous les antécédents de la photographie (la chambre obscure de Porta, les essais de Wedgwood et de Davy, les silhouettes de Charles) prouvent une orientation de l'esprit européen vers l'enregistrement automatique des faits. La photographie n'est qu'une des formes multiples du vaste mouvement naturaliste dont le Baroque est le point de départ, et l'École Impressionniste française l'aboutissement extrême.

Notre intention n'est pas de nier l'apport de Niepce ou de ravaler un savant inventeur comme Daguerre au niveau d'un simple agent d'exécution. Nous prétendons seulement découvrir la genèse et le principe premier de la photographie dans l'ensemble des idées générales de l'époque. L'avènement de la photographie coïncide avec la gestation de l'Ecole de Barbizon et devance de quelques années à peine Courbet et l'Ecole Réaliste. C'est dire qu'elle est la manifestation d'un état de la sensibilité et de l'intelligence qui rend l'homme tributaire des données de la vision. En tant qu'expression d'une culture, l'invention de la photographie est aussi inconcevable dans l'Inde qu'elle l'eut été dans l'Europe Médiévale.

MODE d'enregistrement des impressions visuelles, la photographie serait une forme mécanique perfectible. Son destin présenterait certaines analogies avec l'histoire du ciné-

5

4.24 The special issue of the French graphics journal, *Arts et Métiers Graphiques*, devoted to Typophoto, 1930.

not idealized. A good art director would have brought to Hohlwein from America the right type of people or models and would have helped him in the expressions of the idea without influencing his ideas.[20]

Even if the observation that Hohlwein's figures were not idealized is questionable, market specificity and a more advanced division of labour underlay this debate. Frenzel concluded that 'the art director is also an institution hitherto almost unknown here [in Germany]' and he sought to promote it continually.

The French practice contrasted strongly with the American stress on business organization. In 1927, Charles Peignot of the printers Deberny and Peignot began publication of the journal *Arts et Métiers Graphiques* in Paris.[21] Its base meant that it paid particular attention to the *'livres d'artistes' de luxe* editions associated with the School of Paris painters and illustrators. This also meant that its critical language was predominantly based in aesthetic judgment, with evaluations derived from a post-Cubist understanding of space and form, unlike *Gebrauchsgraphik*, in which the emphasis was on judging design by its suitability for commercial application.

Figures associated with the French modern poster style, such as A.M. Cassandre, Paul Colin and Jean Carlu, all members of Alliance Graphique, were given high profile in its pages. Otherwise, attention turned to figures in other countries, such as the English letter-artist and sculptor Eric Gill.[22] As an example of ideas from Germany being disseminated in France, Jan Tschichold contributed 'Qu'est-ce que c'est la nouvelle typographie et que veut elle?'.[23] The coverage also spread to include publicity in Los Angeles or modern posters in Hungary, for example, but some of the most stunning pages in the magazine were devoted to advertisements for Deberny and Peignot's own studio, experimenting with 'typophoto' at the time. A further indication of the proximity of interest between France and Germany was illustrated in 1930 when *Arts et Métiers Graphiques* published a special photography issue in which The New Objectivity dominated, coinciding with the widespread attention being given to it in Central Europe.[24]

Gebrauchsgraphik succeeded in establishing a pattern of journalism, review articles, national and international coverage and informative reports, with a confident editorial style, which was workable and free from external restrictions. By the beginning of 1933 it was celebrating its tenth year of publication with contributions by poster and graphic designers from many countries. Indicative of its international recognition was the British perspective as expressed by the prominent poster designer, E. McKnight Kauffer:

> Gebrauchsgraphik *can look back upon its ten years of service with pride and glory. It has fulfilled a purpose with which no other magazine can compare and in its ten years of duty has done more than anything else to raise the standard of advertising art – INTERNATIONALLY. Without* Gebrauchsgraphik *the advanced school of Paris would have been delayed – our best type faces might not have been created and photographic montage would still be an isolated peculiarity. Such features continue through* Gebrauchsgraphik *to make new paths for advertising art.*[25]

4.25 

4.25 An aerial view of Pressa, by Raab-Katzenstein Flugzeugwerk.

The Exhibition Pressa, Cologne 1928

Touted as the greatest international exhibition since the end of the war, Pressa was held between May and October 1928 on the east bank of the Rhine in the neighbourhood of Deutz, exactly facing the historic centre of the city of Cologne. Approached by the Mühlheimer Bridge, it was a site adapted from a combination of barracks (occupied by British troops between 1918 and 1927), the remaining buildings from the 1914 German Werkbund exhibition, and new purpose-built pavilions.[26] It was such a large site that it was necessary to build a miniature railway to convey visitors from one hall to another. What it offered was an opportunity for designers to present work alongside each other. Contemporary reviews indicated that opinions were divided on the appropriateness of exhibiting such items of everyday culture and questions were raised about the vast amounts spent on the site and its temporary nature.

The largest part of the exhibition was provided by German concerns and featured national interests in press and publications, a range of regional printers of newspapers and books, typefoundries, and historical sections on the newspaper and the art of the book.

Unlike smaller contemporary exhibitions in related areas, which were often the product of lobbies or representations of partisan interests, this mainstream exhibition cut across the apparent polarities of Modernist and traditionalist design to present a wide range of production, organized in commercial rather than artistic, stylistic or ideological categories.

In its timing Pressa was positioned between the 1925 Paris Exposition Internationale des Arts Décoratifs et Industriels Modernes and the Stockholm Exhibition of 1930. The Paris exhibition, from which the Germans were barred, was regarded as a triumph for the decorative arts, the luxury and craft nature of the majority of pavilions undermining the reference to industry and modernity in the title. Although a specialist exhibition, Pressa created space for much that was modern, and in that sense was closer to the Swedish event to follow two years

4.26

4.27

4.28

4.26 The modern interpretation of the House of Nations put Pressa on a level with other Weimar international architectural exhibitions.

4.27 – 4.28 The west front and tower of the Pressa exhibition in expressive brick idiom and the main Museum building were designed by Alfred Abel.

later. The Cologne and Stockholm exhibitions each had pavilions with illuminated advertisements seen across water, and in both, the mass-production of many of the exhibits was accepted.[27]

Pressa could be seen as a strategic step towards international recognition for Germany in the fields of design and architecture. It provided German publishers with an opportunity to define themselves in an international context at a sensitive time. In the early Weimar years Germany had lost ground significantly in its art industries. After the 1925 Treaty of Locarno, the German Chancellor Stresemann had a vision that his country would bring east and west together in the development of a peaceful Europe. Germany's membership in the League of Nations had been formally ratified in 1926 and one year later Allied troops had evacuated the Rhine region.[28] The Pressa exhibition was one manifestation of a commercial wish for international cooperation, however much such claims were compromised by the knowledge of Stresemann's secret rearmament.[29] Germany had made several moves to re-enter world trade and, as if to testify to this, the newly established cartels and conglomerates, such as IG Farbenindustrie, Siemens, AEG and MAN industrial machinery, were all exhibitors or advertisers at Cologne.

The prominent historian of the book and typographic traditions of Leipzig, Albert Kapr, has suggested that each German city has its own cultural aura or identity.[30] Writing about Leipzig, he suggested that this comprised its trade fairs, music and books. Cologne's identity, while not historically grounded in book publishing, was also distinctly cultural and it had developed as the museum city of the area, in contrast to Düsseldorf, which was cast as the 'art city', and Bonn the 'university city'. The collections of Cologne's museums were extremely rich in the fine and applied arts of the fourteenth and fifteenth centuries and it was these that the city Kunstgewerbemuseum displayed on its opening in 1900 rather than contemporary design.[31] Perhaps more significantly for modern developments was the move of the Sonderbund, an association responsible for promoting

Post-Impressionism and other new aesthetic ideas, from Düsseldorf to Cologne in 1912. Most crucially, as a precedent for Pressa in its concern with modern design, the Werkbund exhibition of 1914 had placed Cologne centrally in the art and industry debate.

Cologne was no more a 'press city' than many other German cities, but the exhibition seems to have played an important political role in reasserting north-west Germany, as the record of its cultural politics shows. Pressa and similar cultural and industrial initiatives developed by Cologne shortly afterwards were intended to signal that it was a world city, worthy of comparison with others of international significance in trade and culture, ranked alongside Berlin, Paris or Chicago. Not previously linked with the artists' colonies and the enlightened patronage of key industrialists as at Darmstadt, Hagen or Munich, Cologne profited from the 1914 Werkbund exhibition by being associated with such figures. By the time of Pressa, the legacy of the 'Werkbund Debate' was evident in the acceptance of mechanization: the proliferation of information on systems of production; the use of statistical evidence in charts, diagrams or graphs of circulation figures, as well as the general use of photography as the major illustrative source.

4.29

4.29 The Egyptian section at Pressa indicated how far removed some of the contributions were from graphic design.

The culture of Cologne in 1928 was largely conservative and stable, discouraging particular association with the radical, avant-garde artistic ideas of other cities during the Weimar Republic. The city's administration was led by Konrad Adenauer, a prominent conservative Catholic who provided a figure of continuity between 1914 and 1928. Appointed Mayor of Cologne in 1917, he wrote in the catalogue of 'an international pageant of civilization' and of Pressa as an 'instrument of PEACE!'.[32]

Appropriately for its subject, the exhibition was given the attention of a house-style, with the official catalogue, poster and publicity overseen by Fritz Ehmcke. Among his more prominent Cologne commissions, Ehmcke had worked for Feinhals, the tobacco company, and the publicity for Pressa followed a characteristic commercial graphic approach: a poster with 'trademark', a diagrammatic representation of the pavilions and a publicity leaflet, maps and signage for visitors, as well as the design of flags along the banks of the Rhine.

In addition, the event was accompanied by a high-quality commemorative book with professional architectural photographs and an official catalogue, which was filled with advertisements and lists of displays and worked as a trade index to the exhibitors.[33] As to the arrangement of the site, the visitor would pass through 42 buildings altogether. Three main buildings formed the focus. The exhibition hall, by architect Alfred Abel, Director of Urban Planning for the city of Cologne, was monumental in approach, featuring brick and reminiscent of much factory and municipal building, albeit on a grander scale.

By contrast, the museum building was in a neo-classical idiom treated in faced stone. Here the German displays were housed, including an exhibition of 'Contemporary European Book Arts', as well as 'Publicity of the German Government and the German Administration' organized by Dr Erwin Redslob, the State Minister of Art. The State Railways, the State Post Office, and the German paper industry all took the opportunity to display their press and publicity operations and to explain their functions in international news services through contemporary developments in telegraph and radio transmission.

The third of the main exhibition buildings was the House of Nations, with a modern exterior, which contained displays from twenty-four countries, including Britain, China and Japan, Norway and Turkey, flanked by contributions from the major powers of the Soviet Union and the USA.[34] Installation photographs and commentaries in catalogues and reviews reveal that many countries saw Pressa as an opportunity to provide a broad range of materials, including newspaper, magazine and book publishing, displays of posters and advertising and, more straightforwardly, environments which evoked national characteristics, enticing tourism through their decorative and atmospheric effects. But these were not always welcomed. According to one German commentator the national pavilions,

4.30

4.31

with their eye on business, unnecessarily stressed press advertising sections, while not offering the wider cultural perspective expected by the organizers of the event. 'For what have toothpaste and Bemberg silk to do with a Press exhibition?', this commentator complained; 'all these countries have devoted their attention in the main to displaying their market territory, that is, they have paid more attention to the advertisement section of the newspapers than to the newspapers themselves.'[35]

4.30 Advertisement for the *Kölnische Zeitung*, showing the pavilion designed by Rolf Lange for the publisher M. Du Mont Schauberg.

4.31 The *Kölnische Zeitung* pavilion photographed at night by Werner Mantz.

4.32 

4.32 Pavilion designed for the publisher Rudolf Mosse by the Berlin architect Erich Mendelsohn.

Upstairs in the House of Nations, themes such as Youth and the Press, Women and the Press, Science, Religion, the Colonies and Sport were addressed by individual thematic displays. Each was organized by the specialists in their field. For example, the Women and the Press, under Dr Emmy Wingerath, presented an historical view of women's professional involvement in publishing and journalism, beginning with examples of calligraphy from early religious orders and moving to cover much contemporary journalism for and by women. The section posed questions about women's employment in these areas, as well as asking what a 'women's press' might be – an interesting extension of the debate opened in Leipzig in 1914.

The House of Nations faced the Street of Newspapers, where a number of individual newspaper publishers had their purpose-built pavilions, including Rudolf Mosse, publisher of *Das Berliner Tageblatt*, and DuMont Schauberg, publisher of art books as well as *Die Kölnische Zeitung*, the main daily newspaper of the host city. Alongside these and other cultural exhibits were straightforward trade displays of advanced German printing industries, including machinery for chromolithography, new type designs and the latest developments in mechanical typesetting. Most notable among these were the Typograph composing machines, aimed to attract the European market in competition with the Anglo-American Lanston Monotype and the American Linotype companies.

Light played a major role in completing the spectacle. Already an important feature of the 1925 Paris Exposition, integrated lighting designs had become a characteristic external feature of many modern buildings for retail design in Germany and the subject of several publications at the time.[36] Finally, there were tea-rooms, a wine terrace and the Rheinland restaurant as well as the obligatory funfair, something that residents in the host cities of international exhibitions had come to expect for their weekend or evening entertainment.

Journalism and Newspapers

To assess internationalism in German publishing and printing in the '20s meant largely to gauge how successful firms had been in adapting to American systems of scale and ambition. In 1927 Ullstein, the largest European publishing house, opened its new building designed by Eugen Schmoll in American factory style in Tempelhof, Berlin. According to one commentator, Ullstein at its height 'employed 10,000 editors, correspondents, employees and workmen, it housed seventy-eight composing machines, sixty-five rotary presses, thirty-seven illustration presses, fifty-nine power presses, eight intaglio presses, and extensive book binding machinery. The average daily production was over twelve million 4-page and magazine sheets, 15,000 books and pamphlets.'[37] In the late '20s international photo agencies were established in London, New York, Berlin and Paris and reportage in weekly illustrated magazines led to the proliferation of information as part of everyday street life.[38] By the time of Pressa, an estimated 7,000 periodicals, 4,000 daily or weekly newspapers and 30,000 book titles appeared annually in Germany. (By contrast, the Soviet Union had 559 newspapers with 8.5 million issues.)[39] A crucial feature of Germany's printing industry and presses was its regionalism. Unlike Britain, for instance, where the London *Times* and the *Manchester Guardian* provided national daily papers at the quality end of the range, in Germany there was no such newspaper. Attempts were made to create one, but each city still maintained several dailies. For instance, Berlin had twenty, Hamburg ten and Cologne eight. Readers turned to the independent city newspapers such as *Das Berliner Tageblatt* or *Die Kölnische Zeitung* for national reporting, but in the end their regional or party affiliations made them unsuitable as national papers

For a visiting international audience, Pressa would have been of interest as an indicator of how Germans were responding to the 'Gothic or Roman question' in design. While the historical convention of printing in Fraktur was undergoing constant review and challenge, Philipp Th. Bertheau claims that Fraktur was still used for approximately 57 per cent of all books and 60 per cent of all magazines in 1928.[40]

By the late '20s arguments for romanization of many commercial publications were being put forward on the basis that they would be more accessible to a non-German readership in the growing international context for trade. In the forum of the Werkbund debates, such commercial incentives were supplemented by aesthetic reasons and the appeal to standardization: using newly designed lower-case letterforms in internationally accepted typefaces was seen to elevate German design from its nationally and culturally narrow linguistic grouping. Commenting on newspaper design at the time, the typographer Paul Renner interpreted Germany as the land of *Vorgestern* or *Übermorgen* (day before yesterday or day after tomorrow).[41] While recognizing Germany's rich historical traditions, he admired American and British newspapers and criticized their German counterparts for treating design as a fancy-dress box. Among Renner's examples of good practice were pages from the *New York Times*, the *Saturday Evening Post* and the London *Times*. He approved of them because of their visual compatability between editorial and advertising pages and layouts, their overall clarity of design and restrained use of good, modern typefaces.

Modern Book Design at Pressa

Pressa was held one year after the International Book Exhibition at Leipzig, where thirty-seven countries had exhibited the arts of the book.[42] An element of competition may have existed between Leipzig and Cologne, although the overall regionalism makes it seem more likely that their attitudes were complementary rather than competitive. Indeed, Hugo Steiner-Prag, the leading Leipzig book illustrator and designer, also contributed to Pressa, overseeing 'The European Contemporary Book Arts Exhibition' and designing the official Pressa book.

Typographers and book artists of the pre-war generation interpreted classical typography as being based on an aesthetic harmony of layout. Legibility and

4.33 House of the Workers' Press by Hans Schumacher, with an interior overseen by the graphic designer Max Burchartz of Bochum.

4.34 The display of the workers' press. 'Statistics, Schools and the Press' designed by students of Fritz Ehmcke

beauty were guiding principles aimed at comfort of reading. By 1928, however, the impact of typographic reform was not confined to bibliophile work. Among designers interested in Leftist cultural activities, it was also felt that good typography served an important service in non-élite publishing. In the *Gebrauchsbuch*, the utilitarian book, which was partly the subject of the 'House of the Workers' Press', arguments were made for legibility as a central strategy for democracy.

This pavilion was organized jointly by the Social Democratic Party and the General Association of German Trade Unions. Inside the pavilion was a display of publications from the German workers' movement and a reading room of nearly two hundred newspapers, the entire range of current newspapers aimed at the country's working class. The most obvious international precedent to this room had been the Workers' Club by the architect Konstantin Melnikov in the Soviet pavilion at the 1925 Paris Exhibition. Especially designed desks and chairs by Alexander Rodchenko equipped a reading room with selections of Constructivist-inspired publications.[43] Additionally at Pressa, examples of five hundred books by publishers with divisions aimed at working-class readership were displayed, as well as a film programme, *'Im Anfang war das Wort'* (In the Beginning was the

Word), which traced the German workers' movement since 1848. The recently founded book clubs were main exhibitors. The first, Büchergilde Gutenberg, had been established in 1924 in Leipzig by the Educational Division of the Union of German Letterpress Printers (*Bildungsverband der deutschen Drucker*) to promote affordable and well-designed books. The Bücherkreis, affiliated to the Social Democratic Party, and the Universum Bücherkreis für Alle (Universum Book Guild for All), had followed in 1927.[44]

Jan Tschichold, whose designs were represented in the Pavilion of Workers' Presses, advocated an alternative to the luxury of the book artist, indicating both a generational and ideological shift. In *Die Neue Typographie* of 1928, perhaps the most significant argument for modern design in printing and published by one of the book clubs, he wrote: 'the new typography distinguishes itself from the earlier in attempting foremost to develop its appearance from the function of the text. Clean and direct expression must be rendered to the contents of the printed material. The "form" must be brought out from the function, just as in the workings of technology and nature.'[45]

That Modernism was associated with progressive politics in this pavilion was made clear by the exhibits with their abundant use of new typography and photomontage. This was reinforced by the approach taken to the setting, the architectural design of the pavilion by Fritz Schumacher and the exhibition design by Max Burchartz. The interior was distinguished from other parts of Pressa by signage in sans-serif capitals, an open-tread staircase finished with industrial materials, panels and cases arranged according to abstract principles and large-scale geometrically composed murals.

The English and Soviet Pavilions

A contrast between the English and Soviet pavilions illustrates the diverse interpretations and range of styles within print culture on display at Pressa and indicates how quickly national and political stereotypes came to be formed

4.35

4.35 The English pavilion at Pressa

in response to them. The English pavilion was organized by the author and journalist Mark Neven du Mont to illustrate the tradition of the 'English' art of printing and the newspaper trades. Historical examples were shown from the collections of the Victoria and Albert Museum, His Majesty's Stationery Office, the St Bride Institute and the Sell collection of early newspapers. Also included was a display of emergency newspapers from the General Strike of 1926, a stand for the London *Times* and the press for *The News of the World*, a newspaper with a circulation of 3.5 million.

Separately, English book arts were interpreted by Oliver Simon, director of the Curwen Press and editor of *The Fleuron*, who suggested in the small catalogue that they 'can fairly claim to be typical of contemporary fine printing and book illustration, where the English reputation for "sanity, common sense and honest materials is obstinately maintained".'[46] The pavilion featured the Golden Cockerel, Shakespeare Head and Gregynog presses, which demonstrated the continuing Arts and Crafts lineage of the private presses in hand-composition. Otherwise all designs were for mechanical setting by Lanston Monotype, using typefaces such as Caslon, Imprint, Baskerville and Poliphilus. By contrast with the work of German contributors, illustrations were distinctly in favour of line-blocks and wood-engravings. The majority of British exhibits comprised examples of contemporary fine printing and book illustration, with some posters for London Transport, works by the Crawfords agency and other established illustrators and commercial artists from within the orbit of the Design and Industries Association.

The designs for Pressa by the Soviet designer El Lissitzky are perhaps the most celebrated in existing literature. Lissitzky devised a montage environment, which commented on the role of design in the press and publishing of the new Soviet society in a challenging and experimental manner. Although this pavilion has been well located in the sequence of Lissitzky's own work, less is known about how it compared with other exhibits at Cologne. For whereas Pressa claimed significant attention at the time (no doubt because its subject-matter directly

4.36 – 4.38 *Union der sozialistischen Sowjet-Republiken: Katalog des Sowjet-Pavillons auf der Internationalen Presse-Austellung, Köln, 1928*
(Union of Socialist Soviet Republics: Catalogue of the Soviet Pavilion at the International Press Exhibition, Cologne, 1928)

Typography and photomontage by El Lissitzky
Catalogue cover, title page, interior
1928

4.36

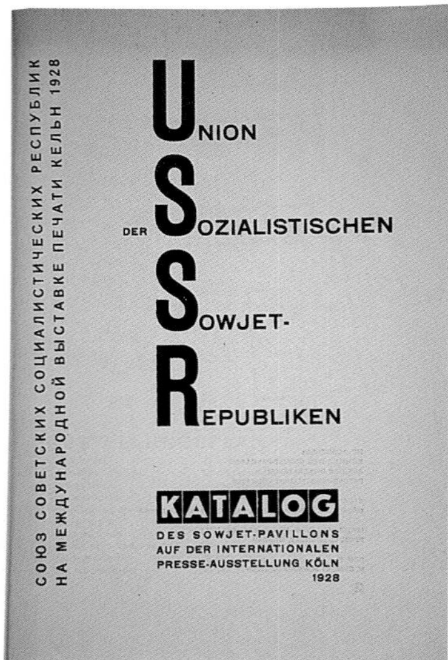

4.37

4.38

4.39

4.39 Part of the photofresco *'The Task of the Press is the Education of the Masses'* designed by El Lissitzky for Pressa, Cologne, 1928.

impinged on reporters' interests), the exhibition has not been extensively interpreted in subsequent years, nor has it been placed in the context of renewed interest in print culture of the Weimar years. A review in the *Berliner Tageblatt* on 26 May 1928 explained the apparent gulf between contributions from England and the Soviet Union:

> *What a contrast between the English and Soviet Russian rooms! Everything that separates the two finds expression when one sees the two brought together under the same roof. England: pious, aristocratic, historically reverent, at peace in its confidence; so it was and so it will be to all eternity...*

And Russia: one must admit, grandeur in its exposition of social conditions, with really mechanical equipment, conveyor belts of great cubistic zig-zags: causing a stir by its enormous steps of progress which are depicted in bold and bragging manner, always in glaring red. Forward! in the struggle and into class-consciousness. [47]

El Lissitzky wrote retrospectively, 'in 1926 my most important work as an artist began: the design of exhibitions'.[48] In December 1927 he was commissioned to design the Soviet contribution to the Pressa by Anatolii Lunacharskii, the Head of Narkompros, the People's Commissariat of the Enlightenment. Previously he had worked on an exhibition to commemorate the Tenth Anniversary of the Revolution in Moscow's Gorky Park, as well as the Soviet contribution to the Dresden 'Hygiene' exhibition of 1926 and the Hanover 1927 Art Exhibition.

Lissitzky headed a thirty-eight member 'collective of creators', who produced most of the display material in the workshop for stage design in the Lenin Hills in Moscow. The centrepiece was a 'photofresco', as Sergei Senkin, one of the collaborators, called it, entitled 'The Task of the Press is the Education of the Masses'. Lissitzky had learnt theories of photomontage from Gustav Klucis with whom he had worked in Moscow.

Even the somewhat reticent German press commented positively on the display:

Soviet Russia wants to make an impression, to win favour, to propagandise. Red is not only the colour of the State but also of excitement. And its combination with white and black, the bizarre primitivism of the models and constructions, the full assault of all the statistics, pictures, slogans are intended to thrill and persuade.[49]

This display has been interpreted by the art historian Benjamin Buchloh as a step in the transition from 'Faktura' to 'Factography'.[50] In aesthetic terms, this can be explained as a shift from photomontage as an artistic device concerned with properties of pictorial representation to a technique of assembling facts as raw data and information for the purposes of communication. In the early '20s many artists were interested in the laboratory nature of their work and investigated the transformative properties of art, by taking the found and everyday and rendering it distinct as 'art'. By 1926-28 Lissitzky and Klucis were applying the principles of the filmic 'montage of attractions' as formulated and practised by the directors Dziga Vertov and Sergei Eisenstein to two-dimensional graphic display as well as exhibition environments. As 'Factography', photomontage attempted to assemble facts; its scientific intention was evident in the term. This shift reflected the political change from the experimental stages of early Soviet Communism to early Stalinism.

Despite the attention it attracted, Lissitzky was unhappy with the results at Pressa. 'It was a big success for us, but aesthetically there is something of a poisoned satisfaction. The extreme hurry and the shortage of time violated my intentions and the necessary completion of the form - so it ended up being basically a theatre decoration.'[51]

Reception of Pressa

> *The aim of the international Pressa exhibition was to give the world a picture of the cultural and economic meaning of the press, to grasp the life of the press in all its manifestations and total sphere of influence, in its living connections with culture and business and with political and social events. Therefore the task was far beyond making an exhibition just for trade people. It should be a show for everyone. The attempt was to step back from the newspaper and magazine as a product to the presentation of their meaning in the life of the population.*[52]

It may be asked what exhibitions can tell us? Can they say anything about the actual state of trade, or do they simply indicate the preoccupations of an industry or national interest group? Are they only a matter of less or more successful propaganda? Three issues arise from Pressa and its reviews. Firstly, the question of how to display products of everyday life was raised in the design press. Konrad Adenauer had spoken in his opening address of a wish to convey 'the world of thought as represented and reproduced in print and picture' and observed that 'The chief danger of such an enterprise was that it should exceed the mental capacity of the visitor.'

Doubts had already been raised by Frenzel in his review of a Berlin 'Advertising Fair' of 1925 on how graphic material might be displayed. His main criticisms were its apparent 'bad taste', unnecessary detail and lack of 'system'.[53] In reviewing the Pressa exhibition he declared:

> *To be sure, it soon becomes apparent that the really important features of the press cannot be put on exhibition – for the attempt to show the spirit of a modern editorial section in five editors' rooms must be regarded as a failure. If the only difference between the local reporter's room and that belonging to the political editor is that one has an upholstered chair and the other not, then even the expert can make nothing of that matter. Neither can one comprehend why precisely the feuilleton or literary editor should have a sofa in his room.*[57]

Frenzel favoured exhibits at Pressa in which process could be understood, as in the printing industry and newspapers with their working displays. It was his view that 'Explanatory and propagandistic exhibitions should really be arranged only for those branches of industry which do not stand in such immediate connection with the public as, for example, the press. An article which I can buy any day at any street corner for two pennies cannot be rendered more familiar by means of an exhibition. It is always said of the press that it is its own best means of advertisement.'

This point of view was not one that all would share, coming as it did from the editor of a prominent magazine with the aim of professionalizing graphic design activities. It is significant that in 1926 Die Neue Sammlung (The New Collection) was established in Munich to collect and exhibit *Alltagskultur,* or everyday culture. Arguing that a new approach to acquisition and display was required in traditional Arts and Crafts museums based on 19th-century principles, Die Neue Sammlung, a body attached to the Bavarian National Museum, aimed to confront 'the tempo of change in diverse media since 1900', to contrast ancient and modern developments in ceramics, metalwork, posters and textiles and to exhibit, for example, 'Finnish knotted carpets or photographs of new American architecture alongside displays of German, Swiss and Austrian products'.[55] The stated priority in this approach was to explain designed objects for consumers as well as producers, and to examine the operation of social and economic forces upon them.

Secondly, the economic viability of exhibitions such as Pressa was questioned in the reviews. For instance, the expenditure was already considered an extravagance:

> *Whether such exhibitions and exertions, so frequently repeated in the various great cities of Germany, are really worthwhile and can cover the enormous costs they entail, not only to the city authorities in question but also to all the firms exhibiting, is to be the subject of international negotiations in the immediate future, and there is no doubt that an attempt will be made to come to an understanding in this direction, for in the next few years great international exhibitions have been announced by a whole series of other countries, in order to induce leaders of industry to send their wares in for exhibition.*[56]

In fact Pressa cleared its costs by September 1928, one month before its close. Just after this, in November, a Paris convention on international exhibitions reported new regulations controlling the number and timing of exhibitions.[57] In a report on a proposed international Werkbund exhibition entitled *Die Neue Zeit* (The New Epoch) for Cologne in 1932 (which was never to take place), it was made clear that two years' notice had to be given before such an exhibition could be opened and that each country would be restricted to hosting an international or 'general' exhibition only once every ten years. Reserved reactions to Pressa were therefore symptomatic of a more general questioning of large-scale exhibitions and their function in a regional or national economy.

Thirdly, there was the issue of what to do with the exhibition site after 1928. The suggestion was made that only exhibitions should be held that had a subsequent use, as at the building exhibitions Am Weissenhof, in Stuttgart in 1927 and that proposed for Breslau in 1929. On this score, Pressa was vindicated. Its main building was to find use as the Rheinisches Museum and proved to be a permanent and valuable addition to the city of Cologne. The other buildings on the site would be used for the planned 1932 exhibition, *Die Neue Zeit*, and for subsequent fairs.

The *ring neuer werbegestalter*

Shortly after the first statements on the new typography were made by Jan Tschichold and Laszlo Moholy-Nagy, their approach entered the curriculum of many art and design schools of Germany. In addition to the activities at the Bauhaus, the prominent new typographers included Max Burchartz in Essen, Willi Baumeister, Hans Leistikow and Grete Leistikow in Frankfurt am Main, Johannes Molzahn in Magdeburg, Paul Renner in Munich, and Georg Trump in Bielefeld. The Circle of New Advertising Designers (*ring neuer werbegestalter*) was a group drawn from this educational context, whose purpose was to promote a shared avant-garde outlook. The association echoed by name a group of architects based in Berlin, Der Ring, which had been formed a few years earlier.

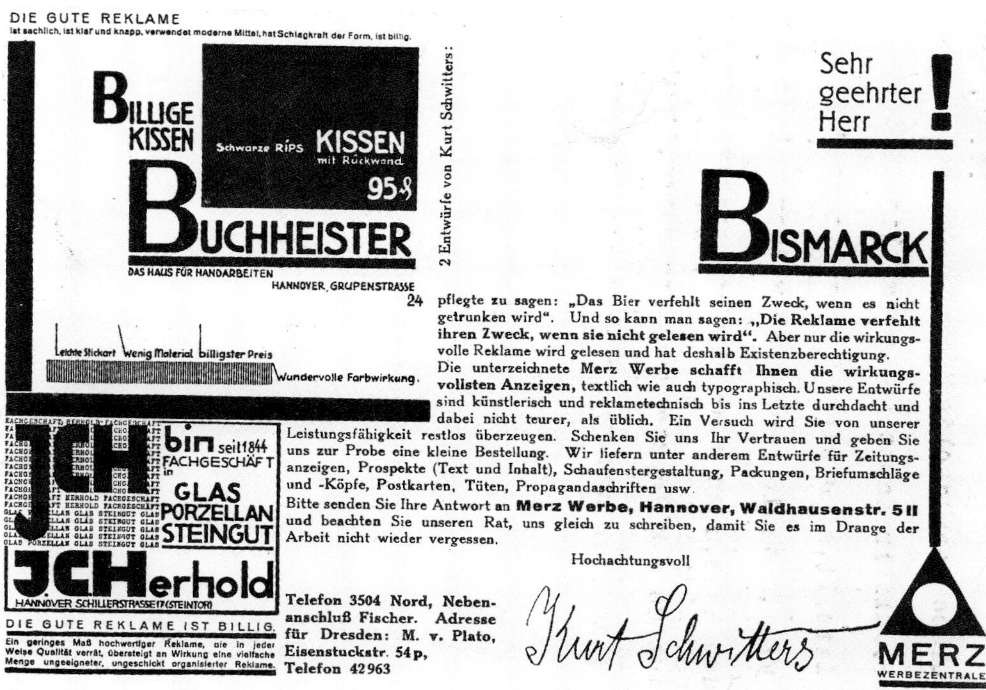

DIE GUTE REKLAME
ist sachlich, ist klar und knapp, verwendet moderne Mittel, hat Schlagkraft der Form, ist billig.

BILLIGE KISSEN
Schwarze RIPS KISSEN mit Rückwand 95 ₰
BUCHHEISTER
DAS HAUS FÜR HANDARBEITEN
HANNOVER, GRUPENSTRASSE 24
Leichte Stickart Wenig Material billigster Preis
Wundervolle Farbwirkung.

2 Entwürfe von Kurt Schwitters:

Sehr geehrter Herr!

BISMARCK pflegte zu sagen: „Das Bier verfehlt seinen Zweck, wenn es nicht getrunken wird". Und so kann man sagen: **„Die Reklame verfehlt ihren Zweck, wenn sie nicht gelesen wird".** Aber nur die wirkungsvolle Reklame wird gelesen und hat deshalb Existenzberechtigung.
Die unterzeichnete **Merz Werbe schafft Ihnen die wirkungsvollsten Anzeigen,** textlich wie auch typographisch. Unsere Entwürfe sind künstlerisch und reklametechnisch bis ins Letzte durchdacht und dabei nicht teurer, als üblich. Ein Versuch wird Sie von unserer Leistungsfähigkeit restlos überzeugen. Schenken Sie uns Ihr Vertrauen und geben Sie uns zur Probe eine kleine Bestellung. Wir liefern unter anderem Entwürfe für Zeitungsanzeigen, Prospekte (Text und Inhalt), Schaufenstergestaltung, Packungen, Briefumschläge und -Köpfe, Postkarten, Tüten, Propagandaschriften usw.
Bitte senden Sie Ihre Antwort an **Merz Werbe, Hannover, Waldhausenstr. 5 II** und beachten Sie unseren Rat, uns gleich zu schreiben, damit Sie es im Drange der Arbeit nicht wieder vergessen.

Hochachtungsvoll

Kurt Schwitters

JCH bin seit 1844 FACHGESCHÄFT in GLAS PORZELLAN STEINGUT
J.C.Herhold
HANNOVER SCHILLERSTRASSE 17 (STEINTOR)

DIE GUTE REKLAME IST BILLIG.
Ein geringes Maß hochwertiger Reklame, die in jeder Weise Qualität verrät, übersteigt an Wirkung eine vielfache Menge ungeeigneter, ungeschickt organisierter Reklame.

Telefon 3504 Nord, Nebenanschluß Fischer. Adresse für Dresden: M. v. Plato, Eisenstuckstr. 54 p, Telefon 42963

MERZ
WERBEZENTRALE

4.40

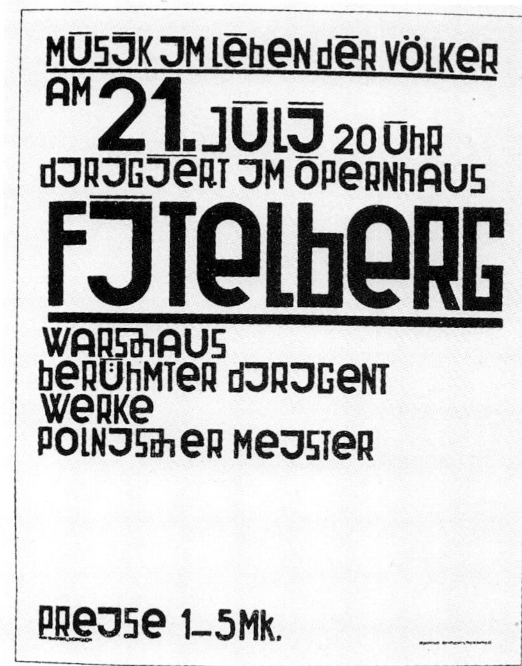

4.41

4.40 The slogan reads, *'The good advertisement is clear and precise, employs modern means, has strength of form and is cheap',* Postcard addressed to Jan Tschichold, 25 July 1928

Designed by Kurt Schwitters
1924

4.41 *Musik im Leben der Völker* (Music in the life of the people)

Designed by Kurt Schwitters
Poster
1924
It employs Systemschrift, an experimental typeface combining lower and upper case letterforms.

The idea came from Kurt Schwitters and was announced in the magazine *Das Kunstblatt* in 1928: 'A group of nine artists active as advertising designers has formed under the presidency of Kurt Schwitters. Baumeister, Burchartz, Dexel, Domela, Michel, Schwitters, Trump, Tschichold and Vordemberge-Gildewart belong to the association.'[58] Before forming the *ring*, Schwitters had broadened his approach to visual art to include graphic design, and had designed a sans-serif typeface. Immediately after the war, he had been a Dada artist, centred in Hanover with international contacts.[59] He was drawn to the idiosyncratic and poetic qualities of typefaces and illustrative styles and made collages in which elements of various periods and styles were juxtaposed in an absurd or lyrical manner. These experimental collages and sculptures, developed from found objects and images, were called *Merzbild* (picture) or *Merzbau* (sculpture), an abbreviated derivation from the German word for commerce, *Kommerz*. As this reference suggests, Schwitters made great play between the meaning of words and images. He published a review, *Merz*, featuring poetry and drawings, initially in Dada style. Issues 8 and 9 of the journal were dedicated to the new typography and were designed in collaboration with El Lissitzky, in a more analytical manner.[60] At this stage Schwitters established a small design studio, called Werbezentrale, in Hanover where he devised a modern house-style

die besten stuhl modelle
der heutigen produktion
ausstellung
der Stuhl
10.–31. märz 1929 offen täglich 10–17 uhr auch sonntags
kunstgewerbemuseum
frankfurt a.m. neue mainzerstrasse 49
eintrittspreis: –.50 pfg
verbunden mit einer
ausstellung moderner gemälde
veranstalter
städt. hochbauamt
kunstgewerbeschule
städt. wirtschaftsamt

4.42

4.42 *Der Stuhl*
(The Chair, the best chairs in production today, an exhibition at Frankfurt on Main Arts and Crafts Museum)

Designed by Willi Baumeister
Poster
1929

4.43

4.43 *Technische Vereinigung, Magdeburg*

Designed by Johannes Molzahn
Leaflet
1929

4.44

4.44 *Der Stuhl* (The Chair)

Edited by Heinz and Bodo Rasch
Catalogue
1928

4.45 *Wohnung und Werkraum* (Dwelling and Workspace)

Designed by Johannes Molzahn
Catalogue
1929

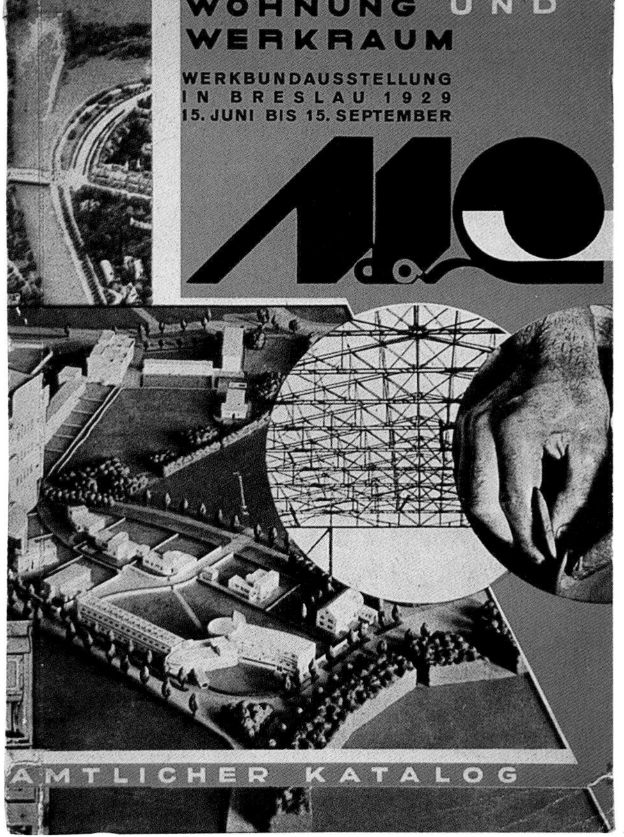

4.45

for the stationery of the City Council as well as designs for Bahlsen biscuits and Pelikan inks.

The affiliation of the *ring* appears to have been loose, its activities consisting mainly of exhibitions, either promoting the group on its own or contributing to larger events. The majority of the original members came from backgrounds in the visual arts and were self-taught in typography. An initial exhibition travelled to Wiesbaden, Barmen, Bochum, Hamburg, Rotterdam, Halle, Dresden, Hanover,

John Heartfield

Zeichner, Berlin-Charlottenburg, Bleibtreustraße 7.

Geboren 19. Juni 1991.

Neue politische Probleme verlangen neue Propagandamittel. Hierfür besitzt die Fotografie die größte Ueberzeugungskraft.

John Heartfield

Buchtitel. Aus dem Titel der Buchstabe „G" geht nichts hervor erst das Bild schafft Gedankenverbindung, läßt erkennen, daß es sich um einen Roman handelt, gibt auch Aufschluß über das Milieu, den vermutlichen Stoff. Die runde Form des „G" steht in Zusammenklang mit den Köpfen. Das Wort „der Buchstabe" steht schräg, tritt erst in zweiter Linie in Erscheinung und stört das Bild, das als solches mit dem „G" zusammenwirken soll, nicht. Auf der Rückseite erscheint nur das große „G", wie eine symbolhafte Zeichnung, als reiner Blickfang. Die Fotomontage gestattet, ausdrucksvolle Köpfe nach Wunsch zusammenzustellen und Steigerungseffekte zu erreichen (vergleiche Richters „G" Umschlag", das verängstigte Gesicht des Mannes am Automobilsteuer und den lachenden Frauenkopf).

53

John Heartfield

4.46

4.46 – 4.49 *Gefesselter Blick: 25 kurze Monographien und Beiträge über neue Werbegestaltung* (The Captured Glance: 25 short monographs on the new publicity design)

Edited by Heinz and Bodo Rasch
Cover and sections on individual designers from the book
1930

Bremen and Magdeburg during 1928 and 1929. In Hanover some works were acquired for the permanent collection of the Landesmuseum by art curator Alexander Dorner. As for larger exhibitions, the *ring* made group contributions to the Berlin Neue Typographie of 1930, where they were shown alongside Bayer, Moholy-Nagy, Karel Teige, van Doesburg and Molzahn, and also to the important Werkbund exhibition of 1929, *Film und Foto*. The members later participated in the exhibitions *Fotomontage* in Berlin in 1931, *Neue Werbegraphik* in the Arts and Crafts Museum in Basel in 1930, the international exhibition *Kunst der Werbung* (Art of Publicity) in Essen in 1931 and the exhibition *Internationaal Reklamedrukwerk* (International Advertising Design) in the Stedelijk Museum Amsterdam in 1931.[61]

By 1930 the number of members had increased to twenty-five and an exhibition and a book, *Gefesselter Blick* (best translated as *The Captured Glance)*, acted as a manifesto.[62] In many ways the format of this book exemplified their approach. The text was set in single-case, Roman type with bold used for emphasis, and it was printed on art paper in red and black inks with a transparent plastic cover sheet. Willi Baumeister's photographic portrait of a woman engaging the reader with staring eyes on the cover expressed the publication's commitment to *Neue Sachlichkeit*. Each short essay or statement from a designer was accompanied by an illustrated work, predominantly an example of what Moholy called Typophoto.

Their point of view was most succinctly defined by the Dutch designer Paul Schuitema, acknowledging that modern design involved the separation of hand and machine which previous generations had so strongly fought against: 'The designer is not a draughtsman, but rather an organizer of optical and technical factors. His work should not be limited to making notes, placing in groups and organizing things technically.'[63]

Another *ring* member, Johannes Molzahn, wrote enthusiastically on the trademark, which is

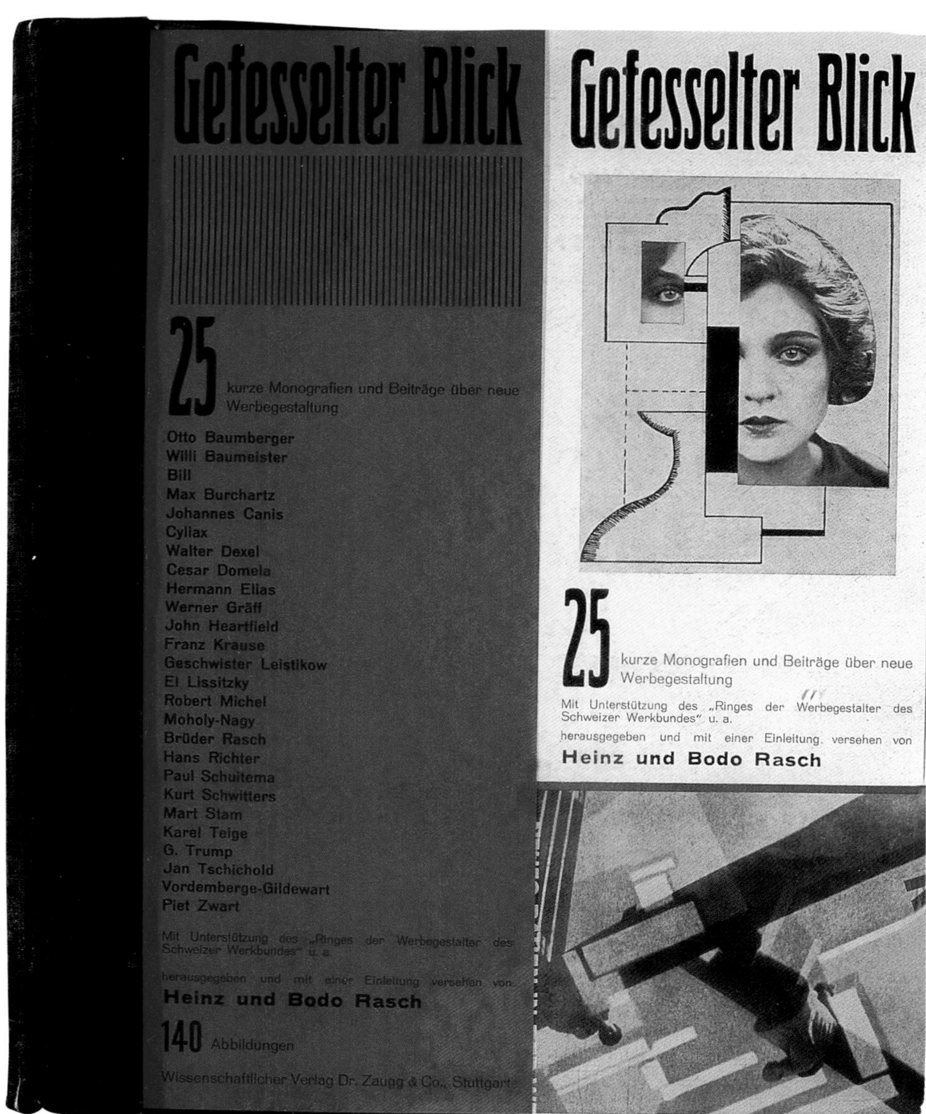

Gefesselter Blick

25 kurze Monografien und Beiträge über neue Werbegestaltung

Otto Baumberger
Willi Baumeister
Bill
Max Burchartz
Johannes Canis
Cyliax
Walter Dexel
Cesar Domela
Hermann Elias
Werner Gräff
John Heartfield
Franz Krause
Geschwister Leistikow
El Lissitzky
Robert Michel
Moholy-Nagy
Brüder Rasch
Hans Richter
Paul Schuitema
Kurt Schwitters
Mart Stam
Karel Teige
G. Trump
Jan Tschichold
Vordemberge-Gildewart
Piet Zwart

Mit Unterstützung des „Ringes der Werbegestalter des Schweizer Werkbundes" u. a.

herausgegeben und mit einer Einleitung versehen von

Heinz und Bodo Rasch

140 Abbildungen

Wissenschaftlicher Verlag Dr. Zaugg & Co., Stuttgart

Gefesselter Blick

25 kurze Monografien und Beiträge über neue Werbegestaltung

Mit Unterstützung des „Ringes der Werbegestalter des Schweizer Werkbundes" u. a.

herausgegeben und mit einer Einleitung versehen von

Heinz und Bodo Rasch

4.47

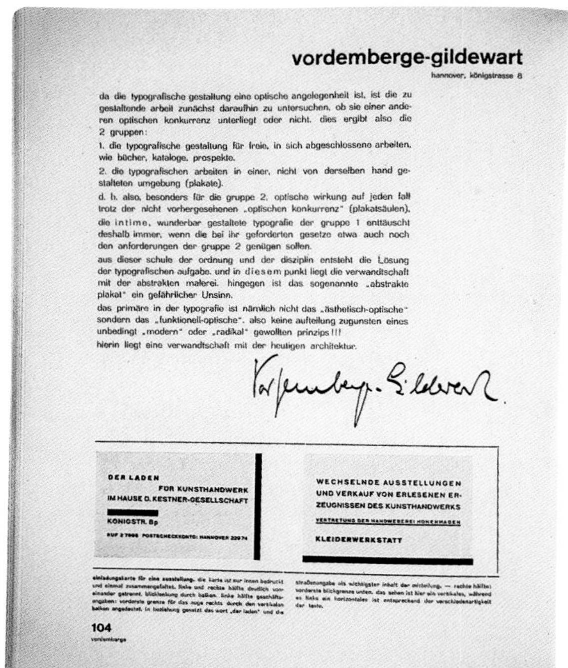

vordemberge-gildewart

hannover, königstrasse 8

da die typografische gestaltung eine optische angelegenheit ist, ist die zu gestaltende arbeit zunächst daraufhin zu untersuchen, ob sie einer anderen optischen konkurrenz unterliegt oder nicht. dies ergibt also die 2 gruppen:

1. die typografische gestaltung für freie, in sich abgeschlossene arbeiten, wie bücher, kataloge, prospekte.

2. die typografischen arbeiten in einer, nicht von derselben hand gestalteten umgebung (plakate).

d. h. also, besonders für die gruppe 2, optische wirkung auf jeden fall trotz der nicht vorhergesehenen „optischen konkurrenz" (plakatsäulen). die intime, wunderbar gestaltete typografie der gruppe 1 enttäuscht deshalb immer, wenn die bei ihr geforderten gesetze etwa auch noch den anforderungen der gruppe 2 genügen sollen.

aus dieser schule der ordnung und der disziplin entsteht die Lösung der typografischen aufgabe. und in diesem punkt liegt die verwandtschaft mit der abstrakten malerei. hingegen ist das sogenannte „abstrakte plakat" ein gefährlicher Unsinn.

das primäre in der typografie ist nämlich nicht das „ästhetisch-optische" sondern das „funktionell-optische". also keine aufteilung zugunsten eines unbedingt „modern" oder „radikal" gewollten prinzips!!!

hierin liegt eine verwandtschaft mit der heutigen architektur.

einladungskarte für eine ausstellung. die karte ist nur innen bedruckt und einmal zusammengefaltet. linke und rechte hälfte deutlich voneinander getrennt. blicklenkung durch balken. linke hälfte geschäftsangaben: vorderste grenze für das auge rechts durch den vertikalen balken angedeutet. in beziehung gesetzt das wort „der laden" und die straßenangabe als wichtigster inhalt der mitteilung. — rechte hälfte: vorderste blickgrenze unten. das sehen ist hier ein vertikales, während es links ein horizontales ist entsprechend der verschiedenartigkeit der texte.

104
vordemberge

4.48

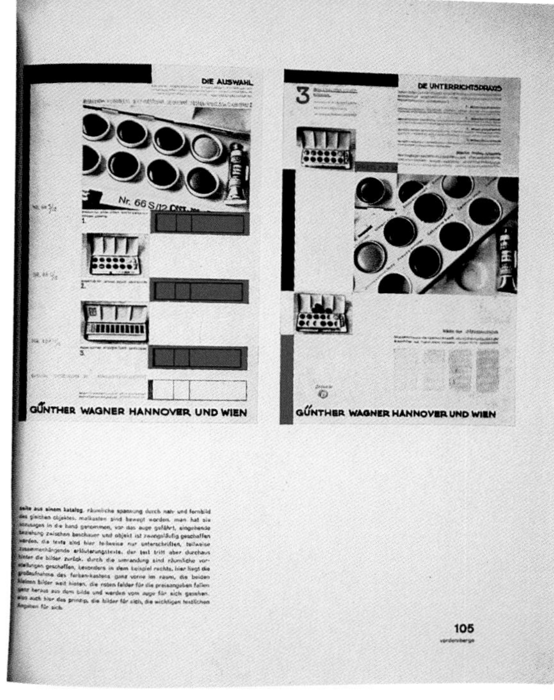

seite aus einem katalog. räumliche spannung durch nah- und fernbild des gleichen objektes. malkasten sind bewegt worden. man hat sie sozusagen in die hand genommen, vor das auge geführt. eingehende beziehung zwischen beschauer und objekt ist zwangsläufig geschaffen worden. die texte sind hier teilweise nur unterschriften, teilweise zusammenhängende erläuterungstexte. der text tritt aber durchaus hinter die bilder zurück. durch die umrandung sind räumliche vorstellungen geschaffen, besonders in dem beispiel rechts. hier liegt die großaufnahme des farben-kastens ganz vorne im raum, die beiden kleinen bilder weit hinten. die roten felder für die preisangaben fallen ganz heraus aus dem bilde und werden vom auge für sich gesehen. also auch hier das prinzip, die bilder für sich, die wichtigen textlichen angaben für sich.

105
vordemberge

4.49

always the elementary means, the link between production and consumption. No organization can exist and expand for long unless it uses such a device as a token to represent it.... The significance of the emblem is absolute, its shape is determined purely according to optical-mechanical laws; the function determines the form just as it does in the construction of a machine.

...But the swift and ever-increasing tempo of life, the rushing traffic, the colossal demands of every second, the age of the cinema and the air-liner, these have not only reshaped our thinking, they have also, and in quite a special way, changed our eyes in their capacity for adjustment and economy, for there is a limit to the amount that can be taken in...[64]

These events and writings were taking place in a period of relative recovery, industrial growth and renewed business confidence. Improved social conditions in the 1920s for white-collar workers and a significant proportion of women were only to be challenged again between 1931 and 1933, when a dramatic growth in unemployment prompted the polarization of political opinion, with support for extreme parties culminating in the National Socialist electoral victory of 1933.

The political implications of the new design were ambiguous. Many of its basic tenets were derived from the Constructivist movement, developed in the Soviet Union under a new, experimental regime in its formative stages. By contrast, after an initial revolutionary struggle, Germany witnessed the reassertion of capitalism and a fragile Social Democratic republic. Although much of the language of the new design was expressed in terms of 'revolutionizing' visual culture, designers' intentions to radicalize political culture were less clearcut. Gradually, as many of the *ring* members found themselves commissioned to produce advertisements and packaging for everyday goods, they adopted an experimental visual language. Some were keen to work for major commercial and industrial companies in the belief that advertising and publicity could act as a benign democratic information service. Others, such as John Heartfield, also a *ring* member, saw all advertising as contributing to capitalist exploitation and developed the new design for specific political reasons in a refusal to compromise.

This becomes more evident if the case of Dutch designers in the group is contrasted. Domela Nieuwenhuis and Vordemberge-Gildewart, resident in Germany at the time, as well as Piet Zwart and Paul Schuitema in their home country, encountered a more stable situation for the new design, '*het nieuwe beelding*', in a country with a greater sense of continuity.[65] In The Netherlands social democracy carried less ideological turmoil than in Weimar and many significant public and corporate services became associated with progressive Modernism at the time.

Heartfield-Monteur

In spite of his anglicized name, changed in 1916 in reaction against the belligerence of Germany, John Heartfield was a Berlin-born artist and political photomontagist. As a young man, still under his real name Helmut Herzfelde, he trained in painting and graphic art at the Munich Arts and Crafts School, where, according to his brother Wieland Herzfelde, he was struck by Ludwig Hohlwein's posters and the graphic works of the Vienna Secessionists, especially Koloman Moser. The brothers founded the Malik Verlag, a Berlin Left-wing publishing house, in 1916. Until 1947 Malik published major Socialist and Communist works in the German language and made other international literature available in translation, notably American progressive political novels. In a similar way to Schwitters, Heartfield's earliest graphic works at Malik were for Dada events he organized with George Grosz, Hans Richter, Raoul Hausmann and others in the Berlin group. Among the Berlin Dada artists there had been a strong programmatic Leftist political commitment and Grosz and Heartfield joined the Communist Party on its foundation in the winter of 1918.[66]

In these early works, the impact of Futurist simultaneity on Heartfield was apparent; as if raiding the compositor's tray, letters, words, expletives, signs, symbols and other devices were spread across the page in the manner of Filippo Marinetti's *Parole in Libertà*. These printed works ranged from single sheets for distribution at street demonstrations or Dada meetings and performances to more consistently published little magazines, such as *Die Neue Jugend* (The New Youth); *Die Pleite* (The Struggle); *Der Gegner* (The Opponent), and *Der Knüppel* (The Cudgel), often working with George Grosz.

While Grosz argued for the effectiveness of the traditional print techniques of etching, engraving and lithography to depict satirical juxtapositions of members of opposing classes, Heartfield argued the case for photography as a modern medium, in his view free from the class connotations of fine-art print techniques. Heartfield's process was in principle that of a designer, cutting and pasting,

4.50

4.51

4.50 and 4.51 Two photomontage book jackets for novels by Upton Sinclair, *Petroleum*, 1927 and *Nach der Sintflut (After the Flood)*, 1925

Designed by John Heartfield

A-I-Z
ERSCHEINT WÖCHENTLICH EINMAL — PREIS 20 PFG., Kc. 1,60, 30 GR., 30 SCHWEIZER RP. — V. b. b. — NEUER DEUTSCHER VERLAG, BERLIN W8 — JAHRGANG XI — NR. 48 — 27. 11. 1932
In Genf, der Stadt des Völkerbundes, wurde mit Maschinengewehren in die gegen den Faschismus demonstrierenden Arbeitermassen geschossen.
15 Tote, über 60 Verwundete blieben auf dem Platze.
(Ausführliche Bildreportage unseres Sonderberichterstatters auf den Innenseiten)
DER SINN VON GENF
Wo das Kapital lebt,
kann der Friede nicht leben!
VÖLKERBUND
Montage: JOHN HEARTFIELD

4.52

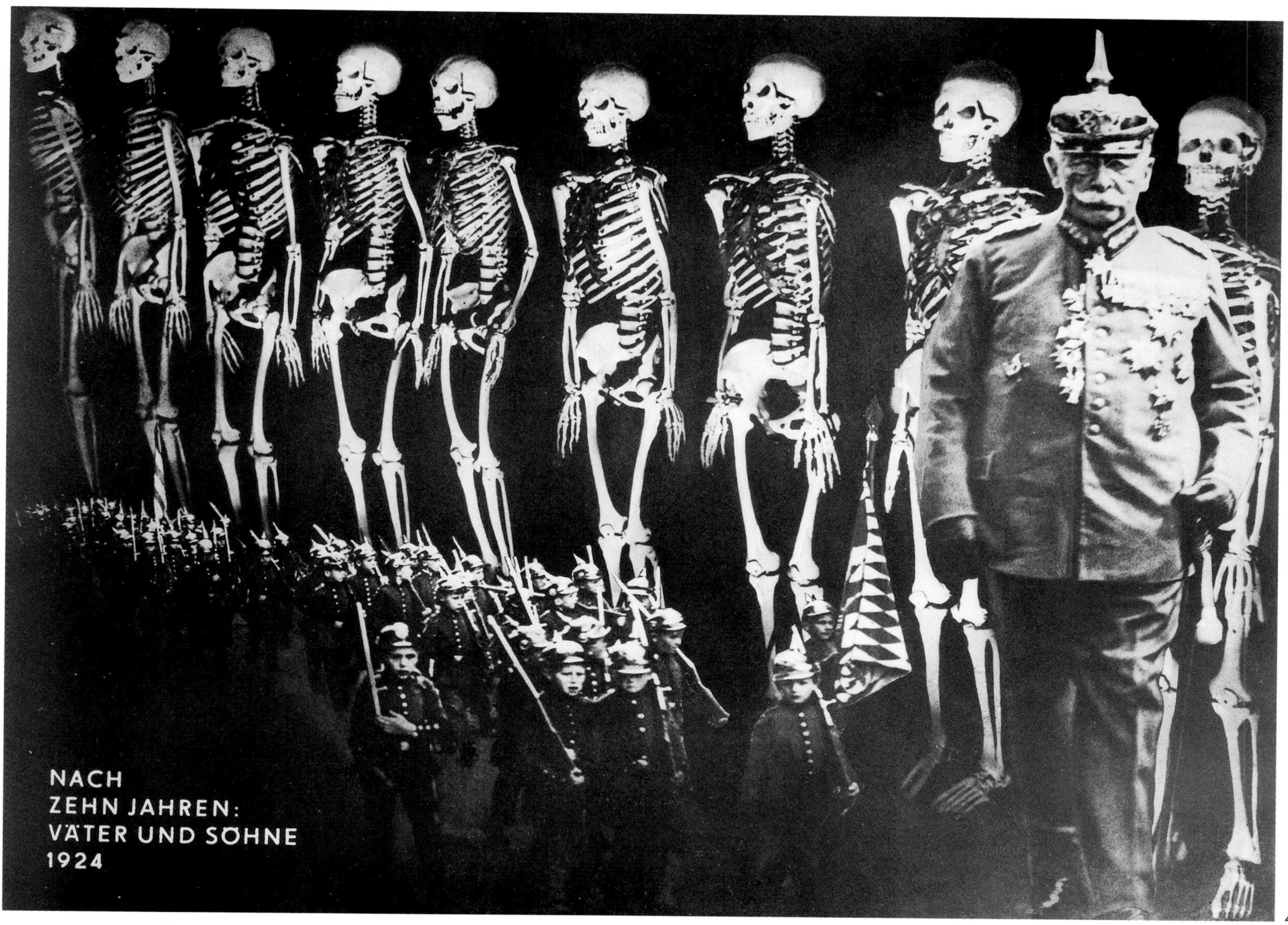

4.53

and later model-making and arranging friends or actors to enact parts which were then photographed. In Dada fashion, he was known as 'Dada-monteur', using the French word for mounter, or arranger, or assembler. Grosz and Heartfield advocated a tendentious machine art which explained its class-position explicitly, and the culmination of this was the publication of *Die Kunst im Gefahr* (Art in Danger) in 1925, in which they made the by then familiar declaration that oil painting, a redundant convention, was dead.[67]

On the tenth anniversary of the outbreak of the First World War, Heartfield arranged a photomontage, 'Fathers and Sons', to be displayed in the Malik Verlag window, depicting young cadets marching, superimposed with the

4.52 *Der Sinn von Genf* (The Meaning of Geneva)

Designed by John Heartfield
Magazine cover
1932

4.53 *Nach Zehn Jahren; Väter und Söhne* (After Ten Years, Fathers and Sons)

Photomontage by John Heartfield
1924

4.54 *Der Sinn der Hitlergrusses: Kleiner Mann bittet um grosse Gaben, Motto: Millionen stehen hinter mir!* (The Meaning of the Hitler Salute: Little man asks for a big donation Motto: Millions stand behind me!)

Designed by John Heartfield
Magazine cover
1932

4.54

skeletons of a previous generation of soldiers and a war veteran, with the caption, 'After Yen Years'. This was a much more programmatic juxtaposition than earlier photomontages, with a message that was constructed by the viewer working on the basis of a visual contradiction and an anchoring text. Heartfield collaborated with the theatre director Erwin Piscator at the Volksbühne at this time and would have become familiar with ideas of Soviet filmic montage in this connection. Following Piscator and Brecht in the theatre, Heartfield's montages operated on a visual dialectic of thesis, antithesis and synthesis, by which the viewer was expected to 'solve' the meaning through recognizing overt contradictions.[68]

Heartfield's contribution to *Gefesselter Blick* was simply the statement, 'New political problems require new means of propaganda. For this, photography has the greatest power of persuasion.' He was on the brink of his most famous work at this stage. From his photomontage book jackets for Malik and other publishers, Heartfield went on to contribute covers to the *Arbeiter Illustrierter Zeitung* (Workers' Illustrated Newspaper), the weekly Communist paper, from 1930 to 1938. Altogether more than two hundred pieces were published, first from Berlin, then, after April 1933, from Prague. At its height in 1932 the print-run amounted to 500,000 copies. AIZ ceased publication on 26 February 1939, by then in Paris.

Walter Benjamin, one of Germany's foremost literary critics and philosophers, championed Heartfield's work, in which he distinguished the different applications of photography in late Weimar society.[69] Alarmed by the National Socialist appropriation of many of the techniques once associated with radical culture, Benjamin argued for the importance of context in his essay 'The Author as Producer'. Originally delivered as a lecture at a conference to study Fascism in 1934, one year into the Third Reich, this advocated the model of John Heartfield, who remained aware of the significance of context in the publication of his designs.

The revolutionary strength of Dadaism lay in testing art for its authenticity. You made still-lifes out of tickets, spools of cotton, cigarette stubs, and mixed

TSCHICHOLD
NAPOLEON
PHOEBUS
PALAST
ANFANGSZEITEN:
4 00 6 15 8 30
SONNTAGS:
1 45 4 00 6 15 8 30
DRUCK: F. BRUCKMANN A.G. MÜNCHEN

4.55

them with pictorial elements. You put a frame round the whole. And in this way you said to the public: look, your picture frame destroys time; the smallest fragment of everyday life says more than painting.

Just as a murderer's bloody fingerprint on a page says more than the words printed on it, much of this revolutionary attitude passed into photomontage. You need only think of the works of John Heartfield, whose technique made the book jacket into a political instrument. But now let us follow the subsequent development of photography. What do you see? It has become more and more subtle, more and more modern, and the result is that it is now impossible to photograph a tenement or a rubbish-heap without transfiguring it. Not to mention a river dam or an electric cable factory: in front of these, photography can now only say, 'How beautiful.' *The World is Beautiful* - that is the title of a well-known picture book by Renger-Patzsch in which we see New Objectivity photography at its peak. It has succeeded in turning abject poverty itself, by handling it in a modish, technically perfect way, into an object of enjoyment.[70]

jan tschichold

münchen 39, vollstraße 8/I

werbegestalter, lehrer an der meisterschule für deutschlands buchdrucker in münchen

geboren 1902. bücher: „die neue typographie", 1928. „foto-auge" (gemeinsam mit franz roh), 1929 „eine stunde druckgestaltung", 1930.

ich versuche, in meinen werbearbeiten ein maximum an zweckmäßigkeit zu erreichen und die einzelnen aufbauelemente harmonisch zu binden — zu gestalten.

Jan Tschichold

plakat, schwarz und rot auf gelb. ein plakat wird wie ein bild gesehen, wird mindestens nicht auf den ersten blick „gelesen". aus diesem grunde ist nötig, das auge zwingend zu lenken. der vordere bildrand ist durch den starken senkrechten balken rechts festgelegt. blickziel und damit ausgangspunkt für den text die stelle „50". der zuerst vom auge erfaßte raum erstreckt sich von hier und dem „M" des namens bis zum schwarzen balken. in noch weiterem blickfeld die näheren angaben: ort und zeit. also klare räumliche trennung zwischen blickfänger, (in diesem fall schlagworte) und näheren angaben. um die näheren angaben zu gewinnen, muß das auge noch einmal weiter ausholen.

102

jan tschichold

4.56

4.55 *Napoleon*
For Phoebus Palast cinema, Munich

Design by Jan Tschichold
Poster
1927

4.56 Opening page on the section on Jan Tschichold from *Gefesselter Blick*, 1930 (see 4.45)

In another essay, 'The Work of Art in the Age of Mechanical Reproduction', Benjamin argued that mass reproduction could avoid what he called the ritualistic tendency of previous art forms. He contrasted the preoccupation with the authentic aura of earlier techniques of art with the ability of the photograph to encourage the reader or viewer to concentrate on the message of the image and not to be constrained by its commodity value. Thus he stressed its relevance to progressive social and political movements.

Jan Tschichold: *Die neue Typographie*

Tschichold was one of the most articulate of the new typographers, not only during the years of the Weimar Republic, but also after his enforced emigration to Switzerland in 1933. In fact, having been a strong advocate of modern functional

4.57 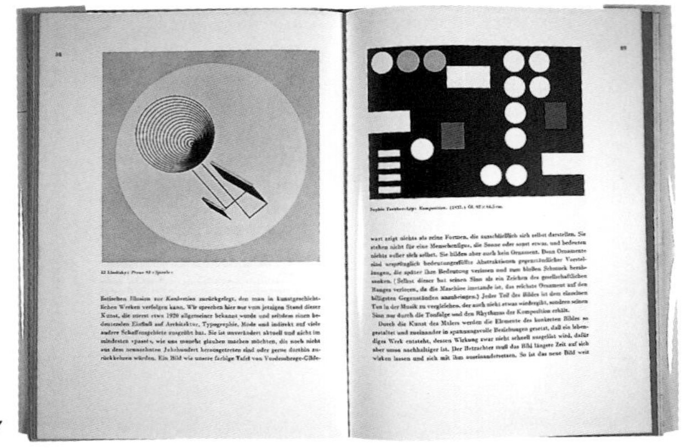

4.57 *Typographische Gestaltung* (Typographic Design)

Written and designed by Jan Tschichold
Page layout from the book
1935

design, he later changed his position in a famous exchange with Max Bill concerning the new typography to take issue with what he saw as its more dogmatic character.[71]

Among the *ring neuer werbegestalter*, Tschichold, like Georg Trump, was unusual for having received a full typographic training as distinct from the more general Arts and Crafts education of many others. He has been described as 'the lucid practitioner'.[72] Consequently, he was drawn to a realistic assessment of the requirements of design for publishers, as well as the practice of reading, which meant that even at its extreme Modernist stage, his design philosophy appeared more restrained and less utopian than that of some of his contemporaries. Tschichold's contribution to *Gefesselter Blick* established his identity as a functionalist. The statement simply ran, 'I attempt to reach the maximum of purpose in my publicity works and to connect the single constructive elements harmoniously – to design.'[73]

Apparently a visit when he was twelve to Bugra, the book arts exhibition in Leipzig, made a strong impression on him. From 1919 to 1921 he studied at the Leipzig Academy under Professor Hermann Delitsch and then as a special student under the director, Walter Tiemann. He ended his training at the Dresden Arts and Crafts School. As a young man he rejected the moderate humanist tradition to which he had been introduced at the Academy. There he had designed calligraphic title pages and colophons according to neo-classical principles for the Insel Verlag. However, inspired by a visit to the 1923 Bauhaus exhibition in Weimar, his meeting with Laszlo Moholy-Nagy and El Lissitzky, and the political and cultural experimentation in the Soviet Union, he adopted the signature 'iwan' for a while and aligned himself with radical Modernism. By 1925 he summarized his thoughts in a manifesto, '*elementare typographie*', and an article, '*Die neue Gestaltung*', for a specialist printers' journal, *Typographische Mitteilungen*.[74]

He chose the word 'elementarist' to apply to the new ideas in design, a term which came from the Dutch De Stijl group where for several years asymmetric typesetting and abstraction had been used in publications mostly associated with art and design. While teaching at the Munich Meisterschule für Deutschlands Buchdrucker (German Master Printers' School), invited there by director Paul Renner, Tschichold continued his advocacy of the new design until his most comprehensive account, *Die neue Typographie*, was published as an educational text in 1928.[75]

The most important book of its time on the new design for communication, it was intended as a practical guide to the new approach. The book exceeded this purpose and instead became a foundation for the interpretation of new typography and a guiding selection of examples of designs which would later contribute to the canon of Modernism.

The book was designed by Tschichold in a black linen cover. Although 240 pages in extent and printed on art paper, it appeared a slim volume. The text was set in both upper and lower cases (unlike many of the prescriptions by other *ring* members), although subheadings were in single-case and certain key words appeared in bold following the visual approach advocated by other new typographers. The text type was Akzidenz Grotesk, an established sans-serif type, and the pages carried integrated illustrations of good practice of modern typography, which were carefully arranged according to principles of asymmetric counterbalance. Footnoting was marked by a disc bullet-point set in the text with the note in lighter type in the margin.

The text consisted of a summary in the form of a handbook of all the areas of jobbing printing and design for publishing for the attention of the typographer, from postcards and stationery to advertising and book design. As well as this methodical exposition, Tschichold provided an art historical introduction to the 'growth and nature' of the new typography, which became a highly influential list of 'pioneer' stages from avant-garde poetry and painting. Interestingly, Tschichold traced a path from the experimental arrangements of poetry of Stéphane Mallarmé and Guillaume Apollinaire's 'calligrammes', which broke with conventional syntax

4.58

4.59

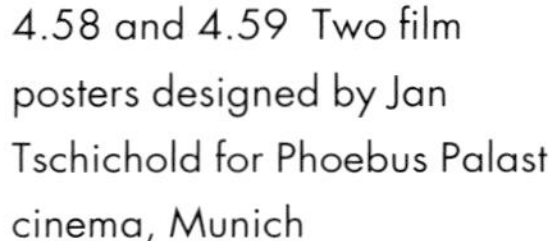

4.58 and 4.59 Two film posters designed by Jan Tschichold for Phoebus Palast cinema, Munich

Laster der Menschheit (The Vice of Humanity) 1927

Die Frau ohne Namen (The Woman without a Name) 1927

and introduced words spread across the blank field of the white page, either to illustrate the text in the form of a rebus or to enhance meaning when read. He placed this interest in 'freeing' the text from traditional book form through Futurism and Dada to De Stijl typography and El Lissitzky. In this manner he located the new typography firmly within the context of literary and avant-garde experimental culture rather than commerce. In choosing this lineage, he possibly overlooked a more mundane tradition which had also started to investigate the properties of typographic symbols for their impact in the form of packaging, advertising and signage.

Max Burchartz: Photomontage for Industry

A successful association between Johannes Canis and Max Burchartz was established in 1924 when they formed a small advertising concern, Werbebau (literally 'building publicity'), which took on commissions from its base in Bochum, in the Ruhr district. Canis was apparently the copywriter and Burchartz the partner who interpreted the designs photographically.[76]

Burchartz had originally trained in commerce, then in Arts and Crafts schools at Elberfeld, Barmen and Düsseldorf. He met Kurt Schwitters in 1918 and contributed an early essay on advertising to the special issue of *Merz* on typographic advertising.[77] Teaching the specialist class *Werbegraphik und Fotografie* (Publicity Graphics and Photography) at the Folkwangschule in Essen, Burchartz was co-signatory to the Weimar Manifesto of International Constructivists in 1922, along with Theo van Doesburg, Hans Richter, El Lissitzky and Karel Maes. In this document Constructivism had been defined as 'new principles of artistic creation – the systematization of the means of expression to produce results that are universally comprehensible.'[78] In later years, 'contemporary means of expression' became for Burchartz photomontage, of which he was an early successful advocate.

The brochures designed for the Bochumer Verein, an industrial association producing mining and cast-steel equipment, were Burchartz's most frequently illustrated work in contemporary articles promoting the new design. They used photomontage to show details of construction techniques: for example, close-ups indicated how railway signals operated, with textual clarification organized in grid boxes. The originals were printed in coloured inks and black on white paper. Burchartz's compositions depended on isolating and grouping. He suggested that three main groups or layers of information were the maximum in a design of one page. While there is a slight awkwardness of arrangement in the first commissions, his later designs become more confident in their layout. Originally derived from the aesthetic principles of Dada and Constructivism, an underlying theme of much design was to lay bare the process: to provide elements which the viewer was encouraged to assimilate. It was an unusual approach to take with the design of an industrial prospectus which did not have the polemical narrative of much artistic and political montage.

Why would a major industrial concern turn to Burchartz to design its identity? At a time when 56 per cent of all manufacturing equipment produced in Germany

4.60 

4.60 *Bochumer Verein für Bergbau und Gußstahlfabrikation* (Bochum Association for Mining and Cast Iron Manufacture)

Designed by 'WERBEBAU' Max Burchartz and Johannes Canis
Industrial prospectus
1924

was for the mining and metallurgical group, this output was crucial for national industry as a whole. The Bochumer Verein was associated with the major metalwork company Thyssen, for whom they manufactured high-grade steels, locomotive wheels, springs, rails, bolts and nuts, as well as tubes, overseeing the chain from raw material to finished components and industrial goods. The idea of the vertical combine of the Trust, modelled on the United States Steel Corporation, led to the formation of three dominant metalwork groups in Germany after 1920, Rhein-Elbe Union with Siemens-Schuckert electrical industries; Thyssen with Bochumer Verein; and Phoenix with AEG. In *The New Economy* the younger Rathenau, Foreign Minister and a modernizer, advocated cartels with State participation: 'These structures are differentiated from the old guild system… no sanction for association of individual and small firms, but a community of production in which all members are organically interwoven…'[79]

Along with Rathenau's influential ideas, Taylorism and scientific management derived from the ideas of the American Frederick Winslow Taylor were also being taken up by some European industries. This could involve re-organization of workshops and the introduction of labour discipline, time-based worker actions, factory planning departments, wage-scales devised on piece work and the application of engineering science to industrial relations.[80]

The exact circumstances of the Bochum commission are not known, nor are the scale of its print-run, circulation and impact on sales. Its feature in the German Werkbund journal *Die Form* suggests that it was through that association that the designers and client met. Burchartz and Canis designed the prospectus in a way which articulated the visual equivalent of a system of production. The 'optical efficiency' was explained by Burchartz in the way the eye would first register images and only read the text once these had been comprehended. This was the most modern and up-to-date concept, presumably a message Bochumer Verein sought to portray.

The move from avant-garde experiment to design for one of Germany's mainstream metallurgical industries was an interesting exception and far from the norm at this time. It was more usual for Modernist design to be favoured by the newer technologies such as Berlin's major electrical companies AEG, Siemens - Schuckert and Osram, as well as by architectural clients, media and cultural sponsors. For them the metaphor of science, rather than evocation of the spirit of arduous labour, was most suitable. Other traditional metallurgical industries continued to present themselves in conventional styles, drawing on the heroism of labour at the furnace, for example. In such designs the heaviness of typeface worked associatively with the industrial qualities of products which were depicted in figurative styles derived from the previous century.

Reception of the New Typography

Even a sympathetic critic such as Gustav Hartlaub indicated the difficulties that modern designers would have in persuading all German companies to commission work from them. 'In fact', he wrote,

> *the modern, objective, constructivist style affects the senses only in advertising for products of the machine industries, the manufacture of instruments and so forth, especially by technical means, and on the other hand by neon-light advertisements; it is by no means to be used for old-fashioned categories of products, such as containers for pipe tobacco or cigars, where the users' conservative taste requires archaic forms and the chilly objectivity of the new style would only irritate the consumer.*[81]

For Germans, a crucial question was whether the new typography was inherently more efficient than traditional typography. An early hostile review of the Bauhaus by Fritz Ehmcke signalled the major issues which would be held against it: its scientism, its 'newness' and its apparent specialization. Noticeable in this

BOCHUMER VEREIN
FÜR BERGBAU UND GUSSSTAHLFABRIKATION
BOCHUM

ABT. FELDBAHNBAU

Muldenkippwagen von 0,5 bis 1 cbm Muldeninhalt mit selbsttätiger Feststellvorrichtung beim Beladen des Wagens. Die Muldenkipper werden hergestellt in Spurweiten von 500 bis 1000 mm.

Die Abteilung Feldbahnbau des Bochumer Vereins ist mit der Entwicklungsgeschichte des Werkes eng verbunden. In etwa 40 Jahren lieferte der Bochumer Verein mehr als 100000 Wagen aller Art. Den Erfolg im Wettbewerb innerhalb der Feldbahnindustrie begünstigte außer der technischen Vollkommenheit der Erzeugnisse der Umstand, daß der Bochumer Verein alle zugehörigen Bauelemente in eigenen Werkstätten herstellen oder aus Konzernwerken beziehen kann.

Bergeversatzwagen (Gruben- und Minenwagen) mit Flacheisenfeststellung

6. 1925.

4.61

4.62

4.61–4.62 Two interior sheets from *Bochumer Verein für Bergbau und Gußstahlfabrikation*

Designed by 'WERBEBAU' Max Burchartz and Johannes Canis 1924

criticism was the lack of any kind of evidence: instead, Ehmcke's article soon slipped into larger cultural questions,

> *The number of catchwords being used in the Bauhaus nowadays begin to sound like some kind of art journalism. Everything we do lacks conviction, clarity and originality. We have become too scientific and too abstract. After all, an arts and crafts workshop is not a chemistry laboratory where exact research can solve a problem down to the tiniest detail, or an operating theatre where the surgeon's knife reveals each individual nerve fibre indispensable for the proper functioning of a healthy organism. Surely it would be preferable for us to try to reconstruct what was once a living entity and to hand it on to coming generations as a vital whole.*[82]

It was perhaps inevitable that the rhetoric of the new typographers would induce such a response from some quarters. The format of manifestos, lists of correct practice, accompanied by geometry and new objective photographs, were open to such interpretation. It is questionable whether Ehmcke's design practice was governed by less need for specification, or any less precise instructions to printers, but his attack was on an emotive level with its appeal to tradition, craft and continuity. He was most caustic about the claims for the new: 'It is no more possible to build a new style in the air than it was before and to begin all over again every five years as if to atone for a new fall. Seen at close quarters, it thus appears that what at first sight seemed like the strength and unity of the Bauhaus, namely the absence of tradition in persons and ideas, has proved to be a weakness.'[83]

As we have seen earlier, Ehmcke often argued for the traditional model of the graphic designer as someone working in a known community and encouraging the public to participate in citizenship by focussing on appropriate sites there. Ehmcke also worked for Pressa and took on large-scale commercial jobs. The contradiction that someone working for one of the peaks of the new mass-media age, having written and spoken consistently for the significance of design as a national activity, could then argue against genuine attempts to modernize, illustrates the difficulties of keeping consistent attitudes in the face of the demands of the new society.

Criticism of the new typography was not the preserve of conservatives alone. As discussed in the case of Walter Benjamin, concern at the ways in which genuinely radical notions could be appropriated by bourgeois structures was being expressed by several cultural commentators. A straightforward political attack on Moholy-Nagy was published in the pages of the Communist *Rote Fahne* in Spring 1933: 'It is you and your kind who sold revolutionary art down the river. With your decadence and your precious experimentation you have destroyed the confidence of the masses in artists and writers. Because you fooled them they don't believe in art any more... Go where you belong before they cut your throat...'[84]

The tenor of this attack, with its sense of disillusion partly explained by its date of publication, also indicated that there had been hopes among political radicals that the new typography could lead to a coherent political approach to design for a new society and that these were about to be dashed.

1938
GROSSE
DEUTSCHE
KUNSTAUSSTELLUNG
1938
IM HAUS DER DEUTSCHEN
KUNST ZU MÜNCHEN
10. JULI – 16. OKTOBER 1938

5.1

5.1 *Grosse Deutsche Kunstausstellung* (Great German Art Exhibition)

Designed by Richard Klein
Poster
1938

5.2 *Ganz Deutschland hört den Führer mit dem Volksempfänger* (All of Germany listens to the Führer with the People's Receiver)

Designed by Leonid
Poster
1936

5 Style and Ideology: Nazification and Its Contradictions in Graphic Design: 1933–1945

Until recently, the dominant interpretation of events under National Socialism in the fields of art, design and architecture was that Nazi ideology called for a return to craft values, *völkisch* ideals of *Handwerk* and small-scale production within the rhetoric of small-town Germany. At the same time, according to this view, neo-classicism was also used as the most appropriate style for official building in the public arena where Adolf Hitler's campaign marked the arrival of significant political change. In many respects, such a view can be seen as a result of the original National Socialist propaganda which offered this as official policy. In a reactive strategy, the Nazis ridiculed what had been seen as characteristic of the Weimar Republic, and consequently Modernism, which had been the most visible development of the preceding years, would be eradicated and styles more generally amenable to the conservative taste of the regime adopted.

5.2

This simplistic interpretation of cultural policy in the Third Reich was first challenged by architectural historians Barbara Miller-Lane and Robert Taylor.[1] They suggested that a more representative view would be that the National Socialists had implemented a selective anti-Modernism, according to industrial and state requirements of art, design and manufacture and that this was far from a straightforward break with the past. Even when craft values were evoked in a building's style, the scale and technology used often indicated that it could only have been produced in the modern age. In other words, a contradiction between form and content or style and ideology emerged. In design history, John Heskett has highlighted complications within the traditional interpretation, especially in relation to industrial design, by showing significant examples of continuity spanning the political change from the Weimar Republic to the Third Reich, as well as the more accepted differences, either in personnel, modes of manufacture or styles.[2]

Developing this theme, the design historian Gert Selle has argued that after 1933 the precepts of design worked on at least two levels, the official and the popular.[3] On the one hand, official design policies allotted a central role to a controlled form of neo-classicism for specifically nationalistic purposes: catalogues of official exhibitions and their posters, for instance. On the other hand, in order to maintain a satisfactory level of consumption in the home market and for the employed urban classes to retain a standard of living to which they had grown accustomed, other German design of this period derived its identity from the *moderne*, from Hollywood and streamlining. This was especially the case for product design in which craft values or neo-classicism were not appropriate, as well as in the realm of entertainment and popular culture. Often the pragmatic recognition that a modern Germany, even under National Socialism, needed a sustained consumer economy was disguised by Party rhetoric and official propaganda.

A thorough analysis of the strategies of advertising under the controlled economy of the Third Reich has yet to be published in the English language. In a recent German study, Uwe Westphal suggests that, rather than regarding political propaganda and commercial graphic practice as antagonistic and mutually exclusive fields, it is more useful to think of official propaganda as learning from and adapting strategies of marketing. A clear instance of this is the way the swastika emblem took on the character of a brand identity.[4]

Furthermore, the aesthetic and stylistic qualities of much advertising design in the Third Reich signify a simplification rather than a total rejection of the modern design which had preceded it, even if greater stress was laid on technique. Qualifying the view that all modern design ceased after 1933, there is evidence of Bauhaus Modernism being used openly in the interests of the National Socialist system, especially, it seems, in the areas of industrial architecture and publicity. Peter Hahn has observed that 'In their attitudes towards the rise and eventual victory of National Socialism, Bauhaus people... were as liable to self-contradiction and compromising entanglements as other artists, not to mention the German population in general.'[5]

With this in mind, we need to make one important distinction between architecture and graphic design. Robert Taylor has used the term 'the word in stone' to describe how architecture was developed as part of National Socialist propaganda, playing a central role in the nazification of public life. Obviously this varied in scale across the typology of architecture: certain types of buildings were more fitted to convey messages than others. Although architecture clearly operated as rhetoric, carrying ideological messages through the choice of material and form, there was a stage when this signification ended and function was addressed; buildings were required to project the longevity of the Third Reich but still had to be useful. By contrast, graphic design was inherently more ephemeral, less controllable and more dependent on diversity. A necessary level of private consumption had to be encouraged by up-to-date and accessible graphic media, as well as the overtly public consumption of posters and leaflets for official Party days and rallies. Graphic design was so implicit in the process of developing the state's ability to function, whether by prompting consumption of political ideas or of commercial products, that it was not invariably advisable to restrict its vocabulary and, as was often the case, many methods were used and possible contradictions overlooked in the search for effective communication.

5.3 

5.3 *Volkswagen-werk GmbH, Berlin*

Illustrated by Thomas Abeking
Catalogue
About 1937

5.4 *Die Kunst im Deutschen Reich*

Edited and published by the NSDAP (Nationale Sozialistische Deutsche Arbeiter Partei)
Periodical
1941

5.5 *Grosse Deutsche Kunstausstellung*

Based on a design by Richard Klein
Catalogue
1940

Cultural Conservatism or Nationalism?

The lobby against the new typography had found voice consistently during the '20s, but it increased in the first years of the new decade. After 1933 it spoke with the authority of national legislation behind it until 1937 when it was deemed no longer necessary. Officially, Modernism was banned and a thing of the past.

Before 1933 cultural conservatives had certainly argued against the new typography and the emergent graphic design. In the pages of *Gebrauchsgraphik*, for instance, Fraktur was occasionally advocated as the preferred typeface and its links with tradition were stressed by several contributors. In 1928, at the height of the promotion of Modernism as a new style for the age, Heinrich Wieynck, Professor of Typography at Dresden, expressed his reservations in a review of the exhibition *Die neue Typographie* in Dresden. He agreed that the new typography could make effective designs for posters, but he was more reserved about its application to book design.[6] Later, he announced a much more thorough rejection of Modernism in typography in a set of rules, also published in *Gebrauchsgraphik*, in 1931. In 'Guiding Principles on the Problem of Contemporary Letterform Design', he countered the manifestos of the new typographers with his own eight-point declaration. Ironically, the level of dogmatism was similar to the object of his criticism: rules set out as commandments with emphasized capitals leading into each paragraph. No doubt unintentionally, the layout with ranged-left titling had a similar clarity to much of the new typography.

Point one stated 'Typography of our day cannot only come from common-sense objectivity; our age, in spite of all the standardization of its many tasks, is looking for a spiritual means of expression and new possibilities for formal riches.'[7]

He then introduced the concept of degeneracy of type or *Schriftentartung*, which was also central to the critique by the National Socialists of Modernist painting and other cultural forms, particularly in propagandistic exhibitions between 1933 and 1937. Degeneracy was first applied to culture by Max Nordau in his book *Entartung* of 1893. According to the art historian Berthold

Hinz, Nordau, one of a generation of theoreticians of cultural decline, was a self-appointed 'educator of the nation'.[8] As the new century progressed, the concept of degeneracy was applied in negative criticism against all modern art, whether Expressionism, Neue Sachlichkeit or Abstraction, to indicate that their tenets were 'unGerman' and alien to the national spirit, even though interest had been shown in the first years of the Third Reich in Expressionism as a possible 'national' style. Between 1933 and 1937, there was 'a battle for art', when exhibitions were organized to ridicule previous modern art while official art, approved by the Party, was exhibited in contrasting exhibitions. Leading up to this, Modernist works were removed from public collections and artists and designers dismissed from their teaching positions. The culmination of the 'battle' was the major exhibition, *Entartete Kunst*, which opened in the Hofgarten in Munich on 19 July 1937. Here modern art was displayed with slogans and juxtapositions wilfully suggesting that it was the art of the insane, the decadent or politically extreme. At the same time the Grosse Deutsche Kunstausstellung showed officially approved art.

It is still unclear how explicit the 'battle' for graphic design was. When applied to typography, degeneracy was interpreted as the tendency to abstract letterforms and to give an overall mechanical appearance. Wieynck, for example, advocated calligraphy and cursive letterforms and predicted a future for Gothic as well as Roman scripts. In his view, the most legible typography was not the geometrical or simplest, as the new typographers had practised, but rather the most expressive, made up from clearly differentiated letterforms. Such a style, he said, *could* be compatible with modern mechanical setting.

In October 1933, in a review of a typographic and lettering exhibition at the Munich Neue Sammlung, Ehmcke also wrote in favour of German script from the point of view of legibility and cultural value: 'The more deep-rootedness there is in the appearance of the letter and sound of language, the richer the clarity of the word pictures. Along with this, in the narrowing of text there can be economic results with the practical advantage of saving space.'[9]

5.4

5.5

Arguments which had once been applied by Functionalists to reform design in favour of Roman typefaces and asymmetric setting were now mobilized by traditionalists suggesting that, in fact, Fraktur letterforms were more economical because of their condensed structure and easier to read because of their expressiveness. Beyond this, Ehmcke saw typography as having a cultural mission, 'For it no longer needs to be stressed... that this exhibition is not only of value for its purely artistic aspects, but that it also has a wider-ranging cultural mission to fulfill concerning the meaning of language and type for our nationhood [*Volkstum*].'[10]

There are no indications that Wieynck or Ehmcke were Party ideologues but they probably represented the conservative lobby in the printing profession which had wide support and was also susceptible to more extreme appropriation.

A further example of an argument against the new typography was made by Dr Albert Giesecke in *Gebrauchsgraphik* in 1930. He drew the distinction between standardization of layout and letterforms themselves. 'Lettering was nothing,' he wrote,

> *is nothing and will be nothing if it can be standardized. One can easily standardize the formats of paper, but not their qualities. Therefore, the print fount sizes have been standardized since the seventeenth century, but not their form. That this movement particularly was proposed by radical revolutionaries, by state Bolshevik typography in Russia, by the Bauhaus in Dessau, by Kurt Schwitters with his Systemtype, by Paul Renner and other Radikalinskis, should make all firm judges sceptical of it.*[11]

Along with cultural degeneracy, Bolshevism was another familiar accusation against the new design. To appeal to a conservative and nationalist audience, Modernism was often portrayed as coming from 'the East', its origins in Communism. Giesecke argued for a popular reaction against the new typography and advocated a regeneration to come from the Volksschulen (elementary schools), once typography and lettering could be taught in these again instead of in the Arts and Crafts schools. In his anti-intellectual stance, he was also opposed to the modern, urban context of much graphic design: 'as long as so much tastelessness abounds in the public realm, on the streets and company signs, inscriptions on buildings, public notices, one cannot yet speak of a culture of lettering of the German people.'[12]

These criticisms all shared a preoccupation with the revival of a German cultural identity. Significantly, they did not advocate a return to small-scale craft typography but favoured mechanization in the belief that the rank-and-file of printers would agree with their anti-Modernist position and produce designs for mass circulation which were more appropriate for a German population.

A final gauge of the impact of the new typography can be taken from the adverse reaction it prompted, in this case in a review three years into the Third Reich, from Gustav Stresow in the *Penrose Annual*. Its author was a supporter of the Rudolf Koch calligraphic revival in Germany and an outspoken opponent of Modernism, although in this article he initially acknowledged the 'superb designs' of Paul Renner's Futura and Kabel. The text is a useful summary of the conservative attitudes towards typography which nationalists were able to share. Stresow first summarized what were for him the characteristics of modern Weimar designs,

> *A few years ago it was not difficult to report on German typography. There were no doubts then about the intentions of the leading typographers. No contradictions, it seemed, marred the picture of a trend which promised to give us an entirely new conception of typography. It claimed to be akin to the important developments in modern art and engineering, with Picasso's cubist paintings and Le Corbusier's concrete architecture, as well as with the industrial design of ships, motor-cars and aeroplanes. According to its industrial models, this new typographical era stood under the password*

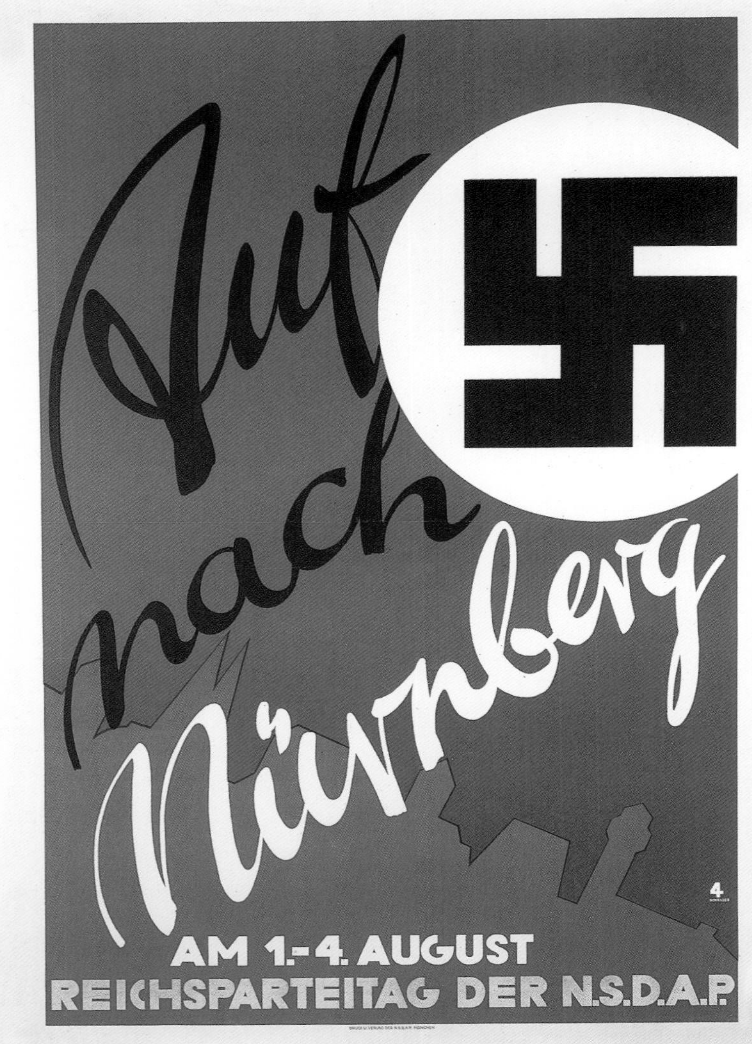

5.6

5.7

5.6 *Auf nach Nürnberg* (Go to Nuremberg!)

Designed by Scheller
Poster
1929

5.7 *Reichssporttag des B.D.M. 23 September 1934* (The Reich Sports Day of the Association of German Girls)

Designed by Ludwig Hohlwein
Poster
1934

'function', though at any time it was a problematic question what bearing the function of 'communication by print' ever had on printing design. ...

In this heroic machine world little room remained, of course, for the human sentiments, most irrational of all qualities. They had to be ignored and suppressed 'for the sake of better function'.[13]

He continued by describing the reaction against Modernism, again locating it in a specific recognition of a national culture,

In Germany, where typographers like Tschichold and his enthusiastic disciples had followed the road of self-denying puritanism for years up to

5.8

5.9

a point of utterly uninteresting 'modern good taste', and where every endeavour for an individual treatment was punished with indignation and contempt, this change came with sudden vehemence that for a time threatened to do away with even the really valuable experiences of the recent past. Fraktur types and typographical arrangements which already had been believed to belong to the past came back – one is tempted to say overnight. The defenders of the 'functional typography', if only true to themselves, had to admit that they had never justly assessed the power of tradition, for the characteristic of this spontaneous turn is the recognition of traditions, where they are still alive in the mind and actions of our generation. So the return to Fraktur, which abroad is so often considered

5.8 *Der Führer versprach: Motorisierungs Deutschlands*
(The Führer promised the motorisation of Germany. The Führer gave 250,000 unemployed bread and work. The Führer achieved the people's car. Therefore German People – thank the Führer on 29th March. Give him your vote!)

Designed by Werner von Axster-Heudtlass
Poster
About 1935

5.9 *Schaffendes Landvolk*
(An agricultural nation at work)

Designed by Anto
Poster
1937

5.10 Stationery for the Nationalsozialistische Deutsche Arbeitspartei. Letter dated 30 November 1935 acknowledging a donation.

Letterhead

5.11 Designs for official swastika metal and rubber stamps

Printer's sample
n.d.

> *wholly reactionary, is nothing but the continuance of an artistic expression which is deeply rooted in national life and mentality, and which has its parallels in folklore and native crafts. And having been connected in their growth so closely with the development and idiosyncrasies of the German language, the Fraktur letter-forms somehow seem to fit it best, just as we may have experience in many things with which we have come to grow up.*

In a footnote, Stresow added: 'The condensed texture of the Fraktur lines reduces the length of the frequently many-syllabled German words, and it harmonizes with the rhythm of vowels and consonants of German orthography; in short, it is "synchronized" with the German language.'

Like other critics of the new typography, Stresow mixed his ideological point of view with practical comments on legibility and cultural symbolism.

Gleichschaltung **– Cultural Alignment in Typography**

After the election on 30 January 1933, a centralized control of the arts and media was imposed during the first months of the Third Reich through the formation of statutory corporations. On 13 March the Reichsministerium für Volksaufklärung und Propaganda (Reich's Ministry for Education and Propaganda) was founded under the direction of Joseph Goebbels. Its responsibilities abroad were to oversee exhibitions and displays of German art, film and sport. Domestically, its divisions incorporated education, the press, the radio, National Socialist pageant days and festivals, art, music and the Deutsche Bücherei in Leipzig – in total, the 'spiritual life' of the nation, or, as it was expressed, '*Die Werbung für Staat, Kultur und Wirtschaft*' (Publicity for the state, culture and the economy).[14]

Graphic design, like all the other aspects of art, was subject to these new forms of legislation. The general number of working designers was published following announcements on the Day of German Art in 1937. These statistics showed that there were approximately 3,500 graphic designers in the country, of whom two-thirds were freelance and one-tenth women.[15] Clearly, the majority of designers were engaged in local, private and commercial work. At its most straightforward, graphic design under National Socialism could mean working on official commissions for Party events, where political content and graphic style were expected to be consistent. For this, Fraktur broken-letter type should be used as the '*Volksschrift*' or national script with the necessary claims made for its origins in German tradition. In the early years of the Reich there was a rash of new black-letter type designs for foundries.[16] There are many signs, however, that it was a matter of what suited the occasion more than a systematically applied and strictly adhered-to policy. Uwe Westphal has noted that 'the aesthetics of the National Socialists were anything but unanimous. Hitler's own preference in architecture and at Party rallies tended towards Classical Roman Imperial letterforms. UFA, the leading German movie studio, followed the successful recipes from Hollywood in its poster designs.'[17]

In the middle of World War II even the policy on Fraktur as the official type was recalled and Gothic types were denounced as 'Jewish-Schwabacher' in a decree from the office of Martin Boormann. The implications for many of the practising graphic designers was that there was a less controlled approach to style than there was to individual circumstance, background and political position. Some designers, for instance Jan Tschichold, were forbidden to practise and forced to emigrate. Many others were persecuted for being Jewish, attacked as 'cultural Bolsheviks', and were murdered or allowed to emigrate.

The serious implications of cultural alignment were immediate for Jewish citizens. Rather than being assimilated, they were put through a forceful period of persecution and exclusion. The boycott of Jewish goods and firms began on 1 April 1933 and Jewish representatives of professional and economic organizations were dismissed. The law of 24 January 1934 prevented Jewish companies from belonging to the *Deutsche Arbeitsfront* (German Labour Front) and after 14 November 1935 Jews could no longer claim state citizenship

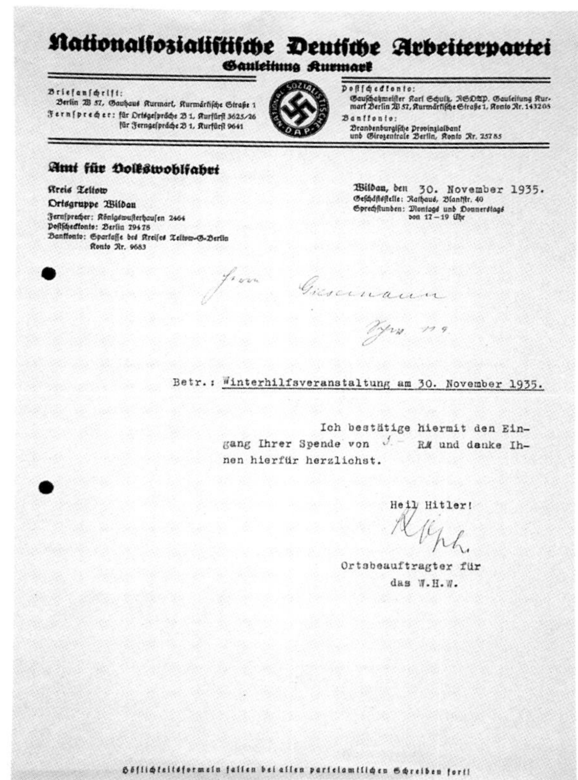

Nationalsozialistische Deutsche Arbeiterpartei
Gauleitung Kurmark

Briefanschrift:
Berlin W 57, Gauhaus Kurmark, Kurmärkische Straße 1
Fernsprecher: für Ortsgespräche B 1, Kurfürst 3625/26
für Ferngespräche B 1, Kurfürst 9641

Postscheckkonto:
Gauschatzmeister Karl Schulz, NSDAP. Gauleitung Kurmark Berlin W 57, Kurmärkische Straße 1, Konto Nr. 143205
Bankkonto:
Brandenburgische Provinzialbank und Girozentrale Berlin, Konto Nr. 25785

Amt für Volkswohlfahrt

Kreis Teltow
Ortsgruppe Wildau
Fernsprecher: Königswusterhausen 2464
Postscheckkonto: Berlin 29478
Bankkonto: Sparkasse des Kreises Teltow-G-Berlin
Konto Nr. 9683

Wildau, den 30. November 1935.
Geschäftsstelle: Rathaus, Blankstr. 40
Sprechstunden: Montags und Donnerstags
von 17–19 Uhr

Betr.: Winterhilfsveranstaltung am 30. November 1935.

Ich bestätige hiermit den Eingang Ihrer Spende von RM und danke Ihnen hierfür herzlichst.

Heil Hitler!

Ortsbeauftragter für
das W.H.W.

Höflichkeitsformeln fallen bei allen parteiamtlichen Schreiben fort!

5.10

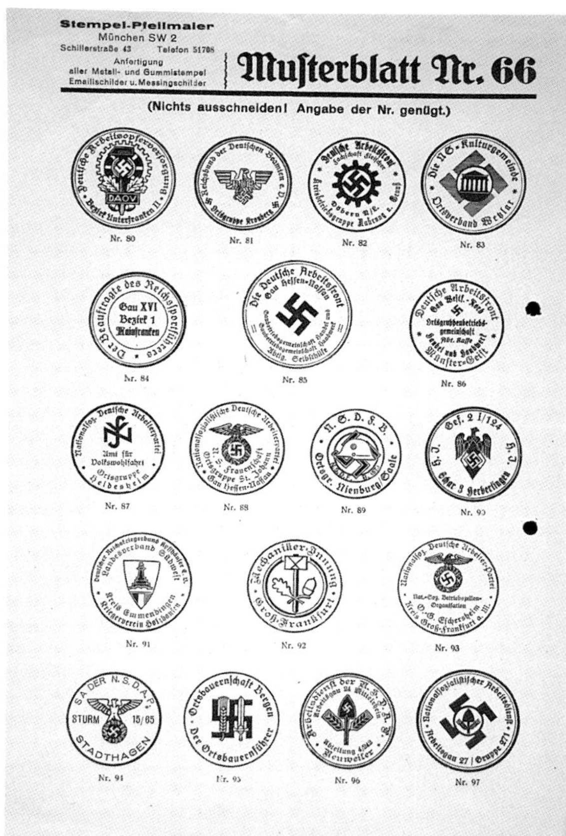

5.11

5.12

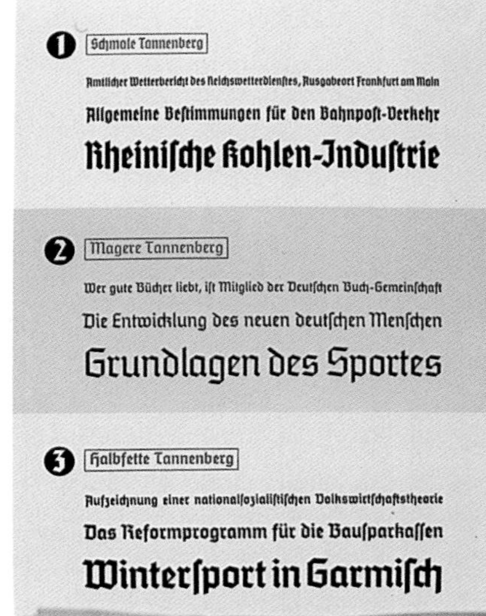

5.15

5.13

5.14

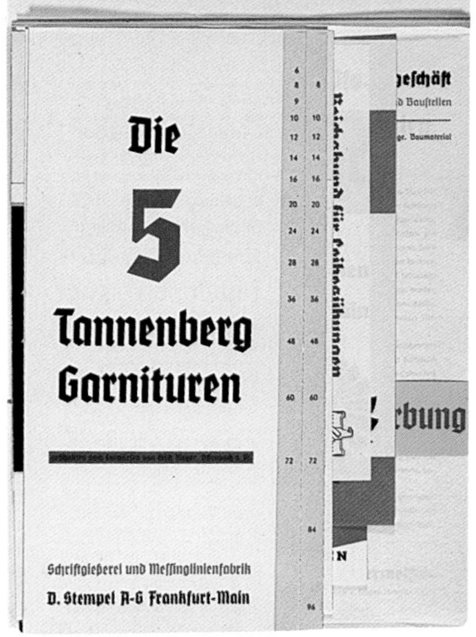

5.16

5.12, 5.14–5.16 *Tannenberg die erfolgreiche deutsche Schrift* (Tannenberg, the successful German type)

Typefoundry booklet
1933

5.13 *Schmalfette Jochheim Deutsch* (Condensed bold Jochheim Deutsch)

Designed by Konrad Jochheim
Typefoundry booklet
1935

5.17 *Früher: Arbeitlosigkeit, Darum deine Stimme dem Führer!* (Before: Unemployment, … Therefore give your vote to the Führer!)

Anonymous
Poster
About 1934

5.18 *Studenten an's Werk* (Students to work!)

Anonymous
Poster
1937

in Germany. Uwe Westphal has listed Georg Adams, Erich Bischof, Lucian Bernhard, Hugo Dachinger, Ernst Deutsch, John Heartfield, Georg Him, Kurt Lade, Max Oppenheimer and Jan Tschichold among identifiable émigré graphic designers who fled for reasons of race or politics. The last exhibition of graphic art, entitled The Jewish Poster, took place at the Jewish Museum in Berlin in March 1937 before the final devastating stage in the obliteration of Jewish Germans in the Kristallnacht pogrom of 9 and 10 November 1938.

Following the formation of the Ministry, the structures by which rights could be administered were announced. On 22 September 1933, the *Reichskulturkammer Gesetz* (Reich's Cultural Chamber Law) established the Reichsminister's ability to organize those active in the areas under his jurisdiction into corporate bodies,

Körperschaften. The six divisions comprised, 1) Literature, 2) Press, 3) Broadcasting, 4) Theatre, 5) Music, and 6) Visual Arts. Within the office for visual arts, individual sections covered specialist groups, such as Department 111. Architecture, Landscape Architecture and Interior Decoration, Department 1V. Painting and the Graphic Arts, Department V. Illustration and Graphic Design, Department V1. Art Promotion, Artists' Associations, and Craft Associations, Department V11. Art Publishing, Art Sales, Art Auctioning.

As art journalism came under control, magazines were also affiliated to state interests and adopted by the appropriate office. Berthold Hinz has detailed the implications for the art journalists, who were expected to provide 'art reports' rather than criticism, especially with regard to the new major journal, *Die Kunst im Dritten Reich,* from 1937.[18] Existing design magazines such as the Werkbund's *Die Form* and *Gebrauchsgraphik* also underwent *Gleichschaltung* and were transformed in editorial and design content.

Hiatus or Continuity in *Gebrauchsgraphik* after 1933?

Another structural change which affected the practice of graphic design was the formation of the *National Sozialistische Reichsfachschaft Deutsche Werbefachleute* (National Socialist Reich Subject Division of German Advertising Experts) announced in August 1933. Under the leadership of Hugo Fischer, Reich Propaganda representative from Munich, its purpose and constitution were described as follows,

> *In order for German advertising and publicity experts to be able to grasp what is permissible in a way that is partisan and professional, it is necessary to put them under unified leadership. Only then will it be possible for German advertising propaganda – be it political, cultural or economic – to give direction to practice agreed to be in the true sense of the National Socialist movement.*

5.17

5.18

5.19 *Gebrauchsgraphik*
November 1937

Designed by Richard Roth
Magazine cover

5.20 *Gebrauchsgraphik*
July 1939

Designed by Otto Hadank
Magazine cover

5.21 *Gebrauchsgraphik*
October 1938

Designed by Herbert Bayer
Magazine cover

In the NS Reich subject division, members of the National Socialist Workers' Party will be taken on, as well as those Friends of the Party of German blood, those who deserve professional advance and those to whom the future of German publicity must be entrusted.[19]

The division was intended to control all aspects of commercial, industrial and state publicity as well as propaganda, teaching and training, window display, and architectural and printed graphics. Membership was shown by a certificate, which had to be displayed at the place of work. Legislation therefore implied that there was a coherent view of how graphic design should continue under the new regime, 'partisan' and 'professional'.

Following the centralization of control of cultural production in the Reich chambers, *Gebrauchsgraphik* came under the *Fachgruppe Gebrauchsgraphiker* (Subject Group for Commercial Art) within the *Reichskammer für bildende Künste*. The *Bund Deutscher Gebrauchsgraphiker* (Association of German Graphic Designers) also became affiliated as the national body for the profession, and through this the magazine became the official organ of the *Fachverband für Gebrauchsgraphike*r, continuing publication on a monthly basis until 1944.

Ludwig Hohlwein's contribution to the tenth anniversary issue of *Gebrauchsgraphik* sounded an ominous tone for its future. 'Today, art, as a cultural factor, is more than ever called upon to take a leading place in building up and conserving cultural values. It must take its place in the front ranks of the legion which Europa has gathered to preserve her individuality against onslaughts from the East.'[20]

An examination of the magazine between 1933 and 1938 supports the view that if not confusion, then certainly pluralism in graphic design was maintained. Editorially the general tendency after 1933 was for shorter reports with more assertions about the quality of the subjects made. A distinction arose between the journalists' articles and official statements, and there were fewer polemical pieces

5.19

5.20

concerning the possible alternative styles for the graphic designer which had become such a characteristic feature of the later Weimar years.

In the early months of the new regime there were no significant changes in the layout design or format, and issues continued to be set in Futura typeface. There are many signs that the magazine sought to satisfy the search for the new, colourful and luxurious both in editorial and advertising coverage. One of its important roles was to indicate to a non-German readership that Germany could compete in quality of design, for which modern approaches were as significant as more indigenous and *völkisch* aspects. The bilingual title was maintained throughout the Third Reich, as were the distribution offices. Foreign design was featured, with articles on events and design in the United States, Britain, France and particular notice was taken of Italy. Such an internationalist attitude was also signalled when a designer such as Herbert Bayer received a major review and was invited to contribute a cover in October 1938.[21]

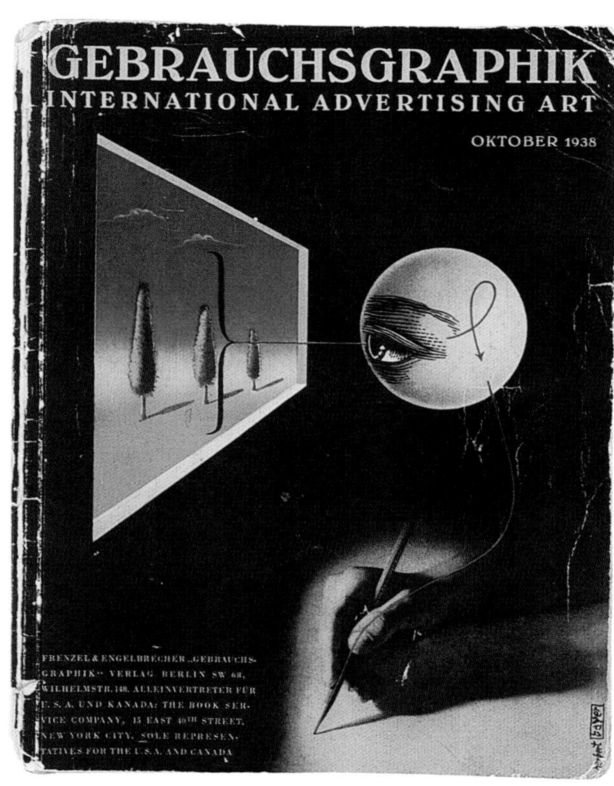

5.21

The pages of small announcements in each issue, where freelance designers were still advertising their services, indicated how eclectic the range of styles was. The magazine continued to publish many articles in English translation, although

5.22

5.23

most of the official material concerning National Socialist legislation was printed in German only, and was often distinguishable for being set in Fraktur typeface. For example, the article 'The Use of the Swastika' by Kurt Bach in the August 1933 issue, set in the home-language only, interpreted a new law protecting the national symbol introduced in May. Changes in legislation and major Party events concerning photography, the press and advertising were also covered.[22] This was the case, for example, with 'Die Kamera', an exhibition of photography presented in Berlin in 1933, and the first major National Socialist advertising exhibition in Germany, 'Deutsche Werbung', in Essen in 1936.[23] This continued with the designs for the Olympic Games in Berlin in 1936 and the important International Handicraft Exhibition in Berlin in 1938.[24]

German designers who were featured tended to be favourites of the regime, such as Tobias Schwab or O.H.W. Hadank. Hadank was Professor of Graphic Art and Design at the Berlin Charlottenburg School of Arts and Crafts. His main work was for Haus Neuerburg, an established Berlin cigar manufacturer, for which he designed the packaging, stationery and publicity, using heavily historicist detail with bronze embossing and heraldic motifs.[25]

The 'report' on another designer, Gerhard Marggraff, indicates the character of much journalism under the new regime:

> *On comparing the examples of the work of the graphic artist, Gerhard Marggraff, which were reproduced some years ago in several of these issues, with what he has produced in recent years and of which we now show a large selection, a decided change in form is visible in the artist's work. This fact, however, finds its natural explanation in the artist's whole development. Gerhard Marggraff started his career as a painter and graphic artist, and so it was not surprising that his early work as an advertising artist should be executed more in the style of drawings and paintings, which method, however, was soon replaced by stricter graphic*

5.24

5.25

forms. This change was due to his efforts to keep to what was eminently practical in his designs. The result is certainly a happy one. Marggraff has developed into an advertising artist whose work shows full maturity and is further distinguished by economy in the use of colours and in clarity of line and form.[26]

5.22–5.23 Designs by Gerhard Marggraff for the official signet of the German Consulate and posters for a performance at the Dietrich-Eckart theatre and Deutsche Lufthansa, 1936.

5.24–5.25 Window display poster for Haus Neuerburg cigar company, Cologne, and hair-tonic packaging design for F. Wohlff and Son, Karlsruhe, 1937.

Designs by Otto Hadank,

The bland comments on his official work, including the national airline Deutsche Lufthansa, indicate how journalism could only provide support for the status-quo and did not engage with any meaningful discourse on the changed political circumstances encountered by designers.

The continuing pluralism in *Gebrauchsgraphik* after 1933 should not mislead the historian into believing that there was an open editorial policy, unchanged by political events. The distinct ideological nature of the overall coverage of official design events warns against this reading.

5.26

5.27

5.26–5.27 The entrance hall and galleries of the exhibition 'Die Kamera' in Berlin 1933.

The Photographic Exhibition 'Die Kamera'

In the summer of 1933 the German public was provided with exhibitions of arts 'loyal to the German tradition'. 'Die Kamera' was the first of the series of National Socialist exhibitions to feature photography. Following it, 'Deutsches Volk Deutsche Arbeit' in Berlin, 1934, 'Gebt Mir Vier Jahre Zeit' in Berlin 1937. 'Schaffendes Volk' held in Düsseldorf, 'Grosse Anti-Bolschewistische Ausstellung', and 'Der ewige Jude', Berlin, all in 1937, were other exhibitions which either used photography as a major medium or displayed photographic objects. In many ways photography was the most difficult of the graphic techniques to dissociate from the Weimar period and obviously also crucial for the development of an effective political or commercial campaign. For example, the National Socialist Party was so impressed by the Communist photojournal *Arbeiter Illustrierte Zeitung* (AIZ) that it set out to publish an imitator, *Arbeit in Bild und Zeit* (ABZ).[27]

Although photography was approaching its centenary year in 1939, the newer developments of light-weight cameras, photojournalism, domestic do-it-yourself amateur and leisure photography, as well as the growth of an entertainment cinema, meant all advanced techniques would inevitably be associated with the Weimar Republic.

Under the Nazi regime, photography was controlled by the Reichskammer-presse. 'Die Kamera' was held at the Funkturm exhibition hall in Berlin in November 1933. Opened by Joseph Goebbels, it claimed a high profile as the first national photographic exhibition under the new regime. Consequently its themes and style of display were significant for the future, but also contrasted with the set of photographic exhibitions that had been held during the last Weimar years.[28]

The Entrance Hall greeted the visitor with a history of the National Socialist movement and the development of photography. Other halls were taken up by such subjects as Face of the German Volk, Face of the German Landscape, and the Hitler Youth. There was also an exhibition of professional photographers, art

5.28

5.28 *Der Ewige Jude* (The Eternal Jew)

Designed by Horst Schlüter
Poster
1937

photography and commercial photography. Photojournalism was now called '*Bildbericht*' (picture report), as the word 'reportage' had been censored as non-German. Photography as Aid to Scientific Research was accompanied by an exhibition of Amateur Work, called Heimat photography in this context.[29] Apart from its propagandistic function, 'Die Kamera' was intended to boost sales of domestic cameras to amateurs as well as to improve exports. The inclusion of amateur photography as an encouragement represented a fundamental challenge to professionals, undermining much of the aesthetic specialization of the previous decade.

Walter Uka has suggested that the exhibition organizers intentionally stepped beyond artistic concerns to deal with all aspects of life.[30] In this way, photography was recast from an artistic, autonomous role within Modernist circles to a more straightforward and transparent reproductive medium. In the accompanying catalogue, this intention was clear:

> *If you compare this exhibition with the propaganda rooms of the Russians that received so much attention during the last years, you will instantly become aware of the direct, unproblematic, and truly grandiose nature of the representation of reality in this room. These pictures address the spectator in a much more direct manner than the confusion of typography, photomontage, and drawings... This hall of honour is so calm and grand that one is almost embarrassed to talk any longer about propaganda in this context.*[31]

On the one hand, traditionalism and craft values could be useful for their associative values in suggesting that little had changed, while on the other, to match the projection of a modern technocracy, there were also demands that an industrialized, competitive graphic tradition be maintained to serve state and industrial interests, and to reinforce German identity.

The Case of Herbert Bayer

The career of Herbert Bayer shows how a Modernist designer could continue to work after the National Socialists came to power in spite of the apparent contradictions of that position. Between 1928 and 1938, when he took up residence in the USA, Bayer was active as an independent designer in Berlin.[32] At Dorland, a small advertising agency, he took on work which was some of the most up-to-date, international and modern of its time. While there, he was also offered the post of art director of the short-lived German edition of *Vogue* by Dr Mehemed Fehmy Agha, who was responsible for modernizing Condé Nast publications at the time. Through his work on *Vogue,* Bayer met Walther Maas of Dorland, who also handled advertising in French *Vogue,* and this in turn led to his meeting Walther Matthess of German Dorland, who invited him to manage all art for the company.[33] At the time when the international agencies on the American and British model arrived in Germany, largely based in Berlin in the mid-'20s, Dorland was already an established name. Formed in 1890, a medium-sized firm employing between eight and twelve people at any one time, it had become successful in London and Paris. Among its designers were Xanti Schwawinsky in the early years, Kurt Kranz, Jupp Ernst, Hein and Hans Ferdinand Neuner, Karl Straub and Walter Funkart. Its German clients included Blendax, Schaub Radio and Olympia typewriters; among its foreign accounts were Elizabeth Arden, Packard cars and the Kellogg company. Bayer was an autonomous art director, and among the commissions there he evidently found new technologies of great interest and challenge. An advertisement from this time explains the agency's interests: 'Dorland avoids the overcrowded streets of everyday life, and goes its own way, although the destination is in so many cases the same – Sales Success! In Good German – an advertisement which is no different from the others, whose "face" has no distinguishing features, means a waste of money.'[34]

In handling Dorland commissions, Bayer adapted his interests in photomontage and retouching, and developed an increasing fascination for Surrealist displacement and illusion. In 1967 he wrote, 'during my years in berlin, i further explored photography and especially the art form of photomontage a technique which advocated the combination of realism with the fantastic and imaginative, particularly as applied to advertising psychology.' [original set in lower case][35]

According to the Bauhaus historian Hans Wingler, 'He transposed principles of surrealistic composition into [commercial] graphics with extraordinary impact.'[36]

5.29–5.32 Four magazine covers for *die neue linie*

Designed by Herbert Bayer May 1930, July 1935, February 1936 and July 1936.

5.29

5.30

5.31

5.32

No doubt, Bayer's contact with fashion magazines offered one route by which he was able to become familiar with Surrealist photography, largely based in Paris, and transfer its strategies to Germany. As we have seen, by 1928 he was finding the formula of functional typography restrictive, and Surrealism offered a way to incorporate figurative elements that went beyond Constructivist testing of visual reality to refer to the subconscious.

One of the founding principles of Surrealism was the 'chance encounter on a dissecting table between an umbrella and a sewing machine', a maxim adapted from the inspirational poem 'Le Chant de Maldoror' by Lautréamont.[37] The juxtaposition of often very ordinary objects to create a new imaginative effect suited the psychological drive in advertising. The Surrealists' aim to lay bare the processes of repressed psychological states (especially desire), and advertising's concern to reach the unconscious wishes of the consumer strangely and fruitfully coincided. Aesthetically, they could also share similar strategies. Bayer built up an iconography of neo-classical heads indebted to *Pittura Metafisica* and parts of figures, often in cross-section, as in the Adrianol advertisements. He transferred the motifs of hand and eye derived from Constructivism, with their original meaning of self-reflexivity of materials and methods of graphic and filmic language, to a novel conceptual solution for various products in which mystery and fantasy were intended. Technically, instead of the deliberate rupture of photomontage, the designs Bayer carried out in the '30s became increasingly sophisticated and their elements were reconciled by airbrush and retouching. These new designs were appealing for their novelty and otherworldliness, and helped form one of the main strategies advertising could use to reach a general public. By transforming his method in this way, Bayer took Constructivist photomontage and made a seamless world which suited the magic properties of advertising and the darker 'magic' of the National Socialists.[38]

The National Socialist Years

Bayer's first exhibition designs were carried out in the late Weimar years. 'at this point [1930] I began to feel that design in two dimensions only is confining and limited', he wrote,

> *and I could no longer accept boundaries which are traditionally drawn between painting, sculpture, design and architecture. exhibition design was discovered to be a new medium of communication, which goes beyond the use of graphics in two dimensions. it embraces all possible visual media,*

5.33

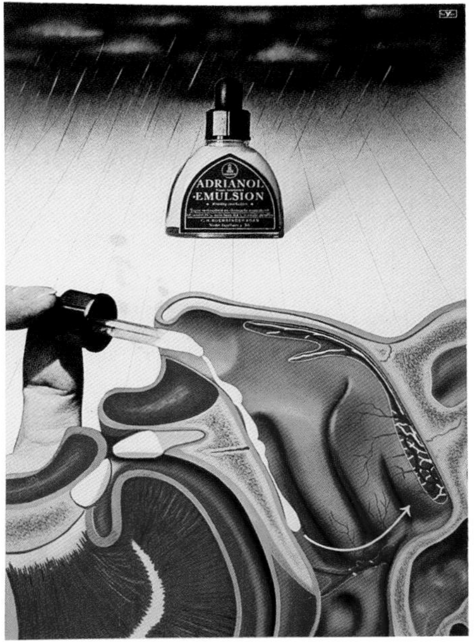

5.34

5.33 *Thymipin forte* (Thymipin nasal drops)

Designed by Herbert Bayer for Dorland Agency, Berlin
Advertisement
About 1935

5.34 *Adrianol-Emulsion*

Designed by Herbert Bayer for Dorland Agency, Berlin
Advertisement
1934

5.35

5.36

5.35 Exhibition of the German Building Workers Unions, Berlin

Designed by Herbert Bayer, Walter Gropius, and Laszlo Moholy-Nagy
1931

5.36 The Deutsche Werkbund section of the *Exposition de la Societé des Artistes Décorateurs,* Paris

Designed by Herbert Bayer and Walter Gropius
1930

5.37 Photograph of an exhibition showing Herbert Bayer's designs for several exhibitions held at the Berlin Radio Tower, including *Die Frau, Sommerblumen, Wasser- und Luft-Sport, Deutsches Volk und Deutsche Arbeit, Das Wunder des Lebens, Internationale Automobil und Motorrad Ausstellung,* and *Grüne Woche.*

5.37

all dimensions of space, and includes oral-aural techniques. it is a new dimension in the art of conveying complex information and has developed through an exciting history with many new discoveries. fascination with optical effects for display purposes, to make exhibits exciting and eye-catching, anticipated some of the optical art of today.[39]

He was a major contributor to the German section at the Exposition de la société des artistes décorateurs at the Grand Palais in Paris in the summer of 1930. He designed not only the poster and exhibition catalogue, but also the arrangement of the rooms displaying Bauhaus architecture and products. He was deeply inspired by the pavilion El Lissitzky had designed for the Cologne Pressa exhibition two years earlier, in which the Russian had produced a montage environment to convey 'the role of the press in the Soviet Union'. Bayer adapted the ideas of a multiple perspective and photocollage.

In a more routine exhibition in 1931 for the Building Workers Unions in Berlin – on this occasion with Moholy and Gropius – he continued these experimental modes, such as large montaged heads; diagrams and statistics; directional diagrams; main text in sans-serif and text type in blackletter. The visitor passed under a bridge and up a ramp, gaining a panoramic as well as close-up view of the display which incorporated movability, animation, peepholes, walls opening up and closing, transparency, glass and perforated sheets.

For a further five years, Bayer worked extensively on exhibitions, designing catalogues and overseeing installation designs, signing himself individually or as a member of Dorland. This activity included a series of thematic exhibitions for Berlin, the new capital of the Reich, among them Die Frau (Woman); Grosse Wassersport und Luftsport (The Great Water- and Airsports); Deutsches Volk Deutsche Arbeit (German Nation German Work); Sommerblumen am Kaiserdamm (Summer Flowers on Kaiserdamm); Grosse Deutsche Funkausstellung (Great Broadcasting Exhibition); the eighth Internationale Büro Ausstellung (International

5.38

5.39

5.40

5.41

5.42

5.43

5.44

5.38 *Deutschland Ausstellung*

Designed by Herbert Bayer
Catalogue
1936

5.41–5.42 *'Germany's peasantry still adhere to the local style of building and wear picturesque local dress.'*

Designed by Herbert Bayer, Pages from *Deutschland Ausstellung*
1936

5.39–5.40 *'Germany's frontiers: the seas in the north and the splendid mountains in the south.'*

Designed by Herbert Bayer, Pages from *Deutschland Ausstellung*
1936

5.43 *Deutsches Volk Deutsche Arbeit* (German People German Work)

Designed by Herbert Bayer
Catalogue
1934

5.44 *Das Wunder des Lebens* (The Wonder of Life)

Designed by Herbert Bayer
Catalogue
1935

5.45 

 5.46

5.45–5.46 *'Classicism, called the Prussian style owing to its severe lines, is found in the purest form in Berlin. The new Germany is creating its own style of architecture.'*

Designed by Herbert Bayer, Pages from *Deutschland Ausstellung*
1936

5.47 

 5.48

5.47–5.48 *'Reich motorways - labour service - holiday trips for all workers - the winter relief work - evidence of the will to reconstruction and unity of the German people.'*

Pages from the catalogue *Deutschland Ausstellung*, 1936

Office Exhibition); Das Wunder des Lebens (The Wonder of Life); Die Grüne Woche (Green Week); Internationale Automobil und Motorrad Ausstellung (International Automobile and Motorcycle Exhibition); Weihnachtsmarkt (Christmas Market) and Deutschlandausstellung (Germany Exhibition).

The main purpose of these exhibitions and fairs was the promotion of German trade and industry. Since 1896 Berlin, like the other prominent cities Hanover, Cologne and Leipzig, had established a tradition of events intended to draw national and international visitors and clients. Uwe Westphal has suggested that, rather than being discontinued under Nazism, these gathered increased significance as a means of propaganda promoting an image of national economic potential for domestic and foreign audiences alike. Accordingly, the most modern exhibition techniques could be justified by the officials responsible for them.[40]

Bayer developed a distinctive square format for the catalogues of these exhibitions which allowed a broad page to include multi-lingual texts. Innovative photocollage was used, as initially devised for the catalogue of the German pavilion at the Chicago World's Fair, A Century of Progress, in 1933. The three exhibitions, Deutsches Volk Deutsche Arbeit (1934), Das Wunder des Lebens (1935), and Deutschland Ausstellung (1936), were interpreted as a trilogy in the German press. Their distinctive design solutions contributed to Bayer's notoriety. All the exhibitions displayed items of German industrial manufacture alongside cultural themes in montaged environments. The first was a collaboration between Bayer, Walter Gropius, Joost Schmidt and Walter Funkart on the various elements of design. All were organized by the association responsible for exhibitions and trade fairs in the city of Berlin and were shown in the exhibition halls by the radio-tower in west Berlin, near the Olympic Stadium which was the city's prime site for exhibitions. It would therefore be a mistake to interpret them as the last bastion of Modernism in retreat, defending itself against National Socialist attack. Deutschland Ausstellung, for example, coincided with the Olympic Games in July and August 1936 and was reported to have attracted 1.3 million visitors.[41]

The catalogue for Deutschland Ausstellung shows, page by page, that it was an important popular manifestation of national and, at times, racist propaganda, in which central concepts of National Socialist ideology were used as organizing principles. Firstly, German cultural and economic expansionism in the form of '*Lebensraum*' was expounded. The text read, 'National socialism consolidates the entire strength of the people for its work of reconstruction in the state, the economy and culture.'

Appeals were made to national cultural history: 'In the area of cultural politics National Socialism realizes its programme in linking the best traditions of German spiritual history,' and 'The large number of picture galleries, museums, theatres and concert halls is evidence of German culture'. The concept of *Heimatschutz*, the protection of German tradition against Modernity, and the suggestion of an unbroken chain of folk customs, in spite of industrialization, were invoked: 'Romantic old towns, built in the Middle Ages with inviting and world famous inns' and 'Germany's frontiers: the seas in the north and the splendid mountains in the south. Germany's peasants still adhere to the local style of building and wear picturesque local dress.'

Although the exhibition and catalogue were clearly designed in Modernist idiom, a spurious German neo-classicism was advocated in the text, 'Classicism, called the Prussian style owing to its severe lines, is found in the purest form in Berlin. The new Germany is creating its own style of architecture'. Interestingly here, Werner March's recent Olympic Stadium was reproduced in sepia by Bayer to imply a continuity and longevity in this building type. Finally, in the area of technology, support for the reorganization of German labour under official Party policies was articulated: 'Reich motorways - labour service - holiday trips for all the workers - winter relief work - evidence of the will to reconstruct and the unity of the German people.'

In terms of graphic style, there *were* certainly continuities between Bayer's Weimar and subsequent work. His use of abrupt and ambiguous space continued, but his elements were more eclectic; more historicist typefaces were incorporated in a still generally rational layout. This, it might be added, reflected a general shift in a wide range of graphic design internationally at this time, often considered to be a softening of Modernism. Decoration and motifs to do with the subject-matter were no doubt a challenge to Bayer's purist side, but they were nevertheless reconciled in the compositions. The most significant difference was that the strangeness in the composition was not used to distance, intrigue and render anew but instead worked with the subject-matter to reinforce its meaning.

'The Way Beyond Art' and Subsequent Interpretations

Bayer's work entered Modernist historiography at an early stage. In *Cubism and*

5.49 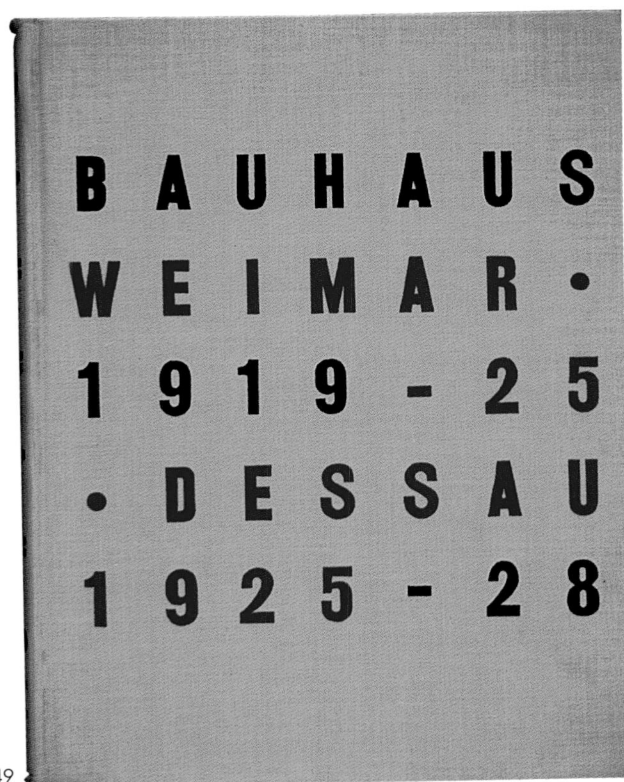

5.49 *Bauhaus 1919-1928*
Edited by Herbert Bayer, Walter Gropius and Ise Gropius.

Cover designed by Herbert Bayer
Catalogue
1938

Abstract Art, the New York Museum of Modern Art seminal analysis of modern art of 1936, mention was made of Bayer along with other designers at the Bauhaus.[42] Alfred Barr stressed the formal connections between Bayer's new typography and the work of De Stijl and Russian Constructivists in his curatorial pursuit of what is now a well-known lineage for Modernism. The next step in Bayer's exposure to New York was the 1938 MoMA Bauhaus exhibition. The idea of the exhibition was formulated during the previous summer, at a meeting with Gropius, Breuer, Moholy-Nagy and John McAndrew, curator at the Museum. The understanding was that Bayer would collect work, organize and design the exhibition, and write the catalogue. For practical reasons it did not deal with work after 1928, for it was by all accounts difficult to locate and export works from Germany in the aftermath of the Degenerate Art exhibitions of 1937. By taking 1928 as its cut-off date, the exhibition concentrated on the Weimar and early Dessau years of craft and what might be termed proto-industrial and commercial graphic design when those four central figures were still there. Although a few outside clients had been reached by them, most of the famous designs were for internal publications: the syllabus, the workshop products, catalogues and posters for the school's exhibitions. Similarly the political significance of the school's closure was not discussed.

The most interesting early interpretation of the more complete range of Bayer's work was made in 1947 in the USA with the publication of Alexander Dorner's *The Way Beyond Art*.[43] A significant and unusual publication in its day, it was the third in the series Problems of Contemporary Art, the others being Wolfgang Paalen's *Form and Sense* and Herbert Read's *The Grass Roots of Art*. In the same year, Wittenborn also published Paul Rand's *Thoughts on Design*, significantly one of the first books about graphic design by an American designer.[44]

One third of Dorner's book was devoted to a study of Bayer. It formed a model and set the tone for subsequent interpretations of the designer, largely in the USA, over the next forty years. Dorner found a way to remove the political complexities of Bayer's position from the account. Having first discussed the changed nature of perception in the 20th century and what he considered the legacy of the Enlightenment and Romanticism, Dorner wanted an example of work which could epitomize the implications of Einstein's 'Restricted Theory of Relativity' of 1905.

Dorner had been Director of the Hanover Landesmuseum from 1923 where he led a progressive collecting policy. His innovative work there had included the commissioning of two rooms, one by El Lissitzky to show the development of painting towards abstraction from Cézanne (it had vertically set strips of tin and a corner mirror reflecting a sculpture by Archipenko) and the other, not realized, was to be by Moholy-Nagy and the 'new vision and its effects upon technical production, such as the abstract movie, cinematography'. As Dorner wrote, both rooms were intended to involve the visitor 'physically and spiritually in the growing process of modern reality'.[45]

Dorner was trained as an art historian in Berlin in the 1900s, in his words, in the tradition of Alois Riegl's dialectical concept of history. This concept harnessed the evolution of art to the traditional eternal polarity of body and spirit – the ideal and the real. Like so much early Modernism in Central Europe, this in turn depended on a Kantian and Hegelian separation of the real and abstract. The 'way' beyond art, alluded to in the title of his book, was Dorner's subsequent re-working of these polarities, after having experienced Weimar experiments in visual communication. He wrote, 'I have chosen Herbert Bayer for this temporary close-up because in him the transformation of the concepts "art" and "artist" into practical energies of autonomous change has happened with unusual intensity.'[46]

His notion of 'autonomous change' stemmed from his familiarity with the philosophy of American Pragmatism. In contradistinction to the German tradition, the philosophy of William James and John Dewey proposed that knowledge was an 'instrument for action, rather than an object of disinterested contemplation'. It also accepted that the propositions of metaphysics can be justified because they contribute to the 'satisfactoriness of, and effectiveness in, the conduct of life',

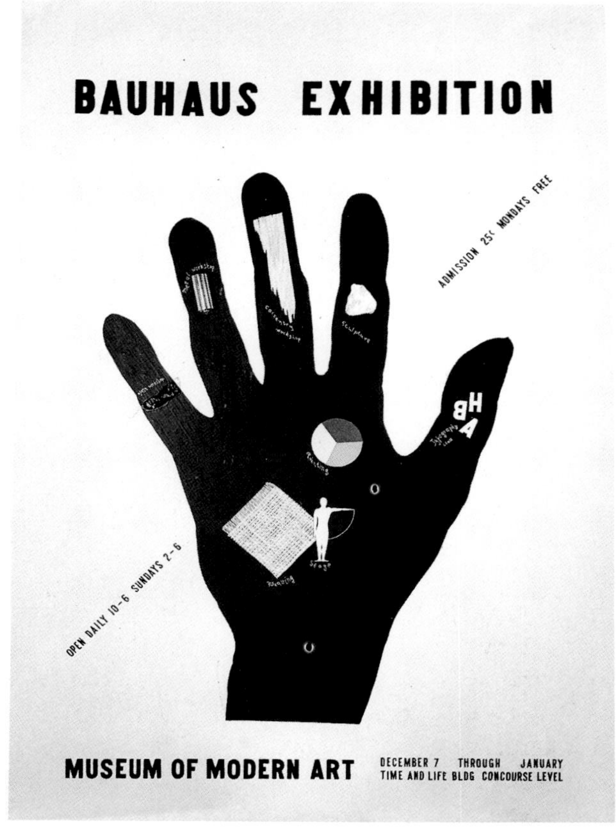

5.50

5.51

5.50 Installation poster from the *'Bauhaus 1919-1928'* exhibition at The Museum of Modern Art, New York, 7 December 1938 to 30 January 1939.

5.51 Walter Gropius, Ise Gropius and Herbert Bayer at the 1938 exhibition, photographed by Soichi Sunami and Hansel Mieth

5.52

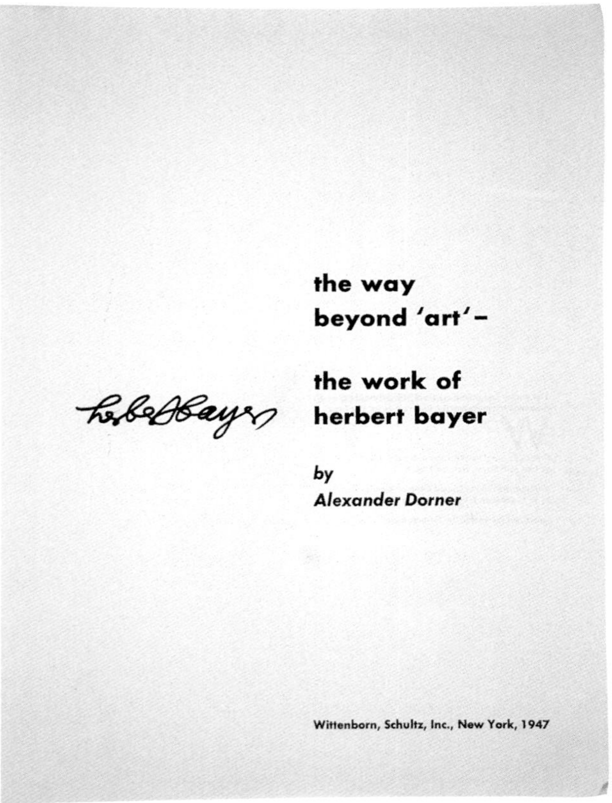

5.52 *the way beyond 'art' - the work of herbert bayer*
Written by Alexander Dorner

Cover and typography
by Herbert Bayer
Book
1947

that is, practice.[47] Dorner was so indebted to this branch of American philosophy that he dedicated *The Way Beyond Art* to John Dewey. Of course, it was a world-view adopted on Dorner's arrival in the USA, which he was imposing *a posteriori* on Bayer's German work.

Dorner's experience of the Third Reich's partial appropriation and rejection of the German idealist tradition no doubt encouraged him to reconsider his view of Bayer in this new context. He was familiar with the teachings of Josef Albers at Black Mountain College in South Carolina and Moholy-Nagy and Kepes at the Chicago Institute of Design, where the European tradition was being extended and adapted. Dorner's interpretation of Bayer justifies the change in outlook from radical photomontage and the transfer of European ideas to the USA.

No doubt after the traumas of fascism and World War II the appeal of a relatively uncomplicated, perhaps intellectually more informal, way of thinking allowed critics and designers to pick up their lives. It was no coincidence that Paul Rand also opened his book, *Thoughts on Design,* with quotes from John Dewey's *Art as Experience.*

This transfer of Modernist ideals to the pragmatic commercial context of the USA has been investigated by James Sloan Allan and Lorraine Wilde.[48] According to Wilde, 'Despite the rise of schools rooted in modernist theory, it is clear, looking back at the dissemination of modernism in design in the United States just before and after World War II, that the look of modern graphic design became much more familiar than the ideas that helped to generate it.'[49]

This separation of content and form in turn permitted a distancing from the political contradictions of Modernism in the Third Reich. Dorner's interpretation locates a change towards everyday life in Bayer's work during the Berlin years.

Following a somewhat iconoclastic and extreme interpretation of the breakdown of formal aesthetics and a description of the alienation of art from modern life, Bayer's work up through the early 1940s was an art of rapprochement.

He interprets it as an art of common signs and symbols, that is, an art that re-establishes connection between ideal and everyday life.[50]

In other words, Bayer's hands, eyes, other body parts and symbols such as directional arrows are taken by Dorner as a reassurance of the pragmatic nature of his activity and he is untroubled by its propagandistic purposes. Historians and critics have often argued that Modernism could have resisted such political persuasion, that Modernism and Nazism were irreconcilable. Dorner wrote:

It is amazing how long Bayer managed to brave the Fascist authorities in Berlin with his utterly anti-absolutistic, visual speeches. Every poster and picture of his proclaimed loudly that art does not become 'healthy' but degenerates if it relapses into traditional, 3 dimensional structures; that when it becomes immune in allegedly eternal, general ideas of racial beauty, physical fortitude and God knows what dead absolutes which force themselves upon life in the guise of brutal, reactionary concepts, it kills life. Bayer fought one of these lonely, hopeless fights and ever more tyrannical enforcements of obsolete reality by those who were afraid of the life of tomorrow. What finally forced him out was his inner conviction that there was no longer any sense fighting against a collapsing mountain. So he came to this country to continue his revolutionary job.'[51]

In 1947 Dorner's shift to pragmatism as an interpretative model allowed a way forward in a new context. However, as a socio-political explanation of Bayer's career in the 1930s, there are some omissions or elisions in this text which can only be corrected by looking elsewhere.

Conclusion

die usa baut
(The USA Builds, an exhibition in the Zürich Arts and Crafts Museum)

Designed by Max Bill
Poster
1945

Graphic Design in a Divided Europe

A mid-century review of German graphic design would have found a devastating situation of a war-torn country, divided by world powers, much in need of the reconstruction of its rich cultural heritage. Access to this, however, was distanced by over twelve years of the worst totalitarian regime the contemporary world has experienced. All designers were faced with the fundamental questions of retrieving their identities and a sense of location, as well as defining their own personal reconstruction of value or tradition. Once again, the style and ideology of graphic design came to the fore, but in 1945, a time known in Germany as zero hour (*Stunde Null*), this reached a level of profound seriousness.

One symptom of the difficulty was a published exchange between Max Bill and Jan Tschichold in 1946. Bill, a Swiss and former Bauhaus student, accused Tschichold of reneging on his former advocacy of Modernism in the new typography.[1] As early as 1937 Tschichold had suggested that the principles of new typography were most suited to display graphics, and he formulated an alternative modern approach for book design which he called the new traditionalism.[2] Forced in 1933 to emigrate from Munich to Basel, Tschichold had reconsidered his former stridency and in Switzerland, working as typographic

kunstgewerbemuseum zürich
USA baut
9. september – 7. oktober 1945

editor on a series of distinguished publishers' lists, his approach indicated continuity with the neo-classical book typography he had so vehemently rejected in his earlier career.

In defending his apparent revisionism, Tschichold wrote about the new typography, 'its intolerant attitude certainly corresponds in particular to the German inclination to the absolute; its military will-to-order and its claim to sole power correspond to those fearful components of German-ness which unleashed Hitler's rule and the Second World War.'[3]

The geography of graphic design was changed by the Third Reich and the war. Whereas many Swiss designers had made their reputation by travelling north before 1933, in the postwar years Switzerland became one of the world's most important centres for a generation of graphic designers. In many respects it was here that the fulfilment of the Weimar debates on modern graphic design were to be realized.

Interest in experimental graphic form had been a crucial part of Zurich-based Dada. In their manifestation in neutral Switzerland from 1915, dadaist experimental combinations of poetry, collage and performance challenged the conventions, and their central protagonists Jean (Hans) Arp and Sophie Täuber-Arp maintained a strong presence in that country. Their art of organic abstraction contributed to the groups called Cercle et Carré and Abstraction - Création.[4] These in turn provided a significant catalyst for the next generation of Swiss designers, among them Max Bill and Herbert Matter.

In more mainstream graphic arts, Switzerland gained a reputation in the 1920s for large format posters. These celebrated the tradition of the *affichiste*, the poster art convention of highly individualized autographed posters which employed the breadth of graphic styles. Their format was standardized for prominent public display and praised by visiting commentators. As early as 1927 Fritz Ehmcke heralded Switzerland as the venue of an impressive graphic tradition. 'The fine days have passed when the walls of the Berlin underground offered a display of good posters, which gave the effect of an underground public art exhibition, as it were. Today, one has to go to little Switzerland to see so many good posters on one wall, just as we have become used to seeing bad ones everywhere in Germany now.'[5]

Likewise, H.K. Frenzel, in the catalogue to the large International Poster Exhibition in Munich in 1929, claimed that Switzerland was the 'classic country of poster advertising'.[6]

To this Swiss identity came a third force which possibly united the two traditions of Modernism and traditionalism. Through its position as a pacifist, then neutral country, Switzerland provided a base for the continuity of modern graphic design, and significant émigrés and exiles were to establish themselves there. Increasingly the art schools of Zurich, under Joseph Müller-Brockmann, and Basel, under Emil Ruder, taught an approach to graphic design which applied mathematical systems, grids and abstraction, an approach which became recognized internationally as Swiss Typography.

In 1944 the international journal *Graphis* was launched from Zurich. Its first editorial, written by Walter Amstutz and Walter Herdeg, explained its aims:

> *The war has entered its decisive phase, and the spirit of reconstruction is already abroad. Plans made for an uncertain future can now begin to take on solid form. European culture revives from the ordeal of war; and for this revival it is essential that there should be some centre at which the truly creative forces can unite and find coordination.*
>
> *Lying at the meeting point of several cultures and itself a synthesis of three of them, Switzerland is ideally placed for the encouragement of that atmosphere which is salutary, if not indispensable, for intellectual discussion and the exchange of cultural and artistic ideas. It is in the hope of providing some such European focus in artistic fields that Graphis*

> *now appears, a magazine published in Switzerland and concerned with all problems attaching to free and applied arts.*[7]

Anyone reading this old enough to remember the launch of *Gebrauchsgraphik* twenty years earlier would have found the list of interests that the magazine set out to cover reminiscent of that German publication.

> *The aim which Graphis sets itself is that of enriching practical life with the seeds of creative inspiration; of helping to bring art into touch with every-day life, and enduing [sic] the forms of that life with artistic significance and value. Our articles and criticism will deal not only with pure art, not only with the graphic arts in a narrower sense, but also with every sphere of applied art. Collaborators, artists, and writers, scholars and experts here and abroad will give their views in these pages on all vital problems of the artistic world.*[8]

There were, however, significant differences in the stress on the European context of *Graphis*. In many ways this predicted the role Switzerland would adopt in the years to follow as the forum for French, Italian and German designers to formulate a design language, appropriate for corporate clients and international information or transport systems, that was particularly successfully received in the USA.

The German magazine was to restart publication in 1950 from Munich as *novumGebrauchsgraphik*. The situation of Germany by then was further complicated by its division into two zones – the Eastern and the Western – following the Warsaw Pact of 1948. Graphic design, once again called upon to define ideological differences, formed one expression of the Cold War conflict. Significantly, under the command economy of Soviet-style Communism, design in the German Democractic Republic returned to early 20th-century precedent. The book arts were the most respected area of activity, promoted through Leipzig, where the fairs and book exhibitions continued. While the state undertook to provide reasonably priced books of approved literature, the broader range of commercial graphics was continued in a much more restricted, if not frozen, manner. The GDR saw itself as the inheritor of the restrained humanist tradition. By contrast, experimental Modernism was one option in graphic design for the Western publishing houses which were also in a better position to modernize their equipment. Many embraced Swiss Typography as the preferred style.

One important centre for continuity between the Weimar Republic and the postwar world was the Ulm Hochschule für Gestaltung in the Federal Republic which opened in 1953.[9] Initially under Max Bill, this school reformulated many of the precepts of the Bauhaus for the next generation. At this stage, rather than graphic design, a broader sense of visual communication was defined which led to a stronger focus on systems design, corporate identity schemes and design for television and film. Ulm was often defined as the equivalent of a 'design monastery', with an austere and critical response to wider consumer society.

However, in the broader commercial and industrial field in these years, the Federal Republic of Germany braced itself for a much more comprehensive stage of Americanization than any previously experienced. In the years of 'the economic miracle' and 'Coca-Colanization', real inroads into German print culture were made through the growth of international design groups and advertising agencies. In this, the relationship between design professionals, industrialists and the consumer took on a new configuration and many of the questions about the character of graphic design raised in the first half of the century were presented to the next generation.

Notes to the text

(Full entries for the abbreviated references below will be found in the Bibliography under BOOKS, CATALOGUES, PERIODICALS *or* ARTICLES.)

Chapter One

1. F.H. Ehmcke, from the article 'Deutsche Gebrauchsgraphik', originally in *Klimschs Jahrbuch*, Frankfurt am Main, 1927 and reprinted in the anthology edited by Ehmcke, *Persönliches und Sachliches* (1928).
2. Ellen Mazur Thomson.
3. Gordon Craig.
4. S.H. Steinberg, p. 17.
5. Marshall McLuhan.
6. Eric Hobsbawm.
7. John Heskett, pp.11–12.
8. *Deutsche Kunst und Dekoration* (Darmstadt: Alexander Koch, 1897–1932), quoted in Alan Windsor.
9. Peter Bain and Paul Shaw.
10. Steinberg, p. 288.
11. James Shand, 'German Typefounders and German Type Design', *Penrose Annual*, 1952, pp. 31–33.
12. Rudolf Conrad, in *Gebrauchsgraphik*.
13. For print technologies in Germany see the journal *Offset, Buch und Werbekunst*.
14. William Morris, *Art and Beauty of the Earth*, London: Longman, 1898, was translated by M. Schwabe as *Die Kunst und Schönheit der Erde*, Leipzig: Hermann Seemann, 1901; and a lecture given by Morris at the Birmingham School of Arts and Crafts on 21 February 1894 was translated by M. Schwabe as *Kunstgewerbliches Sendschreiben*, Leipzig: Hermann Seemann, 1901.
15. Kathryn Bloom Hiesinger.
16. The journals were *Jugend, Münchener illustrierte Wochenschrift für Kunst und Leben*, Munich: Georg Hirth, 1896–1940; *Pan*, Berlin: Genossenschaft Pan, 1895–1900, and *Simplicissimus*, Munich: Albert Langen, 1895–1939.
17. For a commentary see Maria Makela. A contrast between the two cities' graphic traditions was made in Walter F. Schubert.
18. Nikolaus Pevsner. In the case of the South Kensington Museum (known as the Victoria and Albert Museum since 1899), the museum followed the schools. In 1837 the School for Design was established in Somerset House, London, and later became known as the Royal College of Art. In 1841 seventeen local schools of design in manufacturing towns around the country followed, mainly staffed by former students of the South Kensington school.
19. Friedrich Nietzsche, *Also Sprach Zarathustra: ein Buch für Alle und Keinen*, Leipzig: Insel Verlag, 1908.
20. Henry van de Velde.
21. Otto Bettmann (1930).
22. Hermann Wündrich.
23. These comments are based on research in the Graphische Sammlung of the Berlin Kunstbibliothek, where the student work of classes run by Rudolf Koch, Max Hertwig and Fritz Ehmcke are held.
24. Shulamit Volkov.
25. Roger Marx was publisher of *Les Maîtres de l'Affiche* from 1896. Jules Chéret was recognized as 'father of the poster' in *Pan* while the first issue of *Ver Sacrum* also dealt with the poster. See Hanna Gagel.
26. Jean Louis Sponsel.
27. Hans J. Sachs, in *Das Plakat* (1914), p. 68. See also Sachs, *Die Plakatsammlung von Hans Sachs*. A recent summary is provided by René Grohnert, 'Hans Sachs - der Plakatfreund', in the catalogue *Kunst! Kommerz! Visionen!* (ed. Christoph Stölz). In English see Hans J. Sachs (1957).
28. By 1922, when it was dissolved on account of rapid inflation, there were 12,000 members of the Verein der Plakatfreunde. Its natural successor was the Bund Deutscher Gebrauchsgraphiker, founded in the same year. See Sachs (1914)
29. Nancy Troy, pp. 30–31.
30. DWB membership was 492 by its first annual meeting in 1908 and 1,870 by 1914; see Lucius Burckhardt, and Joan Campbell.
31. Frederic J. Schwartz.
32. *Ibid.*, p. 50, originally in 'Wirtschaftsformen im Kunstgewerbe', in *Volkswirtschaftliche Zeitfragen*, No. 233, Berlin: Simion, 1908, p.11.
33. *Ibid.*, p.102.
34. Ulrich Conrads, pp. 28–33.
35. Catalogue *Das Schöne und der Alltag* (1998).
36. The idea of the Folkwangschule was eventually transferred to Essen, where the Arts and Crafts school changed its name to the Folkwangschule für Gestaltung, Handwerker - und Kunstgewerbe in 1925. By this time the town had also bought the contents of the Hagen Museum.
37. *Meyer-Schönbrunn*.
38. Carl Czok, and the catalogue *Leipzigs Wirken am Buch* (1927).
39. Albert Kapr, 'Die Buchgestaltung an unserer Hochschule, ihre Geschichte und Bedeutung für die deutsche Buchkunst', in Peter Pachnicke, *et al.*
40. See the catalogues *A General Guide to the International Exhibition*, Leipzig: Breitkopf and Härtel, 1914, and Verein Deutscher Werbekünstler, *Neuzeitlicher Buchkunst und Angewandte Kunst*, Leipzig: Rudolf Schick, 1914.

41. Dr Volkmann in the catalogue *International Exhibition for the Book Industry and the Graphic Arts* (1914).
42. Anneliese Hübscher, 'Walter Tiemann' in Albert Kapr, and Julius Zeitler, 'Walter Tiemann zu seinem 60. Geburtstag', in *Gebrauchsgraphik*, v. 13, No. 3, March 1936. For a more general commentary on the book arts see Jürgen Eyssen. Interestingly, this interpretation was offered when Leipzig was incorporated in the German Democratic Republic between 1948 and 1989: see Albert Kapr, *op. cit.*
43. See the catalogue *Haus der Frau* (1914).
44. They were Marianne Amthor, Hamburg; Dore Mönkmeyer-Corty, Dresden; Elisabeth von Sydow, Berlin and Munich, and Käthe Wolff; see *Unsere Reklamekünstler, Selbstkenntnisse und Selbstbildnisse*, Berlin: Verlag des Plakat, 1920, 2 volumes. This figure can be compared with 10% female membership of the Graphic Designers Subject Group (Fachgruppe Gebrauchsgraphiker) in the Reichskammer der bildenden Künste in 1936. (See Chapter Five.)
45. Leo Colze, *Berliner Warenhäuser*, Berlin and Leipzig: Ostwald, 1908, reprinted in Jürgen Schutte and Peter Sprengel, pp. 104–10.
46. Walter Rathenau, 'Die schönste Stadt der Welt', from *Impressionen*, Leipzig: Hirzel, 1902 in Schutte and Sprengel, *op. cit.*, pp. 100–04.
47. Iain Boyd Whyte, 'Berlin 1870–1945: an introduction framed by architecture', in Irit Rogoff.
48. Dirk Reinhardt.
49. Hans Franzke.
50. Uwe Westphal.
51. Ernst Growald, in Paul Ruben.

Chapter Two

1. See Tilmann Buddensieg, and Hans Georg Pfeiffer. For Behrens's early career see Alan Windsor, and Gisela Moeller.
2. Windsor, *op. cit.*, pp.14–25.
3. Rainer Maria Rilke.
4. Julius Meier Graefe, *Die Zukunft*, v. 35, p.478, 1901, quoted in Windsor, *op. cit.*
5. Peter Behrens.
6. Peter Behrens, 'Von der Entwicklung der Schrift', quoted in Windsor, *op. cit.*, p.40.
7. F. Meyer-Schönbrunn, *Peter Behrens*, v. 5 in the series *Monographien Deutscher Reklamekünstler*.
8. Tilmann Buddensieg, *op. cit.*, p.8.
9. *Ibid.*, p.9.
10. *Ibid.*, p. 242, originally published in *Die Hilfe*, v. 16, No.18, 8 May 1910, p. 289.
11. Windsor, *op. cit.*, p. 62.
12. Alois Riegl,*Stilfragen*, 1893, published in English translation as *Problems of Style: Foundations for a History of Ornament*, Princeton: Princeton University Press, 1992. For a commentary see Michael Podro.
13. Alois Riegl, *Spätrömische Kunstindustrie*, 1901, published as *Late Roman Art Industry*, Rome: G. Bretschnieder, 1985.
14. Tilmann Buddensieg, *op. cit.*, p. 242.
15. Meyer-Schönbrunn.
16. Ehmcke's own writings are extensive. For his early career see Fritz Ehmcke, 'Rückblick und Ausblick', 1924, in *Persönliches und Sachliches*. The second anthology of his writings was published as *Geordnetes und Gültiges*.
17. Fritz Ehmcke, *op. cit.* For a contemporary commentary see Jean (Hans) Loubier, 'Die Steglitzer Werkstatt', in *Deutsche Kunst und Dekoration*, Darmstadt, v. 13, 1903–04, p. 63, and for a recent article see C. Arthur Croyle, 'The Steglitz Studio in Berlin: 1900–1903' in *The Journal of Decorative and Propaganda Arts*, Miami: The Wolfsonian Foundation, No.14, Fall 1989, pp. 79–93.
18. Other examples of work for Syndetikon are illustrated in the catalogue, *Das Schöne und der Alltag* (1998), p. 209.
19. The manifesto is reprinted in Jürgen Eyssen, p. 9.
20. For Clara Ehmcke see *Monographien Deutscher Reklamekünstler*.
21. Gisela Moeller, pp. 90–103.
22. Edward Johnston.
23. Deutscher Werkbund.
24. Rudolf von Larisch, and a later commentary by Eberhard Hölscher (*q.v.*).
25. For Secessionist graphics see Werner Schweiger.
26. Hans Loubier.
27. On Heimatschutz, see Joachim Petsch, 'The Deutscher Werkbund from 1903 to 1933 and the Movements for the "Reform of Life and Culture"', in Lucius Burckhardt, and Richard Merker, pp. 84–91.
28. *Das Zelt*, 1926–28.
29. *Festschrift der Druckerei Hollerbaum und Schmidt*, Berlin: Hollerbaum und Schmidt, 1920.
30. Hanna Gagel.
31. Paul Ruben.
32. Ernst Growald, 'Amerikanische und Deutsche Reklame', in Paul Ruben, *op. cit.*, v. 1, pp. 57–59.
33. Paul Scheurich.
34. Kurt Friedländer. A second book inspired by these sources in German was Theodor König.
35. 'Lucian Bernhard in NewYork, ein Interview von Oskar M. Hahn', *Gebrauchsgraphik*, v. 3, No. 2, February 1926.

Chapter Three

1. Paul Renner, 'Die Schrift unserer Zeit', in *Die Form*, 1927, Year 2, No.3, pp.109–10.
2. Article by John Elderfield (1970). Also Joan Weinstein.
3. Jeffrey Herf, p. 22.
4. Hans Georg, 'Unser Stand vor dem Abgrund', in *Deutsche Handelswacht. Zeitschrift des deutschnationalen Handlungsgehilfen-Verbandes*, No. 3, January 1921, published in English translation as 'Our Stand at the Abyss' in Anton Kaes, Martin Jay and Edward Dimendberg, pp. 182–83.
5. Wieland Schmied. For the photographic context of Neue Sachlichkeit see David Mellor.
6. Siegfried Kracauer, 'The Mass Ornament', translated by Thomas Y. Levin, in *The Mass Ornament, Weimar Essays*, Cambridge, Mass., Harvard University Press, 1995, pp. 75–76.
7. Siegfried Kracauer, 'Asyl für Obdachlose', originally published in *Die Angestellten*, Frankfurt: Societätsverlag, 1930, and published in English translation in Anton Kaes *et al*, *op. cit.*, pp. 189–91.
8. Hans Wingler (1978), and Gillian Naylor. Specifically on typography and graphics at the school see Ute Brüning (ed.), *Das A und O des Bauhauses, Bauhaus-werbung: Schriftbilder, Drucksachen, Ausstellungdesign*, Berlin: Bauhausarchiv Museum für Gestaltung, 1995.
9. Walter Gropius.
10. Walter Gropius, 'Bauhaus Dessau — Principles of Bauhaus Production', printed sheet, published by Bauhaus Dessau in March 1926, reprinted in Wingler (1978), *op. cit.*, p. 110.
11. For the circumstances of the closure, *ibid.*, p. 176.
12. Hans Wingler (1968).
13. Sibyl Moholy-Nagy, and Krisztina Passuth.
14. Laszlo Moholy-Nagy, 'Constructivism and the Proletariat', in *MA*, May 1922, reprinted in translation in Charlotte Benton, Tim Benton and Dennis Sharp, pp. 95–96.
15. Yves Alain-Bois (1979).
16. Laszlo Moholy-Nagy, *Malerei, Fotografie, Film*, published as v. 8 in the Bauhausbücher series and reprinted in English as *Painting, Photography, Film*, 1969 (which is the source of this quote).
17. *Ibid.*, p. 7.
18. *Ibid.*, p. 38, original in bold as shown.
19. Wingler (1978), p. 106.
20. Gerd Fleischmann, p. 199.
21. For a full review of Bauhaus photography see Jeannine Fiedler.
22. Heinz Loew and Helene Nonne-Schmidt.
23. See Robin Kinross for the fullest account in English of the move to typographic standards in Germany.
24. Fleischmann, p. 7.
25. Jakob Erbar's design was announced in *Gebrauchsgraphik*, v. 3, No. 8, August 1926.
26. This sample booklet was composed in 1927 and appeared in *Gebrauchsgraphik*, v. 7, No. 8, August 1930. For a full account of Futura typeface, see Christopher Burke, Chapter 4.
27. Advertised in *Gebrauchsgraphik*, v. 7, No. 9, September 1930.
28. See the article on Georg Trump by Georg Bettmann, in *Gebrauchsgraphik*, v. 8, No. 9, September 1931, pp. 33–45.
29. Walter Porstmann, in *Gebrauchsgraphik* (1925).
30. J. Scott Taylor.
31. The statement was first published as a contribution to a special issue on the new typography edited by Jan Tschichold and entitled 'elementare typographie', *Typographische Mitteilungen*, Leipzig, Year 22, No. 10, October 1925, p.198.
32. Herbert Bayer, 'Typography and Commercial Art Forms', in *bauhaus*, Dessau: v. 2, No. 1, 1928, reprinted in Hans Wingler (1978).
33. Albert Reimann (ed.), *Farbe und Form, Monatsschrift für Kunst und Kunstgewerbe*, Berlin: Reimannschule, 1927.
34. *Ibid.*
35. Natasha Kroll, former student and teacher at the Reimannschule, in conversation with the author in London 1998.
36. This comparison was first made in Hans Wingler (1977), p. 17.
37. Albert Reimann, *op. cit.*, v. 12, No. 2, February 1927.
38. Max Hertwig, *ibid.*, pp. 75–82.
39. Carl Gadau, *ibid.*, pp. 83–87.
40. Elsa Taterka, *ibid.*, pp. 88–89.
41. Werner Graeff.

Chapter Four

1. Ute Eskildsen and Jan-Christopher Horak, and the chapter on Film und Foto in the catalogue *Stationen der Moderne* (1988). This exhibition, which was organized by the Stuttgart division of the German Werkbund under Gustaf Stolz, celebrated the new techniques and aesthetic ideas concerning photography, photomontage and the new typography, as well as film. There were some common elements between Film und Foto and Pressa, including a Soviet room organized by El Lissitzky. Instead of an avant-garde exception, as at Pressa, in Stuttgart Lissitzky was joined by Piet Zwart as representative for The Netherlands, Karel Teige for Czechoslovakia, F.T. Gubler and Siegfried Giedion for Switzerland

and Edward Steichen and Edward Weston for the USA. Jan Tschichold, architect Bernhard Pankok and art historian Hans Hildebrandt all acted as advisors. The exhibition travelled to several German cities as well as Tokyo and Osaka.

2. Lucian Bernhard interviewed in New York by Oskar M. Hahn in *Gebrauchsgraphik*, v. 3, No. 2, February 1926.
3. The magazine was relaunched in 1950, by which time *Graphis*, the Swiss magazine published from Zürich, was in its sixth year.
4. Hanns Eisler. For a consideration of radical work see the catalogue *Wem Gehört die Welt* (1977).
5. The main source of this autobiographical information on Frenzel was an obituary section in *Gebrauchsgraphik*, v. 14, No. 11, November 1937.
6. 'Crawfords Reklame Agentur' was announced in *Gebrauchsgraphik*, v. 7, No. 8, August 1930. William Crawford contributed an article reviewing poster design in many countries, 'Das Plakat', *Gebrauchsgraphik*, v. 2, No. 5, 1925. Havinden's campaign was highly regarded for its combination of abstract imagery and detailed copyline. It clearly influenced the work of Max Bittrof for Opel cars shown in *Gebrauchsgraphik*, v. 5, No. 12, December 1928.
7. Frenzel contributed to the *Penrose Annual*, v. 38, 1936, pp. 23–26, with the article 'The Influence of Market Fluctuations on the Demand for Advertising'. An obituary of him was published in the *Penrose Annual*, v. 40, 1938.
8. H.K. Frenzel, *Gebrauchsgraphik*, v. 2, No.1, July 1925.
9. *Ibid.*
10. Special issues on these areas included 'Schrift und Schriftschreiber', No. 1; 'Amtliche Graphik des Reichs', No. 2; two issues on the poster, Nos. 4 and 5, and illustrators in No. 6. In 1926 the emphasis was on cities, however, the business prospectus, No. 5, and travel posters, No. 9, formed subjects of special issues.
11. *Gebrauchsgraphik*, v. 4, No. 1, January 1927.
12. H.K. Frenzel, 'Where is Advertising Going?', *Gebrauchsgraphik*, v. 7, No. 1, January 1930. The main author, Dr W. Puttkammer, also contributed articles on 'The Development of Consumption', No. 1, 'Dwellings and Housekeeping', No. 4, 'Income and Consumption', No. 7, and 'The Clothing Retail Trade', No. 9, all in the first year of this column.
13. *Gebrauchsgraphik*, v. 4, No. 7, July 1928.
14. E. Hölscher, obituary to H.K. Frenzel in *Gebrauchsgraphik*, v. 17, No. 11, November 1937.
15. In *Offset*, No. 3, 1924.
16. A range of articles on the USA in *Gebrauchsgraphik* included: 'Amerikanische Reklamemethoden in Europa,' v. 2, No. 3, 1925–26; 'How American Advertising Agencies Advertise Themselves', v. 7, No. 5, May 1930; 'Wrappings and Boxes of the Wards Company, Chicago', v. 1, No. 3, March 1934; and 'Container Corporation of America', v. 15, No. 7, July 1938.
17. *The Annual of Advertising and Editorial Art*, New York, 1922—. Initially it was published as a catalogue 'for the first Annual Exhibition of Advertising Paintings and Drawings held by the Art Directors Club of New York'. The twelfth annual was advertised in *Gebrauchsgraphik*, v. 11, No. 2, February 1934.
18. B.W. Randolph, 'Amerikanische Universitätsausbildung in Reklame und Marktkunde', *Gebrauchsgraphik*, v. 3, No. 2, February 1926.
19. H.K. Frenzel, 'Vorwort', *Gebrauchsgraphik*, v. 3, No. 10, October 1926.
20. H.K. Frenzel in a conversation with Frederic Suhr, *Gebrauchsgraphik*, v. 5, No. 10, October 1928.
21. *Arts et Métiers Graphiques*, director Charles Peignot, editor Bertrand Guégan, published from 3 Rue Séguier, Paris, 1927–39.
22. *Ibid.*, No. 25, pp. 357–64.
23. *Ibid.*, No. 19, pp. 46–54.
24. *Ibid.*, No. 16.
25. *Gebrauchsgraphik*, v. 10, No. 1, January 1933
26. Contemporary reviews of Pressa included Willy Lotz, 'Die Deutsche Presse und die neue Gestaltung, zur Eröffnung der Pressa', in *Die Form*, v. 3, No. 5, March 1928, and a special issue of *Die Form*, v. 3, No. 7, July 1928, devoted to Pressa with reports by Walter Riezler and Willy Lotz. Subsequent interpretations of El Lissitzky include Sophie Lissitzky-Küppers, *El Lissitzky*, Dresden: VEB Verlag der Kunst, 1967 (for English edition see Bibliography), especially the section, 'Demonstrationsräume' for his ideas on exhibitions, and Norbert Nobis *et al.*, *El Lissitzky 1890–1941, Retrospektive*, Eindhoven: Municipal van Abbemuseum, Berlin and Frankfurt am Main: Propyläen Verlag, 1988. See also the articles by Benjamin Buchloh (1984) and Yves-Alain Bois (1988). Recently in the English language, Matthew Teitelbaum, 1992, has interpreted the politically-engaged wing of designers (see especially the essay by Maud Lavin, 'Photomontage, Mass Culture and Modernity, Utopianism in the Circle of New Advertising Designers').

27. For the Swedish exhibition, see the article 'Stockholm 1930' in *The Architectural Review*, No. 405, London, August 1930.
28. Ernest James Passant, pp. 161–71.
29. For a contemporary commentary on the position of Germany, see Hugh Quigley and Robert Thomson Clark. See also Charles Maier (1970).
30. Albert Kapr.
31. For the context of the 1914 exhibition, see the catalogue *Der Westdeutsche Impuls* (1984).
32. Konrad Adenauer in *Pressa* (1928), p. 16.
33. As well as an official catalogue, a commemorative volume was published in the form of *Pressa, Kulturschau am Rhein, Köln 1928*, Berlin: Schröder Verlag, 1928.
34. A full list of participating countries included in the House of Nations Austria, Belgium, China, Czechoslovakia, Denmark, Egypt, France, Greece, Hungary, Italy, Japan, The Netherlands, Norway, Poland, Rumania, Sweden, Switzerland, the Soviet Union, Spain, the countries of South America, Turkey, the United Kingdom and the United States of America.
35. H.K. Frenzel, 'Pressa, Cologne 1928' in *Gebrauchsgraphik*, v. 5, No. 7, July 1928.
36. The subject reached the pages of *The Architectural Review*, No. 384, London, November 1928, in an issue on shopfronts (see, for example, the article by R. Waldo Maitland, 'The Lighted Shopfront'). A more remarkable summary of these interests was presented by Frederik Kiesler in *Contemporary Art Applied to the Store and its Display*, London: Pitman, 1930.
37. Hellmut Lehmann-Haupt, from 'Berlin Commentary' in *Print*, New York, v. 5, No. 2, February 1947. The National Socialists expelled the Ullstein family and took over the company, renaming it Deutscher Verlag. During the war the central publishing offices in the newspaper district of Berlin were destroyed. The Druckhaus Tempelhof survived the war and workers resumed activities while much of the specialist printing equipment was transported to the Soviet Union. See also *Ullstein, Ein Industriebau*, Berlin: Bauwelt Verlag, 1927.
38. Tim Gidal, and Diethart Kerbs *et al.*
39. These figures were published in *Pressa. Amtlicher Katalog* (1928). For the German newspaper industry, see Peter de Mendelssohn. Members of the publishing élite were associated in the Verein Deutscher Zeitungsverleger (League of German Newspaper Publishers), who put on a display of the modern daily paper at Pressa in conjunction with the Reichsverband der deutschen Presse (National League of the German Press). The latter was largely composed of editors and journalists, led by Emil Dovifat of the Institute of Journalism at the University of Berlin. During the '20s there had been a huge dispute between these organizations over the rights and responsibilities of form and content of the newspaper and the continuing state-imposed censorship of the press.
40. Philipp Th. Bertheau, 'The German Language and the Two Faces of Its Script: A Genuine Expression of European Culture?' in Peter Bain and Paul Shaw.
41. Paul Renner, 1931.
42. Albert Kapr, *op. cit.*
43. Christina Lodder, p. 156.
44. Horst Bunke and Hans Stern.
45. Jan Tschichold (1928).
46. *Catalogue of the English Section of the International Press Exhibition*, 1928. For a commentary see Grant Shipcott.
47. The catalogue *Pressa, Internationale Presse Ausstellung Komitee des Sowjet Pavillons, Union der sozialistischen Sowjetrepubliken*, Cologne: Du Mont Schauberg, 1928.
48. Lissitzky quoted in Benjamin Buchloh, *op. cit.* On the collaboration between Klucis and Lissitzky see Margarita Tupitsyn, 'From Politics of Montage to Montage of Politics', in Teitelbaum, *op. cit.*, pp. 82–127.
49. Quoted in the catalogue *Union der sozialistischen Sowjetrepubliken*, *op. cit.*
50. Buchloh, *op. cit.*
51. El Lissitzky in a letter to J.J.P. Oud, 26.12.1928, in Sophie Lissitzky-Küppers and Jen Lissitzky (eds), *El Lissitzky: Proun und Wolkenbügel. Schriften, Briefe und Dokumente*, Dresden: VEB Verlag, 1977, p.135. I am indebted to Victor Margolin for drawing my attention to this source.
52. Dr Ernst Esch in *Amtlicher Katalog* (1928), p. 61.
53. H.K. Frenzel, 'Betrachtungen zur Reichsreklamemesse', in *Gebrauchsgraphik*, v. 1, No.9.
54. H.K. Frenzel, 'Pressa, Cologne 1928', *op. cit.*
55. Hermann Esswein, 'Die Neue Sammlung in München' in *Die Form*, 1929, v. 4, No. 7.
56. H.K. Frenzel, 'Pressa, Cologne 1928', *op. cit.*
57. The Paris convention on international exhibitions of 22 November 1928 was referred to in an article by Ernst Jäckh, 'Idee und Realisierung der internationalen Werkbund-Ausstellung "Die Neue Zeit" Köln 1932', in *Die Form*, v. 4, No. 15, pp. 401–21. The exhibition was intended to celebrate the twenty-fifth year of the German Werkbund and to coincide with the Frankfurt am Main Goethe anniversary exhibitions. The article also suggested

that a link between the themes of the 1933 Chicago world exhibition and Cologne might be developed.

58. *Das Kunstblatt*, Berlin, 1928. By 1930 their numbers included Otto Baumberger, Zurich; Willi Baumeister, Frankfurt; Max Bill, Zurich; Max Burchartz, Essen; Johannes Canis, Bochum; Walter Cyliax, Zurich; Walter Dexel, Jena; Cesar Domela-Nieuwenhuis, Berlin; Hermann Elias, Berlin; Werner Graeff, Berlin; John Heartfield, Berlin; Franz Krause, Bodenbach; Hans and Greta Leistikow, Frankfurt am Main; El Lissitzky, Moscow; Robert Michel, Frankfurt am Main; Moholy-Nagy, Berlin; the brothers Heinz and Bodo Rasch, Stuttgart; Hans Richter, Berlin; Paul Schuitema, Rotterdam; Kurt Schwitters, Hanover; Mart Stam, Frankfurt; Karel Teige, Prague; Georg Trump, München; Jan Tschichold, München; Vordemberge-Gildewart, Hanover; and Piet Zwart, Wassenar.
59. John Elderfield.
60. For a list of the contents of *Merz* see Dawn Ades, *Dada and Surrealism Reviewed*, London: Arts Council of Great Britain, 1978, pp.129–30.
61. See the four catalogues to accompany the exhibitions *Typographie kann unter Umständen Kunst sein* (1990).
62. Bodo and Heinz Rasch (1930).
63. *Ibid.*
64. Johannes Molzahn, 'Economics of the Advertising Mechanism', 1925, reprinted in English translation in C. Benton, T. Benton and D. Sharp, *op. cit.*
65. Kees Broos and Paul Hefting.
66. Eckhard Siepmann.
67. George Grosz and Wieland Herzfelde.
68. On the Malik publishing house, see Jo Hauberg.
69. Walter Benjamin, 'The Work of Art in the Age of Mechanical Reproduction' (1936), in *Illuminations*, Hannah Arendt (ed.), Glasgow: Fontana, 1973, and 'The Author as Producer' (1934), in *Understanding Brecht*, Stanley Mitchell (ed.), London: New Left Books, 1973.
70. Mitchell, *ibid.*, pp. 94–95.
71. See Conclusion for a discussion of this.
72. Robin Kinross in Jan Tschichold (1928).
73. Bodo and Heinz Rasch
74. 'die elementare typografie', a special issue of *Typographische Mitteilungen* published in v. 22, No. 10, Leipzig, October 1925.
75. Jan Tschichold (1928) .
76. Among Max Burchartz's writings were 'Neuzeitliche Werbung' in *Die Form*, v. 1, No. 1, 1925, and 'handschrift - type, zeichnung - foto' in *Gebrauchsgraphik*, v. 3, No. 8, August 1926.
77. *Merz*, No. 11, 'Typoreklame', Hanover, 1924.
78. John Willett, pp. 26–27.
79. Walter Rathenau, 'Die Neue Wirtschaft', see commentary in Hugh Quigley and Robert Thomson Clark.
80. Charles Maier (1970).
81. Gustav Hartlaub (1928).
82. F.H. Ehmcke review originally published in *Die Zeit*, 4 January 1924, and republished in English translation in Benton, Benton and Sharp, *op. cit.*, p.128.
83. *Ibid.*
84. As cited in Naylor, *op. cit.*, p.160, originally in Sibyl Moholy-Nagy, *op. cit.*, p. 88.

Chapter Five

1. Barbara Miller-Lane, and Robert Taylor.
2. John Heskett, 'Modernism and Archaism in Design in the Third Reich' (1980), reprinted in Brandon Taylor and Wilfried van der Will, and his essay 'Design in Inter-war Germany' in Wendy Kaplan.
3. Gert Selle.
4. Ute Westphal, *op. cit.*, pp.26–27.
5. Peter Hahn in the catalogue *Exiles and Émigrés* (1997), p. 214. See also Ute Brüning, *op. cit.*
6. Heinrich Wieynck, 'Neue Typographie' in *Gebrauchsgraphik*, v. 5, No. 7, July 1928.
7. Heinrich Wieynck, 'Leitsätze zum Problem Zeitgemässer Druckschriftgestaltung', in *Gebrauchsgraphik*, v. 8, No. 2, February 1931.
8. Berthold Hinz, p. 61, and Brandon Taylor and Wilfried van der Will, *op. cit.*, p.133.
9. Fritz Ehmcke in *Die Form*, v. 8, No. 10, October 1933.
10. *Ibid.*
11. Albert Giesecke in *Gebrauchsgraphik*, v. 7, No. 7, July 1932, p. 19.
12. *Ibid.*
13. Gustav Stresow, 'German Typography Today', in *The Penrose Annual* (1937).
14. Hinz, *op. cit.*
15. The names of all 3,695 graphic designers in the Fachgruppe Gebrauchsgraphiker of the Reichskammer bildenden Künste were given in the catalogue *Ausstellung Deutsche Werbegraphik*, Munich: RKdBK, Fachgruppe Gebrauchsgraphiker, 1936. Among the established names from the Weimar period, the list included Gerhard Marggraff, Paul Scheurich, Georg Trump, Carl Otto Czeschka, Willy Baumeister, Max Burchartz, Herbert Bayer and Otto Hadank.
16. Hans Peter Wilberg, 'Fraktur and Nationalism', in *Blackletter: Type and National Identity* (1998), *op. cit.*, p. 46.
17. Westphal (1989), *op. cit.*, pp.106–07.

18. *Die Kunst im Dritten Reich*, Munich: Nationalsozialistische Deutsche Arbeiter-Partei, Zentralverlag der NSDAP, 1937–1941, changing its name to *Die Kunst im Deutschen Reich* in 1941.
19. Hugo Fischer, *Gebrauchsgraphik*, v. 10, No. 8, August 1933, p. 65.
20. Ludwig Hohlwein, in *Gebrauchsgraphik*, v. 10, No. 1, January 1933.
21. An article on Bayer appeared in the April 1936 issue of *Gebrauchsgraphik* and his cover was published in October 1938.
22. Kurt Bach, 'Über die Anwendung des Hakenkreuzsymbols' in *Gebrauchsgraphik*, v. 10, No. 8, August 1933.
23. *Gebrauchsgraphik*, v. 13, No. 10, October 1936, pp.16–32.
24. The Olympic Games were the subject of a special issue of *Gebrauchsgraphik* in July 1936.
25. Otto Hadank in *Gebrauchsgraphik*, v. 10, No. 11, November 1933.
26. Gerhard Marggraff, *Gebrauchsgraphik*, v. 15, No. 10, October 1938.
27. Diethart Kerbs, Walter Uka and Brigitte Walz-Richter.
28. Willy Lotz, 'Die Kamera' review in *Die Form*, v. 7, 1933, pp. 321–25.
29. While photography of the Weimar period was cast as inaccessible by the National Socialists, the official photography after 1933 was promoted through popular genres as painting. See P.K. Schuster.
30. Diethart Kerbs, Walter Uka and Brigitte Walz-Richter.
31. Catalogue, *Die Kamera*, Berlin: Messeamt, 1933.
32. Major sources are Herbert Bayer, Magdalena Droste (catalogue *Herbert Bayer*, 1982), Arthur Cohen, Gwen Chanzit, catalogue *herbert bayer collection* (1988). For the wider design context see Fleischmann and Brüning.
33. Cohen.
34. Droste.
35. Bayer.
36. Wingler (1978).
37. Franklin Rosemont, *André Breton and the First Principles of Surrealism*, London: Pluto Press, 1978
38. Sally Stein has traced an equivalent adaptation of photomontage in the American context, see '"Good fences make good neighbours," American resistance to Photomontage between the Wars', in Matthew Teitelbaum.
39. Bayer.
40. Westphal (1989), *op. cit.*
41. *Ibid.*
42. Alfred Barr, *Cubism and Abstract Art*, New York: Museum of Modern Art, 1936.
43. Alexander Dorner.
44. Paul Rand.
45. Dorner.
46. *Ibid.*
47. John Dewey, *Art as Experience*, London: G. Allen and Unwin, 1934.
48. James Sloan Allen, *The Romance of Commerce and Culture: Capitalism, Modernism, and the Chicago-Aspen Crusade for Cultural Reform*, Chicago: University of Chicago Press, 1983.
49. Lorraine Wilde, 'Europeans in America', in Mildred Friedman and Phil Freshman, p. 168.
50. Dorner.
51. *Ibid.*

Conclusion

1. Max Bill, 'Über typografie', in *Schweizer Graphische Mitteilungen*, 65, No. 4, April, 1946. The exchange is commented on by Robin Kinross in Tschichold (c. 1995).
2. Jan Tschichold, 'The New Typography', in Leslie J. Martin, Naum Gabo and Ben Nicholson.
3. Jan Tschichold, 'Glaube und Wirklichkeit', *Schweizer Graphische Mitteilungen*, 65, No. 6, June, 1946.
4. For Swiss graphic design see the catalogue *Das Schweizer Plakat*, 1984.
5. F.H. Ehmcke, 'Deutsche Gebrauchsgraphik', *Persönliches und Sachliches*, 1928, originally in *Klimschs Jahrbuch*, Frankfurt am Main, 1927.
6. H.K. Frenzel in the catalogue *Das Internationale Plakat*, 1929.
7. *Graphis - International Advertising Art*, Zurich, v. 1, No. 1, October, 1944.
8. *Ibid.*
9. See the catalogue *Ulm, die Moral der Gegenstände*, 1987.

Bibliography

Books

ADES, DAWN *The Twentieth Century Poster: Design of the Avant-Garde*, New York: Walker Art Center, Minneapolis, and Abbeville Press, 1984

ADORNO, THEODOR AND HORKHEIMER, MAX *Dialectic of the Enlightenment* (New York, 1944), London: Verso, 1986

ANDERSON, PERRY *Considerations on Western Marxism*, London: Verso, 1979

ARATO, A. AND GEBHARD, E. *The Essential Frankfurt School Reader*, Oxford: Blackwell, 1978

ASCHE, KURT *Peter Behrens und die Oldenburger Ausstellung, 1905 - Entwürfe, Bauten, Gebrauchsgraphik*, Berlin: Gebrüder Mann, 1992

BAIN, PETER AND SHAW, PAUL (eds) *Blackletter: Type and National Identity*, New York: Princeton Architectural Press and The Cooper Union for the Advancement of Science and Arts, 1998

BAYER, HERBERT *Herbert Bayer, Painter, Designer, Architect*, New York: Reinhold, 1967

BEHNE, ADOLF *Das politische Plakat, 1919*, Berlin, Charlottenburg: Verlag das Plakat, 1919

BEHRENS, PETER *Feste des Lebens und der Kunst: eine Betrachtung des Theaters also höchsten Kultursymbols*, Berlin: Eugen Diederichs, 1900

BENJAMIN, WALTER *Illuminations*, Hannah Arendt (ed.), Glasgow: Fontana, 1973

BENJAMIN, WALTER *Understanding Brecht*, Stanley Mitchell (ed.), London: NLB, 1977

BENJAMIN, WALTER *Reflections: Essays by Walter Benjamin*, Peter Demetz (ed.), New York: Harcourt, Brace and Jovanovich, 1979

BENTON, CHARLOTTE, TIM BENTON, DENNIS SHARP (eds), *Form and Function: A Sourcebook for the History of Architecture and Design*, Milton Keynes: Open University Press, 1975

BERGHAHN, VOLKER *The Americanisation of West German Industry*, Leamington Spa: Berg, 1986

BERTONATI, EMILIO *Das Experimentelle Photo in Deutschland*, Munich: Galleria del Levante, 1978

BOBERG, JOCHEN AND TILMANN FICHTER (eds) *Die Metropole: Industriekultur in Berlin in 20. Jahrhundert*, Munich: C.H. Beck, 1986

BOETCHER, ROBERT *Kunst und Kunsterziehung in neuen Reich*, Breslau: Ferdinand Hirt, 1933

BÖJKO, SZYMON *New Graphic Design in Revolutionary Russia*, New York: Praeger, 1972

BOSSELT, RUDOLF, HUGO BUSCH AND HERMANN MUTHESIUS (eds) *Kunstgewerbe, ein Bericht über die Entwicklung und Tätigkeit der Handwerker und Kunstgewerbeschulen in Preussen*, Berlin: Ernst Wasmuth, 1922

BRADSHAW, PERCY *Art in Advertising: a Study of British and American Pictorial Publicity*, London: Art School Press, 1925

BRADY, R. *The Rationalisation Movement in German Industry*, Berkeley: University of California, 1933

BROOS, KEES AND PAUL HEFTING *Dutch Graphic Design*, London: Phaidon, 1993

BRÜNING, UTE (ed.) *Bauhaus Moderne im Nationalsocialismus, zwischen Anbiederung und Verfolgung*, Munich: Prestel, 1993

BUDDENSIEG, TILMANN (ed.) *Industriekultur: Peter Behrens und die AEG 1907-1914*, Berlin: Gebr. Mann, 1979, translated into English by Iain Boyd Whyte, *Industriekultur: Peter Behrens and the AEG*, Cambridge MA, MIT Press, 1984

BUND DER KUNSTGEWERBESCHULMÄNNER *Kunstgewerbe. Ein Bericht über Entwicklung und Tätigkeit der Handwerker und Kunstgewerbeschulen in Preussen*, Berlin: Ernst Wasmuth, 1921

BUND DEUTSCHER GEBRAUCHSGRAPHIKER *Das Adressbuch*, Berlin: B.D.G., 1926/7

BUNKE, HORST AND HANS STERN *Buchgestaltung für die Literatur der Arbeiterklasse, 1918–1933*, Leipzig: Deutsche Bücherei, 1982

BURCKHARDT, LUCIUS *The Werkbund: Studies in the History and Ideology of the Deutscher Werkbund*, London: Design Council, 1980

BURKE, CHRISTOPHER *Paul Renner, the Art of Typography*, London: Hyphen Press, 1998

CAMPBELL, JOAN *The German Werkbund — The Politics of Reform in the Applied Arts*, Princeton: Princeton University Press, 1978

CATE, PHILLIP DENNIS *The Graphic Arts and French Society, 1871–1914*, New Brunswick, N.J.: Jane Voorhees Zimmerli Art Museum, 1988

CHANZIT, GWEN *Herbert Bayer and Modernist Design in America*, Ann Arbor, Michigan: UMI Research Press, c.1987

COHEN, ARTHUR *Herbert Bayer: The Complete Work*, Cambridge MA: MIT Press, 1984

CONRADS, ULRICH (ed.) *Programmes and Manifestoes on 20th Century Architecture*, London: Lund Humphries, 1970

COOPER, AUSTIN *Making a Poster*, London: Studio 1938

CRAIG, GORDON *Germany, 1866–1945*, Oxford University Press, 1997

CROUS, ERNST *Fünfzig Jahre Reichsdruckerei, 1879–1929*, Berlin: Reichsdruckerei, 1929

CZOK, CARL (ed.) *500 Jahre Buchstadt Leipzig*, Leipzig: 1981

DEUTSCHER WERKBUND *Die Durchgeistigung der Deutschen Arbeit ein Bericht vom Deutschen Werkbund*, Jena: Eugen Diederichs, 1912

DORNER, ALEXANDER *The Way Beyond Art, The Work of Herbert Bayer*, New York: Wittenborn, Schultz 1947

EHMCKE, FRITZ H. *Ziel des Schriftunterrichts, ein Beitrag zur modernen Schriftbewegung*, Jena: Diederichs 1911

EHMCKE, FRITZ H. *Drei Jahrzehnte deutscher Buchkunst, 1890–1920*, Berlin: Euphorion Verlag 1922

EHMCKE, FRITZ H. *Persönliches und Sachliches, Gesammelte Aufsätze und Arbeiten aus fünfundzwanzig Jahren*, Berlin: Verlag Hermann Reckendorf, 1928

EHMCKE, FRITZ H. *Rudolf von Larisch*, Leipzig: Staatliche Akademie für künstlerischen Reklame, 1926

EHMCKE, FRITZ H. *Ehmcke Antiqua, Type und Ornament*, Frankfurt am Main: Schriftgiesserei Flinsch 1909

EHMCKE, FRITZ H. AND EHMCKE, CLARA *Arbeiten für künstlerischen Reklame*, Dortmund: Fr. Wilhelm Ruhfus, 1926

EHMCKE, FRITZ H. *Geordnetes und Gültiges: Gesammelte Aufsätze und Arbeiten aus den letzten 25 Jahren*, Munich: C.H. Beck, 1955

EISLER, HANNS *A Rebel in Music*, Berlin: Seven Seas, 1978

ELDERFIELD, JOHN *Kurt Schwitters*, London: Thames and Hudson, 1985

ESKILDSEN, UTE AND JAN-CHRISTOPHER HORAK (eds) *Film und Foto der zwanziger Jahre, eine Betrachtung der internationalen Werkbundausstellung Film und Foto 1929*, Stuttgart: Württembergischer Kunstverein, 1979

EYSSEN, JÜRGEN *Buchkunst in Deutschland vom Jugendstil zum Malerbuch, Buchgestalter, Handpressen, Verleger, Illustratoren*, Hanover: Schlütersche Verlag, 1980

FAHR-BECKER, GABRIELE *Wiener Werkstaette, 1903–1932*, Cologne: Taschen, 1995

FIEDLER, JEANNINE (ed.) *Photography at the Bauhaus*, London: Dirk Nishen, 1990

FLEISCHMANN, GERD (ed.) *bauhaus typografie-drucksachen typografie reklame*, Düsseldorf: Edition Marzona, 1984

FRANCISCONO, MARCEL *Walter Gropius and the Creation of the Bauhaus in Weimar*, Urbana: University of Illinois Press, 1971

FRANZKE, HANS *Ernst Litfass: die ersten 100 Jahre, 1855–1955*, Berlin: Elsnerdruck, 1985

FRENZEL, H.K. *Ludwig Hohlwein, Sein Leben und Werk*, Berlin: Phönix Verlag, 1924

FRIEDL, FRIEDRICH, NICOLAUS OTT, AND BERNARD STEIN (eds) *Typography — when who how*, Cologne: Könemann 1998

FRIEDLÄNDER, KURT *Der Weg zum Käufer*, Berlin: Springer, 1923

FRIEDMAN, MILDRED AND PHIL FRESHMAN *Graphic Design in America, a visual language history*, Minneapolis: Walker Art Center and New York: Harry Abrams, Inc., 1989

GAGEL, HANNA *Studien zur Motivengeschichte des Deutschen Plakats, 1900–1914*, Berlin: Freie Universität, unpublished PhD Thesis, 1971

GIDAL, TIM *Modern Photojournalism — Origins and Evolution 1910–1933*, New York: Collier Books, 1973

GLASER, HERMANN (ed.) *Industriekultur in Nürnberg*, Munich: Prestel Verlag, 1983

GRAEFF, WERNER *Es Kommt der neuer Fotograf!*, Berlin: Reckendorf, 1929

GROPIUS, WALTER *Idee und Aufbau des Staatlichen Bauhauses Weimar*, Weimar and Munich: Bauhausverlag, 1923

GROSZ, GEORG AND WIELAND HERZFELDE *Die Kunst ist im Gefahr, ein Orientierungsbuch*, Berlin: Malik Verlag, 1925

HAUBERG, JO *et al*, *Der Malik Verlag 1916–1947*, Kiel: Neuer Malik Verlag, 1986

HAUPT, GEORG *Rudolf Koch der Schreiber*, Leipzig: Insel Verlag, 1936

HERF, JEFFREY *Reactionary Modernism — Technology, Culture, and Politics in Weimar and the Third Reich*, Cambridge: Cambridge University Press, 1984

HERZFELDE, WIELAND *John Heartfield*, Dresden: D.E.V., 1986

HESKETT, JOHN *Design in Germany, 1870–1919*, London: Trefoil Design Library, 1986

HIESINGER, KATHRYN BLOOM (ed.) *Art Nouveau in Munich, Masters of Jugendstil*, Munich: Philadelphia Museum of Art in association with Prestel Verlag, 1988

HILDEBRANDT, MARTIN *25 Jahre Typograph, Gedenkblätter zum 25 jährigen Bestehen der Typograph*, Berlin: Typograph, 1922

HINZ, BERTHOLD *Art in the Third Reich*, Oxford: Blackwell, 1979

HOBSBAWM, ERIC *Nations and Nationalism since 1750 — Programme, Myth, Reality*, Cambridge: Cambridge University Press, 1990

HOFFMANN, HEINRICH *Deutschland in Paris, 1937*, Munich: Heinrich Hoffmann Verlag, 1937

HOFFMANN, HERMANN *Die Geschäfts Anzeige. Ihre Stil und ihre Gestaltung*, Berlin: Berthold, 1920

HÖLSCHER, EBERHARD *Rudolf von Larisch und seine Schule*, Berlin: Verlag für Schriftkunde Heintze and Blankertz, 1938

JOHNSTON, EDWARD *Schreibkunst, Zierschrift und angewandte Kunst*, Leipzig: Klinkhardt und Biermann, 1910

(KA DE WE) *Kaufhaus des Westens, 1907–1932*, Berlin: 1932

KAES, ANTON, MARTIN JAY, AND EDWARD DIMENDBERG (eds) *The Weimar Republic Sourcebook*, Berkeley: University of California Press, 1994

KÄMPFER, FRANK *'Der Rote Keil': Das Politische Plakat, Theorie und Geschichte*, Berlin: Gebr. Mann, 1985

KAPLAN, WENDY (ed.) *Designing Modernity: the Arts of Reform and Persuasion 1885–1945*, London and New York: Thames & Hudson, 1995

KAPR, ALBERT (ed.) *Traditionen Leipziger Buchkunst*, Leipzig: VEB Fachbuchverlag, 1989

KAUFFER, EDWARD MCKNIGHT *The Art of the Poster*, New York: A. and C. Boni, 1925

KERBS, DIETHART, WALTER UKA AND BRIGITTE WALZ-RICHTER (eds) *Die Gleichschaltung der Bilder, Pressefotografie 1930–1936*, Berlin: Frölich und Kaufmann, 1983

KINROSS, ROBIN *Modern Typography: an essay in critical history*, London: Hyphen Press, 1992

KOCH, RUDOLF (ed.) *Klassische Schriften nach Zeichnungen von Gutenberg, Dürer, Morris, König, Kupp, Eckmann, Behrens, u.a.*, Dresden: Gerhard Kühtmann, n.d.

KÖNIG, THEODOR *Reklamepsychologie, ihr gegenwartiger Stand — ihre praktische Bedeutung*, Munich and Berlin: Oldenburg, 1926

KRACAUER, SIEGFRIED *The Mass Ornament*, translated by Thomas Y. Levin, Cambridge MA.: Harvard University Press, 1995

LARISCH, RUDOLF VON *Unterrricht in Ornamentaler Schrift*, Vienna: Kaiserliche und Königliche Hof- und Staatsdruckerei, 1911. First published in 1908

LATHAM, IAN *J.M. Olbrich*, New York: Rizzoli, 1980

LAVIN, MAUD *Cut with the Kitchen Knife, the Weimar Photomontages of Hannah Höch*, New Haven and London: Yale University Press, 1993

LISSITZKY-KÜPPERS, SOPHIE *El Lissitzky — Life Letters Texts*, London and New York: Thames & Hudson, 1968

LODDER, CHRISTINA *Russian Constructivism*, London and New York: Yale University Press, 1983

LOEW, HEINZ AND HELENE NONNE SCHMIDT *Joost Schmidt — Lehre und Arbeit am Bauhaus 1919–1932*, Düsseldorf: Edition Marzona, 1984

LOUBIER, HANS *Die Neue Deutsche Buchkunst*, Stuttgart: Hoffmannschen Buchdruckerei, Felix Krauss, 1921

MARCH, WERNER *Die Schrift in der Baukunst*, Berlin: Heintze and Blanckertz, 1938

MARTIN, J. LESLIE, NAUM GABO AND BEN NICHOLSON (eds) *Circle: An International Survey of Constructive Art*, London: Faber, 1937

MCLEAN, RUARI *Jan Tschichold - Typographer*, London: Lund Humphries, 1975

MCLUHAN, MARSHALL *The Gutenberg Galaxy: the Making of Typographic Man*, London: Routledge, 1962

MAKELA, MARIA *The Munich Secession, Art and Artists in Turn of the Century Munich*, Princeton: Princeton University Press, 1990

MARGOLIN, VICTOR *The Struggle for Utopia: Rodchenko, Lissitzky, Moholy-Nagy 1917–1946*, Chicago and London: University of Chicago Press, 1997

MELLOR, DAVID (ed.) *Germany: The New Photography 1927–1933*, London: Arts Council of Great Britain, 1978

MENDELSOHN, ERICH *Amerika; Bilderbuch eines Architekten*, Berlin: Rudolf Mosse, 1928

DE MENDELSSOHN, PETER *Zeitungsstadt Berlin*, Berlin: Ullstein, 1982

MERKER, RICHARD *Die Bildenden Künste im Nationalsozialismus, Kulturideologie, Kulturpolitik, Kulturproduktion*, Cologne: Du Mont, 1983

MEYER-SCHÖNBRUNN, F. AND OTHERS, *Monographien Deutscher Reklamekunstler*, Hagen and Dortmund: Fr. Wilh. Ruhfus, 1910–13

1 and 2 *Fritz und Clara Ehmcke*, by F. Meyer-Schönbrunn

3 *Julius Klinger, by* F. Meyer-Schönbrunn

4 *Lucian Bernhard*, by Dr Friedrich Plietzsch

5 *Peter Behrens*, by F. Meyer-Schönbrunn

6 *Julius Gipkens*, by Julius Klinger

7 *Emil Preetorius*, by Fritz Sattler

MILLER-LANE, BARBARA *Architecture and Politics in Germany, 1918–1945*, Cambridge MA: Harvard University Press, 1968

MOELLER, GISELA *Peter Behrens in Düsseldorf: die Jahre 1903–07*, Heidelberg Weinheim: VCH, 1991

MOHOLY-NAGY, LASZLO *Malerei-Fotografie-Film*, Munich: Albert Langen,1925, republished in translation as *Painting Photography Film*, London: Lund Humphries, 1969

MOHOLY-NAGY, SIBYL *MOHOLY-NAGY – Experiment in Totality*, Cambridge MA: MIT Press, 1969

MOOS, STANISLAUS VON, AND C. SMEENK (eds) *Avant-Garde und Industrie*, Delft: Delft University Press, 1983

NAYLOR, GILLIAN *The Bauhaus Reassessed*, St Neots: Herbert Press, 1985

PACHNICKE, PETER, WALTER SCHILLER AND GERT WUNDERLICH (eds) *Buchkunst Leipzig, Abteilung Buchgestaltung*, Leipzig: Rudolf Schick, 1914

PARET, PETER *The Berlin Secession: Modernism and Its Enemies in Imperial Germany*, Cambridge MA: Belknap Press of Harvard University Press, 1980

PASSANT, ERNEST JAMES *A Short History of Germany 1815–1945*, Cambridge: Cambridge University Press, 1962

PASSUTH, KRISZTINA *Moholy-Nagy*, London: Thames & Hudson, 1985

PETLEY, JULIAN *Capital and Culture in German Cinema 1933–1945*, London: BFI 1979

PEVSNER, NIKOLAUS *Academies of Art Past and Present* (1940), new ed. New York: Da Capo 1973

PFEIFFER, HANS GEORG (ed.) *Peter Behrens: Architektur, Grafik, Produktgestaltung*, Düsseldorf: Beton Verlag, 1990

PFEIFFER, HEINRICH *Die Eisenbahnreklame*, Berlin: Deutsche Eisenbahnreklame, GmbH, 1922

PLAGEMANN, VOLKER (ed.) *Industriekultur in Hamburg*, Munich: Prestel Verlag, 1984

PODRO, MICHAEL *The Critical Historians of Art*, London: Yale University Press, 1982

PRESSA INTERNATIONALE AUSSTELLUNG *Kulturschau am Rhein, Köln*, Berlin: Verlag Max Schröder, 1928

QUIGLEY, HUGH AND ROBERT THOMSON CLARK *Republican Germany: a political and economic study*, London: Methuen, 1928

RADEMACHER, HELLMUTT *Deutsche Plakatkunst und ihre Meister*, Hanau/M: Dansien, 1965

RAND, PAUL *Thoughts on Design*, New York: Wittenborn, Schultz, 1947

RASCH, BODO AND HEINZ RASCH *Der Stuhl*, Stuttgart: Verlag Fr. Wedekind, 1928

RASCH, BODO AND HEINZ RASCH *Gefesselter Blick*, Stuttgart: Wissenschaftliche Verlag Dr Zaugg, 1930

RASCH, BODO AND HEINZ RASCH *Wie Bauen?*, Stuttgart: Verlag Fr. Wedekind, 1928

REIMANN, ALBERT *Die Reimannschule in Berlin*, Berlin: Verlag Bruno Hessling, 1966

REIMANN, ALBERT *25 Jahre Schule Reimann*, Special issue of *Farbe und Form*, Berlin: Reimannschule, 1927

REINHARDT, DIRK *Von der Reklame zum Marketing: die Geschichte der Werbung in Deutschland*, Berlin: Akademie Verlag, 1993

RENGER-PATZSCH, ALBERT *Die Welt ist Schön*, Munich: Einhorn Verlag, 1928

RENNER, PAUL *Typografie als Kunst*, Munich: Georg Muller, 1922

RENNER, PAUL *Mechanisierte Grafik — Schrift Typo Foto Film Farbe*, Berlin: Reckendorf, 1931

RILKE, RAINER MARIA *Worpswede, Monographie einer Landschaft*, Bremen: Carl Schünemann, 1951

ROGOFF, IRIT (ed.) *The Divided Heritage, Themes and Problems in German Modernism*, Cambridge: Cambridge University Press, 1991

ROTHSCHILD, DEBORAH, ELLEN LUPTON, AND DARRA GOLDSTEIN *Graphic Design in the Mechanical Age, selections from the Merrill C. Berman collection*, New Haven: Yale University Press, 1998

RUBEN, PAUL *Die Reklame, Ihre Kunst und Wissenschaft*, Berlin: Hermann Pätel, Verlag für Sozialpolitik, 1914, 2 vols.

SACHS, HANS *Die Plakatsammlung von Hans Sachs*, Görlitz: C.A. Stacke, 1908

SACHS, HANS J. *The World's Largest Poster Collection, 1896–1938, how it came about ... and disappeared from the face of the earth*, New York: Hans Sachs, 1957

SACHSSE, ROLF *Lucia Moholy*, Düsseldorf: Ed. Marzona, 1985

SARKOWSKI, HEINZ *Fünfzig Jahre Insel Bücherei, 1912–1962*, Frankfurt am Main: Insel Verlag 1962

SCHEURICH, PAUL *Manoli, Festschrift zur Feier des 25 jährigen Bestehens der Manoli Fabrik in Berlin*, Berlin: Manoli, 1919

SCHMIED, WIELAND *Neue Sachlichkeit und magischer Realismus in Deutschland 1918–1933*, Hanover: Fackelträgerverlag 1961

SCHORSKE, CARL *Fin de Siecle Vienna — Politics and Culture*, Cambridge: Cambridge University Press, 1981

SCHUBERT, WALTER F. *Die Deutsche Werbe Graphik*, Berlin: Verlag Francken und Lang, 1927

SCHUSTER, PETER-KLAUS (ed.) *Die Kunststadt Munchen 1937, Nationalsozialismus und Entartete Kunst*, Munich: Prestel Verlag, 1987

SCHUTTE, JÜRGEN AND PETER SPRENGEL *Die Berliner Moderne, 1885–1914*, Stuttgart: Reclam, 1987

SCHWARTZ, FREDERIC J. *The Werkbund, Design Theory and Mass Culture before the First World War*, New Haven and London: Yale University Press, 1996

SCHWEIGER, WERNER *Aufbruch und Erfüllung: Gebrauchsgraphik der Wiener Moderne*, Munich and Vienna: Edition Christian Brandstätter, 1992

SELLE, GERT *Geschichte des Design in Deutschland von 1870 bis Heute: Entwicklung der industriellen Produktkultur*, Cologne: Verlag M. Du Mont Schauberg, 1973

SHIPCOTT, GRANT *Typographical Periodicals between the Wars*, Oxford: Oxford Polytechnic Press, 1980

SIEPMANN, ECKHARD *John Heartfield Monteur*, Berlin: Elefanten Press, 1977

SLOAN, JAMES *The Romance of Commerce and Culture: Capitalism, Modernism and the Chicago-Aspen Crusade for Cultural Reform*, Chicago: University of Chicago Press, 1983

SPENCER, HERBERT *Pioneers of Modern Typography*, London: Lund Humphries, 1970

SPONSEL, JEAN LOUIS *Das Moderne Plakat*, Dresden: Gerhard Kühtmann, 1897

STARK, BARBARA *Emil Rudolf Weiss*, Lahr: Ernst Kaufmann Verlag, 1994

STEINBERG, S.H. *Five Hundred Years of Printing* (1955), Harmondsworth: Penguin Books, 1979

STERN, J.P. *The Politics of Cultural Despair: A Study in the Rise of Germanic Ideology*, New York: Doubleday, Anchor, 1965

TAYLOR, BRANDON AND WILFRIED VAN DER WILL (eds) *The Nazification of Art, art, design, music, architecture and film in the Third Reich*, Winchester: Winchester Press, 1990

TAYLOR, ROBERT *The Word in Stone, the role of architecture in the National Socialist Ideology*, Berkeley: University of California Press, 1974

TAYLOR, J. SCOTT *A Simple Explanation of the Ostwald Colour System*, London: Windsor and Newton, 1935

TEITELBAUM, MATTHEW (ed.) *Montage and Modern Life 1919–1942*, Boston: ICA, and Cambridge MA.: MIT Press, 1992

THOMSON, ELLEN MAZUR *The Origins of Graphic Design in America, 1870–1920*, New Haven and London: Yale University Press, 1997

TROY, NANCY *Modernism and the Decorative Arts in France, Art Nouveau to Le Corbusier*, New Haven and London: Yale University Press, 1991

Tschichold, Jan and Franz Roh *Foto-Auge: 76 Fotos der Zeit*, Stuttgart: Wedekind, 1929

Tschichold, Jan *Die Neue Typographie, ein Handbuch für zeitgemäss Schaffende*, Berlin: Verlag des Bildungsverbandes der Deutschen Buchdrucker, 1928

Tschichold, Jan *The New Typography: a handbook for modern designers*, Berkeley: University of California Press, c. 1995, translated by Ruari McLean with an introduction by Robin Kinross

Tschichold, Jan *Eine Stunde Druckgestaltung, Grundbegriffe der neuen Typografie in Bildbeispielen für Setzer*, Stuttgart: Fritz Wedekind, 1930

Tschichold, Jan *Typographische Gestaltung*, Basel: Benno Schwabe und Co., 1935

Tucholsky, Kurt *Deutschland, Deutschland über Alles!*, Hamburg: Rowohlt, 1964. Facsimile originally published Berlin: Neuer Deutscher Verlag, Berlin, 1929

(Ullstein) *Ein Industriebau*, Berlin: Bauwelt Verlag, 1927

Velde, Henry van de *Geschichte meines Lebens*, Munich: Piper, 1962

Verein der Plakatfreunde *Handbücher der Reklamekunst*, Berlin: Verlag des Plakat, 1920

Verein der Plakatfreunde *Unsere Reklamekünstler, Selbstkenntnisse und Selbstbildnisse*, 2 vols, Berlin: Verlag des Plakat, 1920

Verein Deutscher Reklamefachleute *Handbuch*, vols 1 and 2, Berlin: VDR, 1925

Volkov, Shulamit *The Rise of Popular Antimodernism in Germany, the urban master artisan, 1873*, Princeton: Princeton University Press, 1978

Waetzoldt, Wilhlem *Gedanken zur Kunstschulreform*, Leipzig: Quelle und Meyer, 1921

Weidenmüller, Johannes *Der Werbe Unterricht*, Hanover: König & Ebhardt, 1917

Weinstein, Joan *The End of Expressionism: Art and the November Revolution in Germany 1918–1919*, Chicago: University of Chicago Press, 1990

Weisser, Michael *Die Frau in der Reklame*, Münster: Coppenrath, 1981

Westen, Walter von zur *Berlins Graphische Gelegenheitskunst*, 2 vols, Berlin: Otto von Holten, 1912

Westen, Walter von zur *Reklamekunst*, Bielefeld: Verlag von Velhagen and Klasing, 1914

Westen, Walter von zur *Zur Entwicklung der Deutschen Gebrauchsgraphik*, Berlin: Verein für Ex libris und Gebrauchsgraphiker, 1927

Westphal, Uwe *Werbung im Dritten Reich*, Berlin: Transit Verlag, 1989

Willett, John *The New Sobriety: Art and Politics in the Weimar Period 1917–1933*, London: Thames & Hudson, 1978

Windsor, Alan *Peter Behrens: Architect and Designer, 1868–1940*, London: The Architectural Press, 1981

Wingler, Hans M. *Graphic Work from the Bauhaus*, London: Lund Humphries, 1968

Wingler, Hans M. (ed.) *Kunstschulreform, 1900–1933*, Berlin: Gebr. Mann, 1977

Wingler, Hans M. *The Bauhaus, Weimar, Dessau, Berlin and Chicago*, revised English language edition Cambridge MA: MIT Press, 1978

Wolff, Hans *Die Geschichte der königlichen Akademie für Graphische Künste und Kunstgewerbe, 1764–1901*, Leipzig: Hans Wolff, 1914

Worringer, Wilhelm *Abstraction and Empathy, a contribution to the psychology of style* (transl. by Michael Bullock), London: Routledge and Kegan Paul, 1967

Wündrich, Hermann *Das Plakat als Werbemittel und Kunstprodukt*, Düsseldorf: Monumental- und Plakatreklame GmbH, 1979

Catalogues

(in chronological order)

Deutsche Buchgewerbeausstellung, Paris, 1900

Official Catalogue, International Exposition St Louis, 1904, Exhibition of the German Empire, St Louis, 1904

Ausstellung der Kunstkolonie vom 15 Juli, Darmstadt, 1904

Österreichische Ausstellung in London, London, 1906

Sonderausstellung von Arbeiten einer Gruppe Englischer Künstler, Königliches Kunstgewerbemuseum, Berlin, 1908

Sonderausstellung: Schulerarbeiten aus Englischen und Amerikanischen Fach und Kunstschulen, Königliches Kunstgewerbemuseum, Berlin, 1909

Lehr und Versuch Ateliers Debschitz Schule, München Königliches Kunstgewerbemuseum, Berlin, 1913

International Exhibition for the Book Industry and the Graphic Arts, Internationale Buchgewerbeausstellung, Leipzig, 1914

Haus der Frau: Sonderausstellung auf der buchgewerblichen Weltausstellung, Leipzig, Die Frau im Buchgewerbe und in der Graphik e.V., Leipzig, 1914

Leitfaden für Film Reklame, Club der Filmindustrie, Berlin, 1924

Form ohne Ornament, Deutscher Werkbund, Stuttgart, 1924

Reichsreklamemesse, Berliner Messe Amt, Berlin, 1925

Leipzigs Wirken am Buch, Internationale Buch Ausstellung, Leipzig, 1927

Pressa, Amtlicher Katalog, Internationale Pressa Ausstellung, Cologne, 1928

Union der sozialistischen Sowjetrepubliken, Internationale Pressa Ausstellung, Cologne, 1928

Catalogue of the English Section of the International Press, Exhibition Cologne, Cologne, 1928 (London: Curwen Press, 1928)

Reklameschau, Berlin: Reichsverband Deutsche Reklame Messe e.V., Berlin, 1929

Das Internationale Plakat, Munich, 1929

Film und Foto, Kunstbibliothek, Berlin, 1929

Wohin geht die Neue Typografie?, Kunstbibliothek, Berlin, 1929

Ausstellung Neue Graphik, Staatliche Akademie für Graphische Künste, Leipzig, 1930

Fotomontage, Kunstbibliothek, Berlin 1931

Ein Jahrhundert des Fortschritts: Was und wo sie ist, ein deutscher Führer zur und durch die Ausstellung, Chicago Worlds Fair, Chicago, 1933

Die Kamera, Messehalle, Berlin, 1933

Deutsches Volk Deutsche Arbeit, Messehalle, Berlin, 1934

Das Wunder des Lebens, Messehalle, Berlin, 1935

Cubism and Modern Art, Museum of Modern Art, New York, 1936

Deutsche Werbegraphik, Fachgruppe Gebrauchsgraphiker in der Reichskammer der bildende Künste, Berlin, 1936

Deutschland Ausstellung, Messehalle, Berlin, 1936

Schaffendes Volk, Düsseldorf, 1937

Bauhaus 1919–28, Museum of Modern Art, New York, 1938

Gutenberg Reich Exhibition, Quincentenary of the Invention of Printing, Leipzig, 1940

50 Jahre Folkwangschule Essen, Essen, 1961

Die Jugend der Plakate, 1887–1917, Kaiser Wilhelm Museum, Krefeld, 1961

50 Years Bauhaus, Royal Academy, London, 1968

The Other Twenties: Themes in Art and Advertising, Carpenter Center, Cambridge MA., 1975

Zwischen Kunst und Industrie - Der Deutsche Werkbund, Die Neue Sammlung, Munich, 1975

Kunst im Dritten Reich: Dokumente der Unterwerfung, Frankfurter Kunstverein, Frankfurt, 1975

Das frühe Pelikan Plakat, 1898–1930, Stadtisches Museum, Göttingen, 1975

Wem Gehört die Welt - Kunst und Gesellschaft in der Weimarer Republik, Neue Gesellschaft für Bildende Kunst, Berlin, 1977

The New Objectivity, German Realism in the Twenties, Arts Council of Great Britain, London, 1977

Plakate der 20er Jahre, Kunstbibliothek, Berlin, 1977

Tendenzen der 20er Jahre, Neue Nationalgalerie, Berlin, 1977

El Lissitzky 1890–1941, Museum of Modern Art, Oxford, 1977

Dada and Surrealism Reviewed, Arts Council of Great Britain, London, 1978

Paris-Berlin 1900–30, Centre Georges Pompidou, Paris, 1978

Thirties: British Art and Design before the War, Arts Council of Great Britain, London, 1979

Paris-Moscou 1900–1930, Centre Georges Pompidou, Paris, 1979

Otto Arpke, Kunstbibliothek, Berlin, 1979

Les Réalismes 1919–1939: Entre Révolution et Réaction, Centre Georges Pompidou, Paris, 1980

Werbestil 1930–1940, Die alltägliche Bildersprache eines Jahrzehnts, Kunstgewerbemuseum, Zurich, 1981

Bauhaus Sammlungs Archiv, Bauhaus Archive, Berlin, 1981

Herbert Bayer: Das künstlerische Werk 1918–1938, Bauhaus Archiv, Berlin, 1982

Jan Tschichold, National Library of Scotland, Edinburgh, 1982

Simplicissimus and the Weimar Republic, Goethe Institute, Munich, 1984

Das Schweizer Plakat, Gewerbemuseum, Basel, 1984

Rationalisierung, Kunsthalle, Berlin, 1984

Der Westdeutsche Impuls 1900–1914, Kunst und Umweltgestaltung im Industriegebiet, Die deutsche Werkbund-Ausstellung Cöln 1914, Kölnischer Kunstverein, Cologne, 1984

Erich Salomon — Fotografien 1928–1938, Berlinische Galerie, Berlin, 1986

Die Aesthetik Faszination der Faschismus, Neue Gesellschaft für Bildende Kunst, Berlin, 1987

Herbert Bayer: Kunst und Design in Amerika 1938–1985, Bauhaus Archiv, Berlin, 1987

Herzblut: Populäre Gestaltung aus der Schweiz, Kunstgewerbemuseum, Zurich, 1987

Ulm: die Moral der Gegenstände, Bauhaus Archiv, Berlin, 1987

Stationen der Moderne, die bedeutenden Kunstausstellungen des 20 Jahrhunderts in Deutschland, Berlinische Galerie, Berlin, 1988

herbert bayer collection and archive at the denver art museum, Denver Art Museum, Denver, 1988

Typografie kann unter Umständen Kunst Sein (eds Volker Rattemeyer and Dietrich Helms),
1) *Kurt Schwitters, Typographie und Werbegestaltung*
2) *Vordemberge-Gildewart*
3) *Ring 'neue werbegestalter', die amsterdamer Ausstellung 1931*
4) *Ring 'neuer werbegestalter' ein Überblick 1928–1933,*
Landesmuseum, Wiesbaden and Sprengel Museum, Hanover, 1990

El Lissitzky: 1890–1941, Retrospektive, Municipal Van Abbemuseum, Eindhoven, 1990

Moholy-Nagy, IVAM Centro Julio González, Valencia, 1991

Kunst! Kommerz! Visionen! Deutsche Plakate 1888–1933, Deutsches Historisches Museum, Berlin, 1992
John Heartfield, Akademie der Künste, Berlin, 1992
Das A und O des Bauhauses, Bauhaus Archiv Museum für Gestaltung, Berlin, 1995
Die Kunst zu Werben: das Jahrhundert der Reklame, Münchner Stadtmuseum, Munich, 1996
Julius Klinger, Plakatkünstler und Zeichner, Kunstbibliothek, Berlin, 1997
Exiles and Émigrés, The Flight of European Artists from Hitler, Los Angeles County Museum, Los Angeles, 1997
Das Schöne und der Alltag — Deutsches Museum für Kunst in Handel und Gewerbe, Karl Ernst Osthaus-Museum der Stadt Hagen, Hagen, 1998
Verführungen Plakate aus Österreich und Deutschland von 1914 bis 1945, Österreichische Nationalbibliothek, Vienna; Kunstbibliothek, Berlin; and Museum für Kunst und Gewerbe, Hamburg, 1999

Periodicals

Arts et Métiers Graphiques, Paris: Deberny-Peignot, no.1–44, 1927–34
Farbe und Form, Monatsschrift für Kunst und Kunstgewerbe, Berlin: Schule Reimann, 1927–30
Die Form - Zeitschrift fur Gestaltende Arbeit, Organ des Deutschen Gewerbeschau, München, 1922, des deutschen Werkbundes, des Reichskunstwarts, des Verbandes deutscher Kunstgewerbeverein und andere Vereiningungen. Vols 1–5, Berlin: Hermann Reckendorf, 1922–34
*Gebrauchsgraphik, Monatsschrift zur Förderung künstlerischer Reklame,*Berlin: Phönix Illustrations Druck Verlag, 1924–33, and Berlin: Gebrauchsgraphik Druck und Verlag, 1934–44. From 1928 the magazine was the official organ of the Bund Deutscher Gebrauchsgraphiker.
Jahrbuch des deutschen Werkbundes, Jena: Eugen Diederichs 1912–15 and Munich: Bruckmann, 1915–20
Die Kunst im Dritten Reich, Munich: Nationalsozialistische Deutsche Arbeiter-Partei, Zentralverlag der NSDAP, 1937–39 and *Die Kunst im Deutschen Reich,* Munich: Nationalsozialistische Deutsche Arbeiter-Partei, Zentralverlag der NSDAP, 1939–44
Das Kunstblatt, Monatsschrift für künstlerische Entwicklung in Malerei, Skulptur, Baukunst, Literatur, Musik, Weimar: Verlag Gustav Kiepenheuer, 1917–33
MERZ, Nos 1–11, 1923–25, Hanover, publisher Kurt Schwitters
Das Neue Frankfurt Monatsschrift für die Fragen der Groszstadtgestaltung, 1926–34, Frankfurt am Main: Englert and Schlosser, 1926–34
Offset, Buch und Werbekunst, Das Blatt für Drucker, Werbefachleute und Verleger, ed. Siegfried Berg, Leipzig: Offset Verlag, 1–16, 1924–39
The Penrose Annual, London: Lund Humphries, London, Vols 31–37, 1929–39
Das Plakat, Berlin Charlottenburg: Verlag Max Schildberger, 1910–21
Die Reklame, Berlin: Verlag Francken und Lang, GmBH, 1924–25
Seidelsreklame, Das Blatt für Werbewesen und Verkaufstechnik, Berlin: Spaeth and Linde, 1913–19
Typographische Mitteilungen in zwangloser Folge erscheinendes Haus und Fachorgan der Typograph, Berlin: Der Typograph, 1901–33
Das Zelt: Zeitschrift des Ehmcke Kreises (ed. F.H. Ehmcke), Munich: Ehmcke Kreis, Fritz Schmidberger, 1926–30

Articles

Aynsley, Jeremy, '*Gebrauchsgraphik* as an Early Graphic Design Journal, 1924–1938', *Journal of Design History,* Oxford: Oxford University Press, 1992, v. 5, No.1, pp. 53–72
Aynsley, Jeremy, 'Pressa Cologne, 1928: exhibitions and publication design in the Weimar period', *Design Issues,* Cambridge MA, Autumn 1994, v. 10, No. 3, pp. 52–77
Bach, Kurt, 'Über die Anwendung des Hakenkreuzsymbols', *Gebrauchsgraphik,* Berlin, 1933, v. 10, No. 8
Bettmann, Georg, 'Georg Trump', *Gebrauchsgraphik,* Berlin, 1925, v. 1, No. 9, pp. 23–24
Bettmann, Otto, 'Elements of New German Typography', *Penrose Annual,* London, 1930, v. 32, pp. 116–21
Bois, Yves-Alain, 'El Lissitzky: Radical Reversibility', *Art in America,* New York, 1988, v. 76, No. 4, pp.160–81
Bois, Yves-Alain, 'El Lissitzky: Reading Lessons', *October,* Cambridge MA, 1979, No. 11, pp. 77–96
Buchloh, Benjamin, 'From Faktura to Factography', *October,* Cambridge MA, 1984, No. 30, pp. 83–118
Conrad, Rudolf, 'Frankfurt-Offenbach und die Deutsche Schrift Entwicklung seit der Jahrhundertwende', *Gebrauchsgraphik,* Berlin, 1926, v. 3, No. 3, pp. 38–41
Creative Camera, special issue: 'Der Arbeiter-Fotograf', London, May-June, 1981
Elderfield, John 'Dissenting Ideologies and the German Revolution', *Studio International,* London, 1970, No.180, pp. 180–87
Esswein, Hermann, 'Die Neue Sammlung in München', in *Die Form,* Berlin, 1929, v. 4, No. 7

Frenzel, H.K., 'Betrachtungen zur Reichsreklamemesse', *Gebrauchsgraphik*, Berlin, 1924/5, v. 1, No. 9
Frenzel, H.K., 'Pressa, Cologne 1928', *Gebrauchsgraphik*, Berlin, 1928, v. 5, No. 7
Frenzel, H.K. 'Where is Advertising Going?', *Gebrauchsgraphik*, Berlin, 1930, v. 7, No.1
Frenzel, H.K., 'The Influence of Market Fluctuations on the Demand for Advertising', *Penrose Annual*, London, 1936, v. 38, pp. 23–26
Gaunt, William, 'Germany - A Modern Utopia?', *The Studio*, London, 1929, pp. 859–65
Gloag, John, 'Design Marches On', *Penrose Annual*, London, 1938, v. 40, pp. 17–20
Hahn, Oskar M., 'Lucian Bernhard interviewed', *Gebrauchsgraphik*, Berlin, 1926, v. 3, No. 2
Hartlaub, Gustav, 'Kunst als Werbung', *Das Kunstblatt*, Weimar, June 1928, v. 12, pp. 170–76
Heskett, John, 'Art and Design in Nazi Germany', *History Workshop*, Oxford, 1978, No. 6, pp. 139–53
Hölscher, Eberhard, 'Obituary to H. K. Frenzel', in *Gebrauchsgraphik*, Berlin, 1937, v. 17, No.11
Horn, F.A., 'Print, Politics and Propaganda', *Penrose Annual*, London, 1939, v. 41, pp. 37–41
Krauss, Rosalind, 'Jump over the Bauhaus', *October*, Cambridge MA, Winter 1980, No.15
Krauss, Rosalind, 'When Words Fail', *October*, Cambridge MA, Fall 1982, No. 22
Lavin, Maud, 'Advertising Utopia: Schwitters as Commerical Designer', *Art in America*, New York, 1985, v. 73, No. 10
Lavin, Maud, 'Androgyny, spectatorship, and the Weimar Photomontages of Hannah Höch', *New German Critique*, New York: Telos Press, No. 51, Fall 1990, pp. 62–86
Lavin, Maud, 'Heartfield in Context', *Art in America*, New York, February, 1985, pp. 84–92
Lavin, Maud, 'Ringl + Pitt: The Representation of Women in Advertising, 1929–33', *The Print Collector's Newsletter*, New York, 1985, v. XVI, No. 3
Lehmann-Haupt, Hellmut, 'Berlin Commentary', *Print*, New York, 1947, v. V, No. 2
Levinger, E., 'The Theory of Hungarian Constructivism', *The Art Bulletin*, Providence, 1987, v. LXIX, No. 3
Lotz, Willy, 'Die Kamera', *Die Form*, Berlin, 1933, v. 7, pp. 321–25
Luckenhaus, H., 'A Comparison of American and German Printing', *The Inland Printer*, Chicago, August 1929, p. 92
Maier, Charles, 'Between Taylorism and Technocracy: European Ideologies and the Vision of Industrial Productivity in the 1920s', *Journal of Contemporary History*, London, Beverly Hills and New Delhi, 1970, v. 5. No.2, pp. 27–61
Molzahn, Johannes, 'Economics of the Advertising Mechanism', reprinted in English translation in Benton, Benton and Sharp (*q.v.*)
Molzahn, Johannes, 'Nicht Mehr Lesen! Sehen', *Das Kunstblatt*, Berlin, 1928, v. 12, pp. 78–82
Pevsner, Nikolaus, 'The Psychology of English and German Posters', *Penrose Annual*, London, 1936, v. 38, pp. 36–38
Porstmann, Walter, 'Kunst und Normung', *Gebrauchsgraphik*, Berlin, 1925, v. 1, No. 9, pp. 23–24
Randolph, B.W,. 'Amerikanische Universitätsausbildung in Reklame und Marktkunde', *Gebrauchsgraphik*, Berlin, 1926, v. 3, No. 2
Read, Herbert, 'A Choice of Extremes', *Penrose Annual*, London, 1937, v. 39, p. 25
Renner, Paul, 'Die Schrift unserer Zeit', *Die Form*, Berlin, 1927 , v. 2, No. 3, pp. 109–10
Rodenberg, J., 'Rudolf Koch, Designer of Letters', *Penrose Annual*, London, 1935, v. 37, p. 27
Sachs, Hans J., 'Address to the Friends of the Poster', in *Das Plakat, Mitteilungen des Vereins der Plakatfreunde*, Berlin, 1914
Schawinski, X., 'Development of Form in Advertising', *Industrial Arts*, London, 1936, v. 1, No. 3
Stein, Sally, 'The Composite Photographic Image and the Composition of Consumer Ideology', *Art Journal*, New York, 1981, v. 41, No. 1, pp. 39–45
Stein, Sally, 'The Graphic Ordering of Desire: Modernization in a Middle-class Women's Magazine, 1919–39', in *The Contest of Meaning, critical histories of photography* (ed. Richard Bolton), Cambridge MA, 1989
Stresow, Gustav, 'The Centenary of the Bauer Type-Foundry', *Penrose Annual*, London, 1938, v. 40, pp. 64–68
Stresow, Gustav, 'German Typography Today', *Penrose Annual*, London, 1937, v. 39, pp. 60–64
Tarr, J.C., 'What Are the Fruits of the New Typography?', *Penrose Annual*, London, 1935, v. 37, pp. 38–41
Tschichold, Jan, 'Abstract Painting and the New Typography', *Industrial Arts*, London, 1936, v. 1, No. 2, pp. 157–64
Westen, Walter von zur, 'Bahnbrecher der deutschen Plakatkunst', in *Das Plakat*, Berlin, 1920, v. 5, p. 231
Wieynck, Heinrich, 'Leitsätze zum Problem Zeitgemässer Druckschriftgestaltung', *Gebrauchsgraphik*, Berlin, 1931, v. 8, No. 2
Zeitler, Julius, 'Walter Tiemann zu seinem 60. Geburtstag', *Gebrauchsgraphik*, Berlin, 1936, v. 13, No. 3
Ziegert, Beate, 'The Debschitz School, Munich, 1902–14', *Design Issues*, Chicago, v. III, No. I

List of Illustrations

Frontispiece

Poster
Vim putzt alles
(Vim cleans everything)
Designed by Julius Gipkens
Printed by Hollerbaum and Schmidt, Berlin, about 1920
Lithograph, 118 x 89 cm
Berlin Kunstbibliothek 14003376

Introduction

0.1
Label for bottle
Designed by Max Hertwig
about 1910
Lithograph, 75 x 97 cm
Berlin Kunstbibliothek Graphische Sammlung 5232(374), 16

0.2
Poster
Kraft Briket
Max Beyer, about 1930
Lithograph, 79.1 x 51.4 cm
The Wolfsonian–FIU XX1990.2825

0.3
Poster
Das Deutsche Lichtbild
Designed by Georg Trump, 1930
Reproduced from Gebrauchsgraphik, September 1931 v. 8 No. 9
Published by Phoenix Verlag, Berlin
Royal College of Art Library, London

0.4
Poster
30. Januar 1933 Adolf Hitler gründet das Dritte Reich!
(Reintroduction of general conscription! Protection of German borders! Protection of national work! Occupation of the German Rhineland! The German Reich against the world market!)
Anonymous
Letterpress, 84.5 x 122.9 cm
The Wolfsonian–FIU TD1989.184.28
Photo: Peter Harholdt

Chapter One

1.1
Poster
Grosse Berliner Kunst Ausstellung
Designed by T. Lucius, 1902
Printed by M. Fischer
Kunstverlaganstalt, Berlin
Lithograph, 69.9 x 48.3 cm
The Wolfsonian–FIU 85.4.77
Photo: Willard Associates

1.2
Photograph of Fritz Hellmut Ehmcke
Reproduced from *Paul Ruben, Die Reklame: ihre Kunst und Wissenschaft Berlin:*
Hermann Pätel, 1914
V&A Museum NAL GC 94.L.22

1.3 and 1.4
Official catalogue of the Exhibition of the German Empire: International Exposition, St Louis, 1904
Designed by Peter Behrens
Published by Georg Stilke, Berlin
Number 101 in an edition of 300
Letterpress, 24 x 19 cm
© DACS 2000
The Wolfsonian–FIU 85.2.174

1.5
Opening of the essay *'An die Deutschen Künstler und Kunstfreunde!'* by Alexander Koch
Deutsche Kunst und Dekoration,
1897, v. 1, No.1
Published by Alexander Koch, Berlin and Darmstadt
29.3 x 21 cm
V&A Museum NAL PP43H

1.6
Typefoundry booklet
Behrens Schriften Initialen und Schmuck
Published by Rudhard'sche Giesserei, Offenbach am Main, 1902
Letterpress, 27.3 x 20.4 cm
© DACS 2000
The Wolfsonian–FIU TD1989.116.14

1.7
Catalogue
Österreichische Ausstellung in London, 1906
Designed by Koloman Moser
Published by the Königliche und Kaiserliche Hof- und Staatsdruckerei, Vienna
Letterpress, 21 x 12 cm
The Wolfsonian–FIU XB1990.5

1.8
Announcement
Sonderausstellung Gebr. Klingspor, Offenbach am Main, 14 March–7 April 1907 at the Kunstgewerbemuseum Frankfurt on Main
Designed by Otto Eckmann
Letterpress, 44 x 51 cm
Berlin Kunstbibliothek 4817 Si 145 c.

1.9–1.11
Typefoundry booklet
Behrens Antiqua und Schmuck
Designed by Peter Behrens, 1902
Published by Gebrüder Klingspor, Offenbach on Main
Letterpress, 27.9 x 21.5 cm
© DACS 2000
The Wolfsonian–FIU 83.2.2285

1.12
Typefoundry booklet
Majestic Typeface
Designed by Julius Gipkens
Published by Bauersche Giesserei, Frankfurt on Main, about 1910
Letterpress, 12 x 17 cm
The Wolfsonian–FIU XB1994.83

1.13
Advertisement for Kast und Ehinger, Stuttgart, 1926
Reproduced in *Offset - Buch und Werbekunst Das Blatt für Drucker, Werbefachleute und Verleger,*
No.2, 1926
Private Collection

1.14
Advertisement for
Cröllwitzer paper factory, 1926
Halle-Cröllwitz
Designed by Franz Paul Glass
Printer Offset Werkdruck
Reproduced in *Offset - Buch und Werbekunst Das Blatt für Drucker, Werbefachleute und Verleger,*
No.2, 1926
Private Collection

1.15
Book
Klassische Schriften nach Zeichnungen von Gutenberg, Dürer, Morris, König, Hupp, Eckmann, Behrens u.a.
(Classical Typefaces after drawings by Gutenberg, Dürer, Morris, König, Hupp, Eckmann, Behrens and others)
Edited by Rudolf Koch
Printed by Wilhelm Woellmers foundry, Berlin
Published by Grimme and Trömel, Leipzig, n.d.
Letterpress, 25 x 33 cm
The Wolfsonian–FIU XC1994.3909

1.16
Catalogue
Katalog der Deutschen Buchgewerbeausstellung, Paris 1900
Designed by Johann Vincenz Cissarz
Published by Breitkopf und Hartel, Leipzig on behalf of the Deutsche Buchgewerbeverein, Leipzig
20 x 13 cm
The Wolfsonian–FIU 83.2.7

1.17
Periodical
Pan, 1895 v.1 No.1
Titlepage illustrated by Joseph Sattler
Published by Genossenschaft Pan, Berlin
Lithograph, 38 x 28 cm
Berlin Kunstbibliothek 5842.5 06.96.401

1.18
Periodical
Ver Sacrum, January 1898 v.1, No.1
Published by Gerlach and Schenk, Vienna
30 x 29 cm
The Wolfsonian–FIU XB1990.2123

1.19
Periodical
Archiv für Buchgewerbe,
1900 v. 37 No. 1
Published by Deutsche Buchgewerbeverein, Leipzig
Lithograph, 31 x 24 cm
The Wolfsonian–FIU XC1992.735

1.20
Poster
Richard Strauss Woche
Designed by Ludwig Hohlwein, 1910
Printed by Vereinigte Druckereien und Kunstanstalten, Munich
Lithograph, 120.6 x 90.4 cm
© DACS 2000
V&A Museum E.348–1921

1.21–1.22
Book
Die Nibelungen dem deutschen Volke
Retold by Franz Keim
Designed by Carl Otto Czeschka, 1909
Published by Verlag Gerlach and Wielding, Vienna and Leipzig
16 x 14 cm
The Wolfsonian–FIU 83.2.367

1.23
Book
Also Sprach Zarathustra: ein Buch für Alle und Keinen
Written by Friedrich Wilhelm Nietzsche
Designed by Henry van de Velde
Typeface designed by Georges Lemmen
Published by Insel Verlag, Leipzig 1908
Letterpress and lithograph, 38 x 26 cm
The Wolfsonian–FIU XB1990.94
Photo: Bruce White

1.24
Poster
Tropon, Eiweiss Nahrung
Designed by Henry van de Velde, 1897
Lithograph, 34.5 x 17 cm
V&A Museum Circ.992–1967

1.25
Photograph of a shopwindow with a display of Tropon goods about 1910
Reproduced from the *Deutsche Werkbund Jahrbuch*, 1913
V&A Museum L.2620.1913

1.26
Periodical
Das Plakat
Cover to the 1916 bound volume
Designed by Lucian Bernhard
Ink on linen and board
28 x 23.2 x 4.5 cm
© DACS 2000
V&A Museum L.435.1940

1.27
Book
Das Moderne Plakat
Written by Jean Louis Sponsel
Published by Verlag von Gerhard Kühtmann, Dresden, 1897
Letterpress and lithograph, 30 x 24 cm
The Wolfsonian–FIU 84.2.374
Photo: Peter Harholdt

1.28
Photograph of Hans Sachs in his 'student den' in Berlin, 1901
Deutsches Historisches Museum, Berlin

1.29
Poster
Scholle München XXV. Ausstellung der Sezession, 1905
Designed by Adolf Münzer
Printed by Klein and Volbert, Munich
Lithograph, 94.9 x 66.4 cm
The Wolfsonian–FIU XX1990.3037

1.30
Poster
Deutscher Werkbund Ausstellung Ortsgruppe Crefeld, 5 April–7 Mai 1911
Designed by Fritz Hellmut Ehmcke
Lithograph, 69.9 x 50 cm
The Wolfsonian–FIU TD1988.48.2
Photo: David Joyall

1.31
Tobacco Box
Feinhals, Köln Deutsche Werkbund Ausstellung, 1913–14
Designed by Fritz Hellmut Ehmcke
Manufactured by Joseph Feinhals, Cologne
Wood, paper, lithograph,
4.5 x 30.2 x 26.7 cm
The Wolfsonian–FIU TD1990.99.7
Photo: Bruce White

1.32–1.35
Four packaging labels
Designed by Max Hertwig, about 1910
Lithographs
Berlin Kunstbibliothek Graphische Sammlung 5232(374), 16

Oliven-Oel H. Braas
72 x 117 cm

Radikaal
Hertels Wanzenmittel
82 x 130 cm

Risslinger
89 x 133 cm

Union Celloidin-Postkarten
89 x 125 cm

1.36
Book
Julius Klinger, 1912
Volume III in the series *Monographien Deutscher Reklamekünstler*
Printed and published by Fr.Wilhelm Ruhfus, Hagen and Dortmund under the auspices of the Deutsches Museum für Handel in Kunst und Gewerbe, Hagen
Letterpress, 24 x 19 cm
The Wolfsonian–FIU 83.2.372

1.37
Poster
Kölner Ausstellung, 1907
Designed by Josef Maria Olbrich
Printed by M. Dumont Schauberg, Cologne
Lithograph, 103 x 83.5 cm
The Wolfsonian–FIU TD1990.161.5
Photo: David Joyall

1.38
Photograph of the entrance gallery of the Museum Folkwang, Hagen remodelled by Henry Van de Velde in 1901–2
Karl Ernst Osthaus Museum, Hagen BK 088

1.39
Photograph of the exterior of the Salamander shoe shop Berlin, 1910–11
Designed by August Endell
Karl Ernst Osthaus Museum, Hagen BK031

1.40
The new building of the Academy for Graphic Arts and Books Trades in Leipzig in 1890
Hochschule für Graphik und Buchkunst, Leipzig

1.41
Advertisement for the Leipzig Advertising Fair, 1927
Designed by Georg Baus
Reproduced from *Gebrauchsgraphik*, September 1927, v. 4 No. 9
Royal College of Art, London

1.42–1.43
Book
Das Stundenbuch
Poems by Rainer Maria Rilke
Designed by Walter Tiemann
Published by Insel Presse, Leipzig, 1921
18.8 x 12.2 cm
© DACS 2000
Private collection

1.44
Poster
Kronleuchter Fabrik Möhring
Designed by Julius Klinger, 1909
Printed by Hollerbaum und Schmidt, Berlin
Lithograph, 76.5 x 98.7 cm
The Wolfsonian–FIU 86.4.24
Photo: Willard Associates

1.45
Poster
Oliver Schreibmaschine
Designed by Paul Scheurich, 1909
Printed by Hollerbaum und Schmidt, Berlin
Lithograph, 76.5 x 98.7 cm
The Wolfsonian–FIU TD1990.161.7
Photo: David Joyall

1.46
Tins
Kaffee Hag
Designed by Alfred Runge and Eduard Scotland, about 1910
Manufactured by Kaffee-Handels-Aktiengesellschaft, Bremen
Tinned steel, enamel paint
left, 20.3 x 20.3 x 9.8 cm
centre, 10.2 x 6.4 x 4.1 cm
right, 29.9 x 22.2 21.6 cm
The Wolfsonian–FIU TD1990.270.7a,b; TD1992.9.15; TD1990.95.9
Photo: Bruce White

1.47
Photograph
Friedrichstrasse, Berlin in 1907
Photographed by Max Mischmann
Märkisches Museum, Berlin

1.48
Photograph
The department store Ka De We.
Reproduced from Das Kaufhaus des Westens, 1932, edited by Max Osborn
The Wolfsonian–FIU XC1991.879

1.49
Poster
'200 Plakatsaülen'
Düsseldorf Poster Column Company, 1926
Designed by Germain
Printed by Offset Graf and Schumacher, Düsseldorf
Lithograph
© DACS 2000
Reproduced from *Gebrauchsgraphik*, August 1927, v. 4 No. 8
Royal College of Art Library

1.50
Poster
Plakat Kunst
Poster issued by the Leipzig Advertising Fair, Leipzig
Designed by Fritz Buchholz, about1925
Printed by Naumann, Leipzig
Lithograph, 91 x 60.5 cm
V&A Museum E.1500–1926

1.51
Poster
Garbáty Flaggen gala
Designed by Julius Gipkens, about 1914
Printed by Hollerbaum and Schmidt, Berlin
Lithograph, 115.6 x 87 cm
The Wolfsonian–FIU TD1990.296.4
Photo: David Joyall

1.52
Advertisement
Hamburger Verkehrsreklame
Hoenicke and Kypke, Hamburg
Reproduced from *Gebrauchsgraphik*, November 1931, v. 8 No. 11
Royal College of Art, London

1.53
Photograph
Berlin poster column
Reproduced from *Gebrauchsgraphik*, October 1926, v. 3 No. 10
Royal College of Art, London

1.54
Photograph
Posters on the Berlin underground
Reproduced from *Gebrauchsgraphik*, September 1927, v. 4 No. 9
Royal College of Art, London

Chapter Two

2.1
Print
Der Kuss
Peter Behrens, 1898
Woodcut, 27.3 x 21.7 cm
© DACS 2000
Berlin Kunstbibliothek 5133,1

2.2
Invitation card
Ausstellung Peter Behrens, Frankfurt am Main
Designed by Peter Behrens, 1909 employing his *'Antiqua'* typeface
Letterpress, 10 x 15 cm
© DACS 2000
The Wolfsonian–FIU XB1992.1497

2.3–2.4
Envelopes for the *Wiener Werkstätte* Incorporating the monogram for the *Vienna Neustiftgasse* branch
Designed by Josef Hoffmann and Koloman Moser
11 x 19 cm and 10 x 15 cm
The Wolfsonian–FIU XB1992.1503 and XB1992.1876

2.5
Der Bunte Vogel
Illustration and typographic arrangement for Otto Julius Bierbaum's calendar book
Designed by Peter Behrens
Published by Verlag Schuster and Loeffler, Berlin and Leipzig, 1899
Lithograph, 28.2 x 21.6 cm
© DACS 2000
Berlin Kunstbibliothek 5133,5

2.6
Title page
Feste des Lebens und der Kunst: eine Betrachtung des Theaters als höchsten Kultursymbols
Designed by Peter Behrens
Published by Eugen Diederichs, Berlin 1900
Printed by C. F. Winter'schen Buchdruckerei, Darmstadt
23 x 16.5 cm
© DACS 2000
V&A Museum L.5919–1985

2.7
Poster
Kunstausstellung Darmstadt
Designed by Otto Ubbelohde, 1911
Printed by H. Hohmann Hof Buch und Steindruckerei, Darmstadt
Lithograph, 82.2 x 60.1 cm
The Wolfsonian–FIU TD1989.163.2
Photo: David Joyall

2.8
Poster
Darmstadt, ein Dokument Deutscher Kunst, Die Ausstellung der Künstlerkolonie
Designed by Peter Behrens, 1901
Printed by Jos. Scholz, Mainz
Lithograph, 127 x 43. 8 cm
© DACS 2000
The Wolfsonian–FIU TD1991.134.2
Photo: Bruce White

2.9–2.11 as 1.6
© DACS 2000

2.12
Magazine cover
Die Kunst für Alle
Special issue on Arnold Böcklin
Designed by Peter Behrens employing 'Behrens' typeface
Published by Bruckmann Verlag, Munich 1901
29.4 x 21.1 cm
© DACS 2000
Berlin Kunstbibliothek 5133 7

2.13–2.15
Book
Peter Behrens Monographien Deutscher Reklamekünstler, Volume 5
Written by F. Meyer-Schönbrunn
Published by Deutsches Museum für Handel und Gewerbe, Hagen and Dortmund, 1913
24 x 19 cm
© DACS 2000
The Wolfsonian–FIU XB1990.38

2.16
Poster
Deutsche Werkbund Ausstellung
Designed by Peter Behrens
Printed by A. Molling and Comp. K.-G. Hanover and Berlin
Lithograph, 90 x 63 cm
© DACS 2000
V&A Museum E.279–1982

2.17
Poster
Deutscher Werkbund Cöln
Designed by Fritz Hellmut Ehmcke
Reproduced from F.H. Ehmcke, *Persönliches und Sachliches*
Published by Hermann Reckendorf, Berlin, 1928
The Wolfsonian–FIU TD1989.341.6

2.18–2.19
Book
Sonette nach dem Portugiesischen
Poems by Elizabeth Barrett Browning
Designed by Fritz Hellmut Ehmcke
Published by Eugen Diederichs,
Leipzig, 1903
Printed by Steglitzer Werkstatt, Berlin
Gold ink stamped on vellum
and letterpress, 22 x 18 cm
The Wolfsonian–FIU XB1990.1986

2.20–2.22
Small advertisement, five cut-out dolls and collectors' stamps for *Syndetikon* glue
Designed by Fritz Hellmut Ehmcke, 1903
Lithograph
Berlin Kunstbibliothek Ehmcke, 5213 (575) no.4; 5213 (575) no.15 and 5213 (575) no.18.

2.23–2.25
Book
Unterricht in ornamentaler Schrift
Written by Rudolf von Larisch
Printed by Kaiserliche und Königliche Hof- und Staatsdruckerei, Vienna, 1909
Published by Kaiserliche und Königliche Staatsdruckerei, Vienna
Second revised edition
Letterpress, 24 x 16 cm
The Wolfsonian–FIU XB1989.176

2.26–2.27
Typefoundry booklet
Ehmcke Mediaeval
Designed by Fritz Hellmut Ehmcke, 1926
Published by D. Stempel, Frankfurt am Main, Leipzig and Budapest
Letterpress, 30 x 23 cm
The Wolfsonian–FIU TD1990.331.148

2.28
Typefoundry booklet
Ehmcke Fraktur
Designed by Fritz Hellmut Ehmcke, 1912
Published by W. Drugulin,
Vienna and Leipzig
Letterpress, 20 x 16 cm
The Wolfsonian–FIU TD1990.331.145

2.29
Typefoundry booklet
Ehmcke Elzevir
Designed by Fritz Hellmut Ehmcke, 1928
Published by Ludwig Wagner, Leipzig
Letterpress, 27 x 21 cm
The Wolfsonian–FIU TD1990.331.146

2.30
Poster
Reklameschau Berlin
Designed by Lucian Bernhard
and Fritz Rosen, 1929
Printed by Hans Pusch GmbH, Berlin
Lithograph, 83 x 58.3 cm
© DACS 2000
The Wolfsonian–FIU 85.4.84
Photo: Willard Associates

2.31
Poster
Deutsche Werkstätten Jetzt
Designed by Lucian Bernhard, 1912
Printed by Klein and Volbert, Munich
Lithograph, 104.8 x 70.3 cm
© DACS 2000
The Wolfsonian–FIU TD1991.146.5
Photo: Peter Harholdt

2.32
Poster
Stiller Shoes
Designed by Lucian Bernhard, 1907–08
Printed by Hollerbaum and Schmidt, Berlin
Lithograph, 65.5 x 94.9 cm
© DACS 2000
V&A Museum E.928–1966

2.33
Poster
Oigee Binoculars
Designed by Lucian Bernhard, 1912
Printed by Hollerbaum and Schmidt, Berlin
Lithograph, 83.8 x 62.9 cm
© DACS 2000
V&A Museum Circ.613–1971

2.34
Poster
Die Deutsche Demokratische Partei ist die Partei der Frauen!
Designed by Lucian Bernhard, 1920
Printed by Werbedienst GmbH, Berlin
Lithograph, 69.9 x 96.2 cm
© DACS 2000
The Wolfsonian–FIU TD1990.296.1
Photo: Peter Harholdt

2.35
Poster
Manoli Kardash Cigarettes
Designed by Lucian Bernhard, 1912
Printed by Hollerbaum and Schmidt, Berlin
Lithograph, 69.7 x 94.7 cm
© DACS 2000
V&A Museum E.624–1915

2.36
Poster
Blende nicht - leuchte mit Bosch-Licht!
Designed by Lucian Bernhard and
Fritz Rosen
Reproduced from *Gebrauchsgraphik*,
February 1927, v. 3 No. 2
© DACS 2000
Royal College of Art, London

2.37
Poster
Lärme nicht - warne mit Bosch-Horn
Designed by Lucian Bernhard
and Fritz Rosen
Reproduced from *Gebrauchsgraphik*,
February 1927, v. 3 No. 2
© DACS 2000
Royal College of Art, London

2.38
Magazine
Gebrauchsgraphik,
February 1927, v. 3 No. 2
Designed by Lucian Bernhard
and Fritz Rosen
32 x 24.2 cm
© DACS 2000
Royal College of Art Library, London

2.39
Photograph of Lucian Bernhard (right) with Hans Sachs in New York 1956
Deutsches Historisches Museum

2.40
Poster
Amoco Gas
Designed by Lucian Bernhard, 1949
110 x 69.6 cm, Lithograph
© DACS 2000
V&A Museum E.2934–1980

Chapter Three

3.1
Periodical
Farbe und Form
Ein Bildprospekt der Schule Reimann
Monatsschrift für Kunst und Gewerbe
Reimannschule, Berlin
Edited by Albert Reimann
Published by Reimannschule, Berlin, 1927
Berlin Kunstbibliothek,
Kasten Schule Reimann

3.2
Book
Staatliches Bauhaus Weimar 1919–1923
Written by Walter Gropius
and Laszlo Moholy-Nagy
Cover designed by Herbert Bayer
Interior layout designed by
Laszlo Moholy-Nagy
Published by Bauhaus Verlag,
Weimar, 1923
Printed by F. Bruckmann A.G., Munich
25 x 26 cm
© DACS 2000
The Wolfsonian–FIU TD1988.67.28

3.3
Poster
Arbeiter! Bannt die Gefahr von Rechts! Wählt Sozialisten!
Designed by Joseph Schwingen,
Schlegl and Kötter, 1920
Printed by Kunst im Druck, Munich
Lithograph, 124.8 x 94.9 cm
The Wolfsonian–FIU XX1990.3040
Photo: David Joyall

3.4
Periodical
Das Politische Plakat
Written by Adolf Behne,
Paul Landau and Herbert Löwing
Edited by Heinrich Schwarz
Printed by A. Wohlfeld, Magdeburg
Published by *Das Plakat*, Berlin
Charlottenburg, 1919
Lithograph, 24 x 18 cm
© DACS 2000
The Wolfsonian–FIU 84.2.374

3.5
Poster
Schafft Rote Hilfe!
Fünf Jahre I. R. H. 1923–1928
Designed by Heinrich Vogeler
Printed by Peuvag, Berlin
Lithograph, 79.9 x 53.3 cm
© DACS 2000
The Wolfsonian–FIU TD1990.34.11
Photo: Peter Harholdt

3.6
Poster
Nie Wieder Krieg
Poster for the *Mitteldeutscher Jugendtag*
Designed by Käthe Kollwitz, 1924
Lithograph, 94 x 69.5 cm
© DACS 2000
Berlin Kunstbibliothek 14003587

3.7
Das Illustrierte Blatt
(The Frankfurt Illustrated Newspaper)
v. 6 No. 18 (5 May 1928)
Frankfurt am Main: Frankfurter
Societäts-Druckerei GmbH, 1928
Photograph by Sasha Stone
39 x 28.2 cm
V&A Museum NAL Osman Gidal Archive

3.8
Das Illustrierte Blatt
(The Frankfurt Illustrated Newspaper),
v. 6 No. 36 (8 September 1928)
Frankfurt am Main: Frankfurter Societäts-Druckerei GmbH, 1928
39 x 28.2 cm
V&A Museum NAL Osman Gidal Archive

3.9
Das Illustrierte Blatt
(The Frankfurt Illustrated Newspaper)
v. 6 No. 46 (14 November 1928)
Frankfurt am Main: Frankfurter Societäts-Druckerei GmbH, 1928
39 x 28.2 cm
V&A Museum NAL Osman Gidal Archive

3.10
Berliner Illustrierte Zeitung,
No. 10 (10 March 1929)
Berlin: Verlag Ullstein und co., 1929
Photograph by Riebicke
37.5 x 28 cm
V&A Museum NAL Osman Gidal Archive

3.11
Berliner Illustrierte Zeitung,
No. 4 (27 January 1929)
Berlin: Verlag Ullstein und co., 1929
Photograph Ullstein
37.5 x 28 cm
V&A Museum NAL Osman Gidal Archive

3.12–3.13 as 3.2
© DACS 2000

3.14
Print
Scene from Hoffmann
Paul Klee, 1921
Number 6 from the portfolio,
Neue Europäische Graphik
Erste Mappe, Weimar
Lithograph, 57 x 45.2 cm
© DACS 2000
V&A Museum Circ.134–1951

3.15–3.17 as 3.2

3.18
Photomontage
Jealousy
Laszlo Moholy-Nagy, 1927
30 x 24.6 cm
© DACS 2000
V&A Museum Circ.204–1974

3.19–3.20
Book
Die gegenstandslose Welt
Bauhausbücher 11
Written by Kazimir Malevich
Designed by Laszlo Moholy-Nagy
Published by Albert Langen, Munich, 1927
24 x 19 cm
© DACS 2000
The Wolfsonian–FIU TD1990.331.83

3.21
Book jacket
Malerei Photografie Film
(Bauhausbücher 8)
Written and designed
by Laszlo Moholy-Nagy
Published by Albert Langen Verlag, Munich
Second edition 1927
23 x 55 cm
© DACS 2000
V&A Museum NAL Jobbing Printing Archive

3.22
Book
Kubismus
Bauhausbücher 13
Written by Albert Gleizes
Cover designed by
Laszlo Moholy-Nagy
Published by Albert Langen, Munich, 1928
24 x 19 cm
© DACS 2000
The Wolfsonian–FIU TD1990.331.84

3.23
Leaflet
14 Bauhausbücher
Designed by Laszlo Moholy-Nagy
Published by Albert Langen Verlag,
Munich, 1929
Lithograph, 21 x 15 cm
© DACS 2000
V&A Museum NAL Jobbing Printing Archive

3.24
Periodical cover
Bauhaus magazine, 1928 v. 2 No. 2/3
Designed by Herbert Bayer
Reproduced from *Gebrauchsgraphik*,
July 1930, v. 7, No. 7
© DACS 2000
Royal College of Art, London

3.25–3.27
Announcements
Die Futura,
Typeface designed by Paul Renner
Available from Bauersche Gießerei,
Frankfurt am Main
Reproduced from Satz
und Druck Muster Heft
Published by Verlag der Graphischen
Monatsschrift deutscher Drucker,
Berlin, 1930
Private Collection

3.28
Advertisement
Elementare Typographie
mit Erbar Grotesk
Typeface designed by Jakob Erbar
Available from Ludwig and Mayer,
Frankfurt am Main
Reproduced from *Gebrauchsgraphik*,
August 1927, v. 4, No. 8
Royal College of Art, London

3.29
Advertisement
Berthold Grotesk
Typeface designed by Georg Trump
Available from Berthold, Berlin
Reproduced from *Gebrauchsgraphik*,
January 1930, v. 7, No. 1
Royal College of Art, London

3.30
Advertisement
Kabel Light and Bold
Available from Gebr. Klingspor,
Offenbach am Main
Typeface designed by Rudolf Koch
Reproduced from *Gebrauchsgraphik*,
November 1929, v. 6 No. 11
Royal College of Art, London

3.31
Advertisement
Fabriken Fortschritt for filing cabinet
Designed by Johannes Canis
Reproduced from *Jan Tschichold*
Eine Stunde Druckgestaltung, 1930
Published by Dr Fritz Wedekind & Co.,
Stuttgart
The Wolfsonian–FIU TD1990.194.60

3.32
Announcement
Die Monotype
Universal setting machine
Designed by Herbert Bayer, 1926
Printed by Bauhaus, Dessau
Lithograph, 31 x 23 cm
© DACS 2000
The Wolfsonian–FIU Herbert Bayer Archive

3.33
Announcement
Korallenschrift
For a typeface available from
J.G.Schelter and Giesecke, Leipzig
Designed by Herbert Bayer, 1926
Printed by Bauhaus, Dessau
Lithograph, 31 x 23 cm
© DACS 2000
The Wolfsonian–FIU Herbert Bayer Archive

3.34
Typefoundry booklet
Signal
Designed by Herbert Bayer, 1929
Published by Berthold AG, Berlin
Lithograph, 30 x 21 cm
© DACS 2000
V&A Museum NAL Jobbing Printing Archive

3.35
Printer's proof
'Universal' alphabet
Designed by Herbert Bayer, 1926
Letterpress, 16.2 x 24 cm
© DACS 2000
V&A Museum NAL Jobbing Printing Archive

3.36–3.38
Studies of ornament, 1913–33
Designed by Max Hertwig
Ink on paper, 42 x 30 cm
Berlin Kunstbibliothek, 5233 a,
number 3, 12 and 67

3.39
Four letterheads
Designed by Max Hertwig, about 1913
29.5 x 21 cm
Berlin Kunstbibliothek, 5232 (374) 13

3.40
Periodical
Farbe und Form
Monatsschrift für Kunst und Kunstgewerbe
Designed by Max Hertwig, 1927
Edited by Albert Reimann
Published by Reimannschule, Berlin
Berlin Kunstbibliothek,
Kasten Schule Reimann

Chapter Four

4.1
Poster
Köln, Mai bis Oktober,
Weltschau am Rhein, 1928
Designed by Werkstatt F.H. Ehmcke, René
Binder and Max Eichheim
Printed by Offsetdruck Kölner-Görres-Haus
Lithograph, 70.5 x 50 cm
The Wolfsonian–FIU XX1990.3329
Photo: David Joyall

4.2
Catalogue
Das Internationale Plakat, 1929
Designed by Franz Paul Glass
Published by Städtereklame GmbH, Munich
Lithograph, 19 x 13 cm
The Wolfsonian–FIU XB1990.1812

4.3
Photograph of H. K. Frenzel, editor
of the magazine *Gebrauchsgraphik*
Reproduced from *Gebrauchsgraphik*,
October 1926, v. 3 No. 10
Royal College of Art, London

4.4
Magazine
Gebrauchsgraphik
Titlepage
January 1930, v. 7 No. 1
32 x 24.2 cm
Royal College of Art, London

4.5–4.13
Magazine covers
Gebrauchsgraphik
32 x 24.2 cm
Royal College of Art, London
4.5 Kreuscher, August 1925, v.2 No.8
4.6 Werbebau, Max Burchartz and
Johannes Canis, August 1926,
v. 3 No. 8. © DACS 2000
4.7 Hans Möhring, Leipzig issue,
December 1926, v. 3 No. 12
4.8 Uli Huber, October 1928,
v. 5 No. 10
4.9 Max Bittrof, December 1928,
v. 5 No. 12
4.10 Grit Kallin, June 1930, v. 7 No. 6
4.11 A.M. Cassandre, March 1930,
v. 7 No. 3
4.12 Joseph Binder, June 1931,
v. 8 No. 6
4.13 Stephan Schwarz, July 1931,
v. 7 No. 7

4.14
Poster
Hut ab vor dem neuen Chrysler 65!
Designed by Ashley Havinden, 1929
Printed by Crawfords Reklame-Agentur,
Berlin
Lithograph, 55.9 x 94 cm
The Wolfsonian–FIU 87.1136.4.1
Photo: Willard Associates

4.15
Advertisement for Crawfords Agency
Reproduced from *Gebrauchsgraphik*,
February 1928, v. 5 No. 2
Royal College of Art, London

4.16–4.17
Magazine layout
Article on El Lissitzky
Gebrauchsgraphik,
December 1928, v. 5 No. 12
© DACS 2000
Royal College of Art, London

4.18
Photograph of Otto Arpke
by Martin Höhlig
Reproduced from *Gebrauchsgraphik*,
December 1930, v.7 No. 12
Royal College of Art, London

4.19
Magazine layout
Article on Reynaldo Luza
Gebrauchsgraphik,
February 1930, v. 7 No. 2
Royal College of Art, London

4.20
Magazine layout
Article on Dora Mönkemeyer-Corty
Gebrauchsgraphik,
March 1930, v. 7, No. 3
Royal College of Art, London

4.21
Poster
Adler Turf Cigarettes, Dresden
Designed by
Dora Mönkemeyer-Corty, 1921
Printed by Kunstanstalt Jais, Dresden
Colour lithograph, 120 x 89.6 cm
Berlin Kunstbibiliothek 14050631

4.22
Page of advertisements
Gebrauchsgraphik,
February 1931, v. 8, No. 2
Royal College of Art, London

4.23
Poster
Elektrizität im Haushalt
Designed by Ludwig Hohlwein, 1924
Printed by Kunstanstalt Gebr.
Reichel, Augsburg
Lithograph, 104.5 x 74.9 cm
© DACS 2000
The Wolfsonian–FIU 87.4.32

4.24
Periodical
Arts et Métiers Graphiques,
No.16, 15 March 1930
Edited by A. François Haab
Published by Charles Peignot, Paris
Private Collection

4.25
Aerial view of Pressa taken by
Raab-Katzenstein Flugzeugwerk.
Reproduced from *Pressa: Kulturschau am Rhein, Cologne:*
Verlag Max Schröder, 1928
V&A Museum L.2263–1925

4.26–4.29 as 4.25

4.30
Advertisement
Die Kölnische Zeitung
Designed by Rolf Lange for M. Du Mont Schauberg
Reproduced from *Gebrauchsgraphik*, July 1928, v. 5 No. 7
Royal College of Art, London

4.31–4.35 as 4.25
(4.33 © DACS 2000)

4.36–4.39
Catalogue
Union der sozialistischen Sowjet-Republiken: Katalog des Sowjet-Pavillons auf der Internationalen Presse-Ausstellung, Köln, 1928
Written and printed by the Komitee des Sowjet-Pavillons auf der Internationalen Presse-Ausstellung
Typography and photomontage designed by El Lissitzky
Letterpress and lithograph, 22 x 16 cm
© DACS 2000
The Wolfsonian–FIU XB1990.791

4.40
Postcard addressed to Jan Tschichold, 25 July 1928
Designed by Kurt Schwitters, 1924
10.5 x 14.5 cm
© DACS 2000
V&A Museum NAL Jobbing Printing Archive

4.41
Poster
Musik im Leben der Völker
Designed by Kurt Schwitters, 1924
Reproduced from *Gebrauchsgraphik*, March 1930, v. 7, No. 3
© DACS 2000
Royal College of Art, London

4.42
Poster
Der Stuhl
Designed by Willi Baumeister, 1929
Lithograph, 63 x 86 cm
© DACS 2000
Berlin Kunstbibliothek 14004187

4.43
Advertising leaflet
TVM, Technische Vereinigung Magdeburg
Designed by Johannes Molzahn, 1929
Lithograph, 11 x 15 cm
The Wolfsonian–FIU 86.19.986

4.44
Catalogue
Der Stuhl
Edited by Heinz Rasch and Bodo Rasch
Published by Akademischer Verlag Dr Fritz Wedekind and Co., Stuttgart
25 x 18 cm
The Wolfsonian–FIU TD1990.157.5

4.45
Catalogue
Wohnung und Werkraum
Designed by Johannes Molzahn
Published by Deutsche Werkbund, 1929
22 x 15 cm
The Wolfsonian–FIU XC1991.119

4.46–4.51
Book
Gefesselter Blick: 25 kurze Monographien über neue Werbegestaltung
Edited by Heinz Rasch and Bodo Rasch
Published by Wissenschaftlicher Verlag Dr Zaugg and Co., Stuttgart, 1930
27 x 22 cm
© DACS 2000
The Wolfsonian–FIU TD1990.324.1

4.52
Magazine cover
Der Sinn von Genf
John Heartfield
Published in *Arbeiter Illustrierte Zeitung: das Illustrierte Volksblatt (AIZ)* 27 November 1932, v. XI, No. 48
Published by Neuer Deutscher Verlag
38 x 28 cm
© DACS 2000
The Wolfsonian–FIU XB1990.2047

4.53
Photomontage
Nach Zehn Jahren, Väter und Söhne
John Heartfield, 1924
38.9 x 50.5 cm
© DACS 2000
V&A Museum Ph.295–1980

4.54
Magazine cover
Der Sinn der Hitlergrusses: Kleiner Mann bittet um grosse Gaben, Motto: Millionen stehen hinter mir!
John Heartfield
Published in *Arbeiter Illustrierte Zeitung: das Illustrierte Volksblatt (AIZ)* 16 October 1932, v. 11, No. 42,
Published by Neuer Deutscher Verlag
38 x 28 cm
© DACS 2000
V&A Museum Ph.30–1980

4.55
Poster
Napoleon
Designed by Jan Tschichold, 1927
For Phoebus Palast cinema, Munich
Linocut and half-tone, 119 x 84 cm
Reproduced from *Gebrauchsgraphik*, February 1928, v. 5, No. 2
Royal College of Art, London

4.56 as 4.46

4.57
Book
Typographische Gestaltung
Designed and written by Jan Tschichold, 1935
Published by Benno Schwabe & Co., Basel
22 x 16 cm
The Wolfsonian–FIU TD1990.40.53

4.58
Poster
Laster der Menschheit
A film poster for Phoebus Palast, Munich
Designed by Jan Tschichold, 1927
119 x 84 cm
Reproduced from *Eine Stunde Druckgestaltung*
The Wolfsonian–FIU TD1990.194.60

4.59
Poster
Die Frau ohne Namen
A film poster for Phoebus Palast, Munich
Designed by Jan Tschichold, 1927
Linocut and half-tone, 122 x 86.5 cm
Berlin Kunstbibliothek no, Bi 1928, 21/4

4.60–4.62
Cover and two interior sheets from industrial prospectus
Bochumer Verein für Bergbau und Gußstahlfabrikation
Designed by 'WERBEBAU' Max Burchartz and Johannes Canis, 1925
30 x 21.5 cm
© DACS 2000
V&A Museum NAL Jobbing Printing Archive

Chapter Five

5.1
Poster
Grosse Deutsche Kunstausstellung im Haus der Deutschen Kunst zu München, 1938
Designed by Richard Klein
Printed by Kunst im Druck, Munich
Lithograph, 119.4 x 83.8 cm
The Wolfsonian–FIU XX1992.249
Photo: Peter Harholdt

5.2
Poster
Ganz Deutschland hört den Führer mit dem Volksempfänger
(All of Germany listens to the Führer with the People's Receiver)
Designed by Leonid, 1936
Published by Reichsrundfunkkammer
Printed by Preussischer Druckerei und Verlgs AG, Berlin
Lithograph, 119.4 x 84.8 cm
The Wolfsonian–FIU XX1990.3116
Photo: David Joyall

5.3
Catalogue
Volkswagen-werk GmbH, Berlin
Illustrated by Thomas Abeking
Published by Transart Aktiengesellschaft für Zellglas-Kunstdruck, about 1937
Lithograph, 21 x 30 cm
The Wolfsonian–FIU 84.2.612

5.4
Periodical
Die Kunst im Deutschen Reich, 1941
Published by the Nationalsozialistische Deutsche Arbeiter-Partei
Munich
36 x 29 cm
The Wolfsonian–FIU XC1991.1102

5.5
Catalogue
Grosse Deutsche Kunst Ausstellung 1940: im Haus der deutschen Kunst zu München
Based on a design by Richard Klein
Published by Haus der Deutschen Kunst zu München, Munich, 1940
Lithograph, 21 x 12 cm
The Wolfsonian–FIU XB 1992.1740

5.6
Poster
Auf nach Nürnberg, 1–4 August, 1929 Reichsparteitag der N.S.D.A.P.
Designed by Scheller
Printed by Druck und Verlag der N.S.D.A.P. Munich
Lithograph, 121.9 x 85.7 cm
The Wolfsonian–FIU TD1989.184.25
Photo: David Joyall

5.7
Poster
Reichssporttag des Bund Deutsches Mädchen, 23 September 1934
Designed by Ludwig Hohlwein
Printed by Chromolithographische Anstalt, Munich
Lithograph, 120.3 x 84.8.cm
© DACS 2000
The Wolfsonian–FIU XX1990.2965
Photo: Peter Harholdt

5.8
Poster
Der Führer versprach: Motorisierungs Deutschlands
(The Führer promised the motorisation of Germany)
Der Führer gab 250,000 arbeitslosen Volksgenossen Arbeit und Brot
Der Führer schafft: den Volkswagen
Darum Deutsches Volk - danke dem Führer am 29. März 1936
Gib ihm dein Stimme!
Designed by Werner von Axter-Heudtlass, 1936
Printed by Hugo Fischer, Munich
Lithograph, 104.5 x 86.4 cm
The Wolfsonian–FIU TD1989.184.1

5.9
Poster
Schaffendes Landvolk
An exhibition held in the Nordostseehalle, Kiel 17–25 July 1937
Designed by Anto, 1937
Published by Blut und Boden, Institut für Deutsche Wirtschaftspropaganda
Lithograph, 82.2 x 58.4 cm
The Wolfsonian–FIU TD1991.146.7
Photo: Bruce White

5.10
Stationery
Letter of 30 November 1935 from the Nationalsozialistische Deutsche Arbeitspartei in recognition of a donation showing official letterheading.
30 x 21 cm
The Wolfsonian–FIU TD1988.154.7

5.11
Printer's sample
Designs for official swastika metal and rubber stamps - Display sheet number 66
Published by Stempel Pfeilmaier, Munich
31 x 20 cm
The Wolfsonian–FIU XC1994.4358

5.12, 5.14–5.16
Typefoundry booklet
Tannenberg, die erfolgreiche deutsche Schrift
Published by Stempel AG, Frankfurt am Main, 1933
Lithograph, 30 x 22 cm
The Wolfsonian–FIU XC1994.4360

5.13
Typefoundry booklet
Schmalfette Jochheim Deutsch
Designed by Konrad Jochheim
Published by Wilhelm Woellner typefoundry, 1935
Lithograph, 31 x 22 cm
© DACS 2000
The Wolfsonian–FIU XC1994.4361

5.17
Poster
Früher: Arbeitslosigkeit, Hoffnungslosigkeit, Verwahrlosung, Streik, Aussperrung
Heute: Arbeit, Freude, Zucht, Volkskammeradschaft
Darum deine Stimme dem Führer
(Before: Unemployment,loss of hope, demoralisation, strikes and lock-outs
Today: Work, joy, culture, people's comradeship
Therefore give your vote to the Führer)
Anonymous, about 1934
Publisher, Hugo Fischer, Munich
Lithograph, 84.5 x 59.1 cm
The Wolfsonian–FIU XX1991.516
Photo: Peter Harholdt

5.18
Poster
Studenten an's Werk. Reichsberufsweltkampf 1936/7
Anonymous, 1937
Published by Deutschen GmbH, Berlin
Colour lithograph, 117.8 x 83.2 cm
The Wolfsonian–FIU XX1990.3115
Photo: David Joyall

5.19
Magazine cover
Gebrauchsgraphik, November 1937, v. 14 No. 11
Designed by Richard Roth
32 x 24.2 cm
Private Collection

5.20
Magazine cover
Gebrauchsgraphik, July 1939, v. 14 No. 11
Designed by Otto Hadank
32 x 24.2 cm
Private Collection

5.21
Magazine cover
Gebrauchsgraphik, October 1938, v. 16 No. 12
Designed by Herbert Bayer
© DACS 2000
The Wolfsonian–FIU Herbert Bayer Archive 83.3.165.52

5.22
Signet for the German Consulate
Designed by Gerhard Marggraff, 1936
Reproduced from *Gebrauchsgraphik*, October 1938, v.15 no. 10
Private Collection

5.23
Poster
Dietrich-Eckart theatre, Berlin and a poster for Deutsche Lufthansa
Designed by Gerhard Marggraff, 1936
Reproduced from Gebrauchsgraphik, October 1938, v. 15 No. 10
Private Collection

5.24–5.25
Window display poster for Haus Neuerburg, Cologne
Packaging design for F. Wohlff and Son, Karlsruhe
Designed by Otto Hadank, 1937
Reproduced from *Gebrauchsgraphik*, July 1939, v.16 No. 7
Private Collection

5.26–5.27
Die Kamera, Berlin, 1933
The main entrance hall with photographs by Wilhelm Niemann
Exhibition rooms designed by Winfried Wendland
Reproduced from *Die Form*, 1933, v.8
Published by Hermann Reckendorf, Berlin
Victoria and Albert Museum, London

5.28
Poster
Der Ewige Jude
(The Eternal Jew)
Designed by Horst Schlüter, 1937
Colour lithograph, 84.1 x 60 cm
The Wolfsonian–FIU 1990.3107
Photo: Peter Harholdt

5.29–5.32
Four magazine covers
die neue linie
May 1930, July 1935, February 1936 and July 1936
Designed by Herbert Bayer
36.5 x 26.7 cm
© DACS 2000
The Wolfsonian–FIU Herbert Bayer Archive XB1999.210.3, .23, .25, .28

5.33
Advertisement
Thymipin forte
Chemische Fabrik J. Blaes and Co. GmbH
Designed by Herbert Bayer, Dorland Agency, Berlin, about 1935
Lithograph, 25.3 x 18 cm
© DACS 2000
The Wolfsonian–FIU Herbert Bayer Archive

5.34
Advertisement
Adrianol-Emulsion
Hay-fever drops manufactured by Boehringer
Designed by Herbert Bayer, Dorland Agency, Berlin, 1934
Lithograph, 30 x 21 cm
© DACS 2000
The Wolfsonian–FIU Herbert Bayer Archive

5.35
Photograph of installation of the Exhibition of German Building Workers' Unions, Berlin, 1931
© DACS 2000
The Wolfsonian–FIU Herbert Bayer Archive
Photo: Peter Harholdt

5.36
Photograph of the Deutsche Werkbund section of the Exposition de la Societé des Artistes Décorateurs at the Paris 1930
© DACS 2000
The Wolfsonian–FIU Herbert Bayer Archive
Photo: Peter Harholdt

5.37
Photograph of an exhibition showing Herbert Bayer's designs for several exhibitions held at the Berlin Radio Tower.
© DACS 2000
The Wolfsonian–FIU Herbert Bayer Archive
Photo: Peter Harholdt

5.38–5.42 and 5.45–5.48
Catalogue
Deutschland-Ausstellung, 1936
Designed by Herbert Bayer
From *Gebrauchsgraphik*, April 1936
Lithograph, 21 x 21 cm
© DACS 2000
The Wolfsonian–FIU Herbert Bayer Archive 83.2.165.22

5.43
Catalogue
Deutsches Volk Deutsche Arbeit: Amtlicher Führer durch die Ausstellung, Berlin, 1934
Designed by Herbert Bayer
Published by Ala Anzeigen-Aktiengesellschaft
Lithograph, 21 x 21 cm
© DACS 2000
The Wolfsonian–FIU Herbert Bayer Archive XC1994.3495

5.44
Catalogue
Das Wunder des Lebens, 1935
Designed by Herbert Bayer
Printed by Meissenbach Riffarth and Company, Berlin
Lithograph, 21 x 21 cm
© DACS 2000
The Wolfsonian–FIU Herbert Bayer Archive TD1989.10.6

5.49
Catalogue
Bauhaus 1919–1928
Typography and cover designed by Herbert Bayer
Edited by Herbert Bayer, Walter Gropius and Ise Gropius
Published by the Museum of Modern Art, New York
26 x 20 cm
© DACS 2000
The Wolfsonian–FIU Herbert Bayer Archive 84.2.5

5.50 and 5.51
Photographs
Installation of the Bauhaus exhibition, Museum of Modern Art, New York, 7 December 1938 to 30 January 1939
Soichi Sunami and Hansel Mieth
The Wolfsonian–FIU Herbert Bayer Archive
Photo: Peter Harholdt

5.52
Book
the way beyond 'art' - the work of herbert bayer
Written by Alexander Dorner
Cover and typography Herbert Bayer
Published by Wittenborn, Schultz, New York, 1947
26 x 20 cm
© DACS 2000
The Wolfsonian–FIU XC1993.299
Photo: Peter Harholdt

Conclusion

Poster
'die usa baut'
an exhibition poster issued by the Zürich Arts and Crafts Museum, 1945
Designed by Max Bill
Printed by reproduktionsanstalt l. speich, zürich
Signed and dated, bill, 45.
Lithograph, 127.6 x 90 cm
© DACS 2000
V&A Museum E.217–1982

Picture Credits

Staatliche Museen zu Berlin Preußischer Kulturbesitz, Kunstbibliothek
Frontispiece, 0.1, 1.8, 1.17, 1.32, 1.33, 1.34, 1.35, 2.1, 2.5, 2.12, 2.20, 2.21, 2.22, 3.1, 3.6, 3.36, 3.37, 3.38, 3.39, 3.40, 4.21, 4.42, 4.59

Deutsches Historisches Museum
1.28, 2.39.

Hochschule für Graphik und Buchkunst, Leipzig 1.40

Bildarchiv Foto Marburg
1.38, 1.39

Märkisches Museum, Berlin 1.47

Royal College of Art
0.3, 1.41, 1.49, 1.52, 1.53, 1.54, 2.36, 2.37, 2.38, 3.24, 3.28, 3.29, 3.30, 4.3, 4.4, 4.5, 4.6, 4.7, 4.8, 4.9, 4.10, 4.11, 4.12, 4.12, 4.13, 4.15, 4.16, 4.17, 4.18, 4.19, 4.20, 4.22, 4.30, 4.31, 4.32, 4.33, 4.34, 4.35, 4.41 4.55.

V&A Picture Library
1.2, 1.5, 1.20, 1.24, 1.25, 1.50, 2.6, 2.16, 2.32, 2.33, 2.35, 2.40, 3.7, 3.8, 3.9, 3.10, 3.11, 3.14, 3.18, 3.20, 3.21, 3.23, 3.34, 3.35, 4.25, 4.26, 4.27, 4.28, 4.29, 4.40, 4.53, 4.54, 4.55, 4.60, 4.61, 4.62, 5.26, 5.27, Conclusion 1.

The Wolfsonian-Florida International University
0.2, 0.4, 1.1, 1.3, 1.4, 1.6, 1.7, 1.9, 1.10, 1.11, 1.12, 1.15, 1.16, 1.18, 1.19, 1.21, 1.22, 1.23, 1.27, 1.29, 1.30, 1.31, 1.36, 1.37, 1.44, 1.45, 1.46, 1.48, 1.51, 2.2, 2.3, 2.4, 2.7, 2.8, 2.9, 2.10, 2.11, 2.13, 2.14, 2.15, 2.17, 2.18, 2.19, 2.23, 2.24, 2.25, 2.26, 2.27, 2.28, 2.29, 2.30, 2.31, 2.34, 3.2, 3.3, 3.4, 3.5, 3.12, 3.13, 3.15, 3.16, 3.17, 3.19, 3.20, 3.22, 3.31, 3.32, 3.33, 4.1, 4.2, 4.14, 4.23, 4.36, 4.37, 4.38, 4.39, 4.43, 4.44, 4.45, 4.46, 4.47, 4.48, 4.49, 4.50, 4.51, 4.52, 4.56, 4.57, 4.58, 5.1, 5.2, 5.3, 5.4, 5.5, 5.6, 5.7, 5.8, 5.9, 5.10, 5.11, 5.12, 5.13, 5.14, 5.15, 5.16, 5.17, 5.18, 5.21, 5.28, 5.29, 5.30, 5.31, 5.32, 5.33, 5.34, 5.35, 5.36, 5.37, 5.38, 5.39, 5.40, 5.41, 5.42, 5.43, 5.44, 5.45, 5.46, 5.47, 5.48, 5.49, 5.50, 5.51, 5.52.

Author's Acknowledgments

This book would not have been possible without the extremely generous support of the Wolfsonian-Florida International University. I would like to express my gratitude to Mitchell Wolfson Jr. and the Wolfsonian Director, Cathy Leff. All staff there have contributed to the book and the accompanying exhibition. In particular, I extend my thanks to Wendy Kaplan, Associate Director, Exhibitions and Curatorial Affairs, and Marianne Lamonaca, Curator, for their gracious support and invaluable advice. Others who deserve mention for their considerable assistance are Richard Miltner, Amy Karoly, Neil Harvey, Joel Hoffmann, David Burnhauser, Pedro Figueredo, and Frank Luca.

During the years of research and writing of this book, I have been attached to the History of Design programme jointly run by the Victoria and Albert Museum and Royal College of Art, London. Here, students and fellow staff have encouraged me to think about my approach and challenged assumptions or tested ideas. I would like to thank them all, and especially Marie-Louise Bowallius, Yasuko Suga-Ida, Emily King, Rick Poynor, Lorna Goldsmith, Laurence Mauderli, Viviana Narotzky and Alice Twemlow, whose interests were often close to my own.

The research towards this book originally took the form of a PhD thesis and I am greatly indebted to my supervisor, Professor Gillian Naylor, who sustained her interest throughout. Also, I have been greatly inspired by art and design historians working in related areas, among them Charlotte Benton, Christopher Breward, Christopher Burke, Tag Gronberg, John Heskett, Robin Kinross, Ellen Lupton, Victor Margolin, Frederic Schwartz and Penny Sparke. By their good example, ideas have either fed directly into this book or I have been prompted to approach the subject from new directions. Colleagues in the Research Department of the Victoria and Albert Museum, Marta Ajmar, Helen Clifford, Paul Greenhalgh, Katrina Royall and John Styles, have all shared their interests or offered practical and intellectual stimulus.

In 1997, I organized an exhibition, *Signs of Art and Commerce, Graphic Design in the German Language, 1890–1945,* in the Department of Prints, Drawings and Paintings at the Victoria and Albert Museum. I would like to thank all colleagues who contributed to that event, and in particular Susan Lambert, Julia Bigham, Mark Haworth-Booth and Margaret Timmers, as well as Susannah Robson, then of the National Art Library.

Several bursaries and awards have allowed periods of extended study and opportunities to visit special collections. I was a grateful recipient of a British Council travel award in 1990, which enabled study at the Bauhaus Dessau and the Leipzig Buch und Schrift Museum. In 1997, I was an exchange partner on the International Program among Museums, organized by the American Association of Museums, which gave me an opportunity to become familiar with the collections of The Wolfsonian–FIU. Finally, I would like to acknowledge the financial support of the Research Policy Committee of the Royal College of Art.

Over the last four years, Barbara Berry has been a constantly reliable colleague, always generous in her help. I would like to thank Dominic Sweeney, also of the Royal College of Art, for his expert photography. Staff of the libraries of the Kunstbibliothek, Berlin; the Bauhaus Archiv, Berlin; the Buch und Schrift Museum, Leipzig; the Wolfsonian–FIU; the Royal College of Art, and the National Art Library, have all provided constant assistance in making their collections available.

At Thames & Hudson, I would like to extend my thanks to Stanley Baron, editor, and Andrew Sanigar, designer of the book, for guiding me with their professional judgment and imagination.

Finally, my thanks go to Sarah, my wife, and Agnes and Hugh, our children, who provided continued support and necessary distractions throughout the entire project.

Index

Page numbers in *italics* refer to illustrations in the text.